Producing American Races

NEW AMERICANISTS

A Series Edited by Donald E. Pease

Producing American Races

Henry James,

William Faulkner,

Toni Morrison

Patricia McKee

Duke University Press   Durham & London

1999

© 1999 Duke University Press

All rights reserved

Printed in the United States of America on acid-free paper ∞

Designed by Cherie Westmoreland

Typeset in Palatino with Officina Sans Bold display by

Keystone Typesetting, Inc.

Library of Congress Cataloging-in-Publication Data appear on

the last printed page of this book.

for

Donald Pease

Contents

Acknowledgments

I am grateful to past and present colleagues working in American literature at Dartmouth who have contributed to my thinking about James, Faulkner, and Morrison: especially to William W. Cook, James M. Cox, Chauncey Loomis, and Henry Terrie. I also thank members of the 1997 Humanities Institute at Dartmouth, which was directed by Donald Pease and which focused on "futures of American Studies," for their responses to my thinking about race in James's work. Especially, Robyn Wiegman made a great difference to this work through her critical reading of not only the chapters on James but also the manuscript as a whole.

At Dartmouth, Mary Childers has been an invaluable, thoughtful, and critical presence, and her reading of part of the manuscript was a great help to me.

An earlier version of Chapter 5 appeared in *Modern Fiction Studies* and was reprinted in *Toni Morrison: Critical and Theoretical Approaches,* published by the Johns Hopkins University Press in 1997. I am grateful for permission to reprint.

I thank the anonymous reviewers of the manuscript, for their criticism led to many improvements and clarifications in my argument. I am also grateful to Reynolds Smith and the other people at Duke University Press who have helped so much with this project, particularly Miriam Angress.

Most of all, I thank Donald Pease for reading, thinking about, and criticizing the chapters in their different versions.

Race and Media

Henry James, William Faulkner, and Toni Morrison have, over the course of the twentieth century, produced various fictions of racial identity among white and among black Americans. The common identities of white Americans in works of James and Faulkner and the common identity of black Americans in works of Morrison depend alike on a consistency of public political behavior and individual consciousness. In this study I want to indicate the different forms and degrees of political power available to James's, Faulkner's, and Morrison's racial identities by focusing primarily on the different cultural media that produce those identities.

These media are, in the production of James's and Faulkner's white identities, mostly visual. The media used to produce Morrison's black identities are primarily oral and aural. Visual media include imagery—figures of things and persons—as well as views—the ways people look at things and persons. Oral and aural media include both speech and music. All these means of cultural and racial identity are produced and reproduced not only in public performances and publications but within individual consciousness as well. I emphasize particularly the extension of cultural reproduction to individual consciousness, which is a crucial medium of cultural and racial identity in works by these three authors.

Studies of race in American literature have increased in number over the past two decades, though studies of whiteness are still unusual. Some recent critics of James have focused on his concern with a white identity, as well as on representations of Jews and African Americans that are important to his constructions of whiteness.[1] More numerous critics of race in Faulkner's novels have concentrated primarily on his characterizations of African Americans.[2] Critical studies of race have tended to shift attention away from the dominant American racial group identified as whites to racial groups excluded from whiteness. Indeed, much recent discussion concerns whether whiteness ought to be the direct focus of academic study and whether analyses of whiteness have the political effect of returning white experience to a central position of power from which critics of race have worked to dislodge it.

Many critics of Morrison's fiction have directed attention to her representations of African American identity.[3] Morrison's fiction concerns, almost exclusively, black characters and black culture; white culture in her novels, though powerful in its effects, is usually present only indirectly. Yet Morrison is a pivotal figure for students of whiteness because of *Playing in the Dark: Whiteness and the Literary Imagination.*[4] In these essays, Morrison argues that representations of American whites depend on representations of Africans and African Americans. The black presence in white American literature, though often invisible, means that whiteness cannot be isolated from blackness. Other critics of white identity have followed Morrison in emphasizing the dependence of white on black identities.

My own juxtaposition of six novels by James, Faulkner, and Morrison—*The Wings of the Dove, The Golden Bowl, The Sound and the Fury, Light in August, Sula,* and *Jazz*—is one I have some difficulty locating among more recent studies of race. I have brought these novels together because they demonstrate strategies of racial identity that effect intense interconnections of personal with public meaning. Insofar as their characters search for identity, they search for racial identity; the very structure of individual consciousness is one of race. This interdependence of personal and racial identity makes individual characters virtually inconceivable without their racial and cultural identities. Yet representations of persons as racial constructions in these works also insist that personal and racial identity are made up, if not necessarily by individual choice, by historical developments socially produced.

In general, James, Faulkner, and Morrison recognize as American whites characters who reproduce a visual cultural order: an order that not only corroborates the ways these characters see things but also necessitates visual representations of both things and persons. Visual identities—in representations ranging from commercial advertising to psychoanalytic mirror stages—dominate white culture and identify white characters as distinct and autonomous physical and psychological entities. In Morrison's work, the cultural media most used by black characters are, rather, oral and aural and are media of social response. Morrison has remarked on the importance of music as a medium of black culture,[5] and that medium, in *Jazz,* is important both for its reproduction of traditional works and for the unrecorded and improvisational elements of its history. Such media produce invisible relations of both continuity and change among persons whose individual identity is therefore more responsive to than independent of other persons.

To some extent my focus on cultural media of racial identity corresponds to that of more recent studies of race. My identification of whiteness as a visual culture echoes the emphasis put by many critics on visual representations of race.[6] My discussion of a socially and historically responsive African American culture draws from many critics who have emphasized the communal and historical character both of Morrison's novels and of black American identity.[7] These critical readings of black and white racial identities indicate too the more "abstract" character of whiteness that is central to my discussion of race. But I resist the tendency among current critics to dismiss or set aside abstract characteristics of white racial and cultural identity. For one thing, this tendency has meant that the power and reach of white culture are not always recognized. For another, it has meant that the power and reach of black culture are not always recognized.

Critics of whiteness have argued that the abstractness of whiteness is responsible for the political dominance of whites in modern Western cultures. Abstracted from particular physical attributes as well as from history and cultural practices, whiteness is understood as inclusive, neutral, normal, and unremarkable, difficult to specify or define. The abstractness of racial whiteness can be visibly represented, as Richard Dyer has demonstrated in his analyses of American and British films. He contends that "white power secures its dominance by seeming not to be anything in particular" but that "when whiteness qua whiteness does come into focus, it is often revealed as emptiness, absence, denial or even a kind of death." Such representations of whiteness as a negative but pervasive, even transcendent presence lead to Dyer's recognition that "this property of whiteness, to be everything and nothing, is the source of its representational power."[8] Whites' representations of persons who are not white, however, make those persons and their cultures appear physically marked, unusual, exclusive, and abnormal. Critics of film in particular have discussed the ways that black Americans are represented merely as bodies.

If whites have been made to appear transcendent, and "other" people have been made to appear material entities, this inequity has been addressed by various critics with a call to materialize, mark, or embody whiteness.[9] I take issue with such readings of black and white racial identities and such strategies for altering their political effects. Using James, Faulkner, and Morrison, I emphasize whiteness as a visual culture rather than merely a certain way of visualizing experience. The visuality of white culture is an order of meaning as well as a mechanism of abstraction. "Visual culture," then, has reproduced racial distinctions that privilege whiteness not only because it is produced in the interests of white privilege but also because the kind of symbolic construction that produces whiteness is the sort that produces twentieth-century visual culture. The extent to which visuality structures meaning in white culture is evaded if not obscured, I think, by the repeated critical focus on film as a medium of racial distinctions. The visuality of white culture is more extensive than the imagery of film can indicate.

Rather than particularizing and materializing whiteness, then, I work here to clarify dimensions of abstract visuality that structure and corroborate white American identity. These dimensions cannot be adequately understood as or countered by particular representations; nor can this visuality be understood or countered in terms of visibility. One of my reasons for using James's late and Faulkner's early novels is that they demonstrate the dependence of whiteness on "visual culture" in the early twentieth century, before film and television became the predominant media of white culture. They evidence instead a visuality of whiteness that often works without actually being seen.

The "visual culture" of whiteness in these novels is apparent in exchanges of visual representations among characters—representations not only of images but also of characters' views. Their exchanges constitute whiteness as a comprehensive range or even a symbolic field of likenesses and differences. A community in which differing views are expressed by individuals, in whom consciousness also produces conflicting views, enjoys a theoretical consistency of individual and group. This consistency requires a specific kind of consciousness, which must appear to be internally "free" or "open" to various views; in his constructions of open-minded individuals, James in particular presents a compellingly liberal white identity.

Morrison's constructions of African American consciousness and culture produce a less abstract social order. But her social and historical relations of characters construct black identity in ways equally difficult to mark or particularize. Consideration of the historical strategies of collective identity in *Sula* and *Jazz* indicates that a consistency of African American identity is produced through media of responsiveness and responsibility that nevertheless change over time. Unlike the comprehensiveness that structures whiteness as an open and inclusive symbolic field, here both the double individual consciousness and the collective are open to variation because of pressures exerted within and from outside the community. Consistency develops in social and historical relations rather than within any order of representation that can be abstracted from social relations or from historical change.

Black identity in these novels is produced in exchanges that occur among more often than within characters. Media of call-and-response, for example, instead of authorizing extensions of individualism, express a responsiveness among persons that is understood to move social exchange beyond the bounds of individual consciousness. Both individual consciousness and collective identity, relative and variable, are productions of media that are not necessarily visible or visualizable. Because Morrison's African American communities identify themselves in nonvisual, even antivisual terms, they refute not merely white representations of black persons as objects but also visual orders of representation that have constructed both whites as subjects and blacks as objects.

Whiteness as Visual Media

The dependence of white culture on visuality may seem paradoxical, if whiteness is understood to be an abstraction. Yet the paradox of abstract vision—vision detached from bodily sensations of sight—has been a crucial component of advances in visual technology since at least the early nineteenth century. One of my aims in this volume is to indicate the degree to which visualizations and abstractions of white American identity are tied to "progressive" developments—in the growth of knowledge, the growth of democracy, and economic growth—over the past two centuries. The dimensions of modern visual culture extend well beyond visibility to abstract visual metaphors of knowledge and identity: ranging from Lacan's mirror stage as a representation of the relation of self and other to the expression of individual "views" as the means of political representation in a democracy. Media of visual culture have also been progressively abstracted from sensations of sight in order to function as means of cultural reproduction.

Such abstractions are characteristic of a number of modern media. Jonathan Crary has clarified how, in historical developments culminating in the nineteenth century, European thinkers reconceived vision as an objective, "optical neutrality" of impressions and therefore subject to standardization.[10] The reconception of vision as a mechanical and impersonal process effected its disembodiment and allowed for its reproduction by machines. The idea that a camera "sees" more accurately than can a person had the result of further diminishing the importance of what any particular subject sees to the images of photography. American critics in the 1890s debated how photographic "images seemed to consider the subject (both maker and implied beholder) *secondary* to the visible world."[11]

James Lastra traces this secondariness of the subject in developments that revalued photography as "represented *vision*" rather than art.[12] The recording of various "looks" or views means that film captures more than the human subject can record. And the mobility of looking that increased with "moving pictures" is a mechanical mobility, exceeding any body's capacity to move or see.[13] Jacques Aumont, however, argues that "the history of the eye in film" redefines personal as well as impersonal vision; "we might conclude that the cinema [early in the twentieth century] had developed the theme of the eye's mobilization in two opposing directions: toward the object and toward the subject. . . . [A]s a symbolic machine for producing points of view," film not only abstracts vision from subjective, bodily sight but also represents particular, limited, subjective points of view, as if to cover all possibilities.[14]

One characteristic of white cultures in novels by James and Faulkner is media of representation that provide this kind of inclusiveness. White cultural media represent and therefore reproduce both impersonal likenesses and personal differences. The most important difference between representations of white and nonwhite characters in these novels is not a difference between abstract and embodied identities per se but that between a theoretically open symbolics of white identity, inclusive of both abstracted and embodied characteristics, and representations of limited, exclusive, embodied identity. The abstraction of white culture means that whiteness theoretically includes everything. To be nonwhite or outside the terms of this field is to be limited and partial.

One distinction of white characters in novels by James and Faulkner is their ability to manipulate and profit by media of visual culture. When Milly Theale in James's *The Wings of the Dove* decides to "see" and represent herself as a dove, she adopts an explicitly symbolic identity whose "clarity" allows both her and others to escape much confusion about her identity. Like the "escape" offered by the mobility of cinematic images, Milly's move allows her to escape her bodily identity, which she replaces with an image that is both impersonal and historically transcendent.[15] Moreover, Milly thereby acquires a kind of cultural capital that she would not otherwise possess. To say that Milly is a dove is to identify her not only as a representation but also as a representation that is part of an extensive repertoire of likenesses, accumulated and reproduced over centuries in Christian symbolism, particularly that of European art.

The "dark" Italian prince in James's *The Golden Bowl*, on the other hand, lacks the mobility of vision that characterizes most white Americans in the novel; he thus appears "backward," "as fixed in his place as some statue of one of his forefathers."[16] Similarly, Dilsey and other black characters in Faulkner's *The Sound and the Fury* appear culturally "backward." Although Dilsey exercises transcendent vision when she attends church, for example, the biblical imagery of her vision—"I've seed de first en de last"—seems to complete rather than motivate or mobilize vision.[17] Others in her congregation share her beliefs and see what she sees, bonding through these shared beliefs and visions. But the symbolic dimensions of Dilsey's vision, unlike the symbolic dimensions of Milly Theale's dove, are reproduced without being "seen" as images. This difference marks not only a difference of representation but a difference of production as well. Nonwhite characters appear nonproductive.

The productive character of whiteness that I emphasize means that whiteness is allied to capitalism with particular force. It is not only possession and dispossession that differentiate whites from others. The cultural production of whiteness in these novels identifies whiteness with means of production: not only with money but also with other media. My emphasis is on media that reproduce in abstract visual terms both a theoretically inclusive culture and various individual distinctions which mark the freedom and diversity of that culture. The cultural media that function as cultural capital are both reproduced and used to produce various new forms and images of identity.

The abstract dimensions of whiteness, then, indicate an alliance with capitalistic modes of production and power that cannot be erased by an insistence on differentiating white persons, bodies, or ethnic groups. Rather than particularizing representations of whiteness, it is necessary to identify the ways that whiteness has laid claim to both abstract and particular identities. Representing ethnically differentiated groups of white persons as minorities, what Ruth Frankenberg discusses as "me-too-ism," does little to address the power of whiteness.[18] The assimilationist practices that have occurred in the name of white American identity remain historically powerful.[19] Particularizations of white ethnic groups, moreover, do little to alter the real and nonmaterial privileges afforded to persons identified as white in the United States.[20] Thus it is the abstract character and abstract powers of racial whiteness, along with the discriminatory as well as assimilationist effects of these abstractions, that are the focus of my readings of James and Faulkner.

Whiteness as a Public Sphere

The imagery that both represents and constitutes whiteness in the novels by James and Faulkner which I consider here is in public circulation. In fact, one important distinction between white and "other" identities in these works is that white identities are open to view and openly available for reproduction. Images of whiteness in open circulation become media of exchange with currency not only in visual media, such as painting, theater, and photography, but also in written and spoken representations: in literature and the democratic public sphere.

The abstract identity of individuals who have made up the dominant political class in Western democracies since the eighteenth century has been elaborated by Jürgen Habermas in his discussion of a public sphere in England and France, in which rational debate occurred among private persons who understood themselves to be autonomous. Theoretically, such public debate works something like cinema, with a capacity both to represent and to produce differing "views."

Within the family, Habermas argues, "a private autonomy denying its economic origins . . . seemed to be established voluntarily and by free individuals and to be maintained without coercion." "The three elements of voluntariness, community of love, and cultivation were conjoined in a concept of the humanity that was supposed to inhere in humankind as such and truly to constitute its absoluteness: the emancipation . . . of an inner realm, following its own laws, from extrinsic purposes of any sort."[21] Such autonomous individuals, involved in public debate as rational and critical participants, could understand their own points of view as impartial, free of particular, personal interests and purposes.

Michael Warner has argued that such an abstract identity of the colonial American white male developed specifically in print and publication. "At least in the British American colonies, a style of thinking about print appeared in the culture of republicanism according to which it was possible to consume printed goods with an awareness that the same printed goods were being consumed by an indefinite number of others." The indefinition and depersonalization of this common identity were particularly appealing in "the culture of republicanism, with its categories of disinterested virtue and supervision." As it "perform[ed] the disincorporation of its authors and its readers, public discourse turned persons into a public."[22]

Warner emphasizes, however, that this public was not inclusive. Only certain white males identified their political status in such abstractions, which became, moreover, "a differential resource."

> The ability to abstract oneself in public discussion has always been an unequally available resource. Individuals have to have specific rhetorics of disincorporation; they are not simply rendered bodiless by exercising reason. And it is only possible to operate a discourse based on the claim to self-abstracting disinterestedness in a culture where such unmarked self-abstraction is a differential resource.

Here the "white, male, literate, and propertied" person loses particularity.[23] Whiteness becomes, on the one hand, a common identity of certain persons. Whiteness also becomes what Frankenberg calls "a relational category": "a normative space" that makes it possible to produce and order differences between various racial and cultural identities.[24]

Such "a differential resource" was, as Joan W. Scott has clarified, a paradoxical development. Eighteenth-century conceptions of the democratic individual, she points out, are characterized by a central disparity. The abstract idea of a common humanity, which all human beings share and which therefore can function as the basis for a democratic government, was theoretically inclusive. But although many individual differences were subsumed in an abstract common humanity, differences of race and gender were deemed significant enough to exclude persons from that common concept.[25]

Scott argues that over the past two centuries feminism has elaborated this conflict. And she thereby points to an important differential component of the abstract white male identity.[26] If, according to Habermas, democracy is constituted by rational debate among differing individuals, persons who are not white males owning property may participate in public debate. But they must debate their own right to political powers that white males can take for granted, according to the accepted definition of democracy. This indicates the kind of advantages that accrue for those persons in Western culture unmarked by particular differences.

The "unmarked" character of racial whiteness needs some additional emphasis. In keeping with the abstraction of political subjects from particular bodily and historical identity that is characteristic of the dominant political class in western Europe and the United States, persons identified as "white" are in effect removed from racial categories, identified as unaffected by the historical and social experiences that constitute the racial identity of others. Only "others," then, are identifiable by race. "White" persons are often grouped together as a nonrace, by means of assimilations of various ethnic backgrounds that reinforce or reproduce the abstractions believed necessary to a political subject. Whiteness then becomes the mark of no particular group of persons. Blackness, on the other hand, is seldom identified as an assimilation of persons from various ethnic backgrounds. Instead, blackness is usually understood as a racial and ethnic identity.[27]

For whites, assimilation occurs as abstraction; for blacks, an assimilation of particulars occurs. To particularize a white ethnicity, however, does not clearly lessen the abstractions that produce whites' political identity and political consciousness.

This is again to indicate characteristics of whiteness that allow it to appear as "everything and nothing," as Dyer says. If white persons are "nothing in particular" in racial or ethnic terms, this clearly interferes with their visibility. If they assume indefinite and impersonal identity as their political power, this also resists imagery. The power of whiteness is not visible; it is visualized, and its visualizations both represent and reproduce its cultural power. Whiteness, that is, maintains the properties of media productivity without maintaining properties of physical objects. This removal from the realm of the visible, as bell hooks argues, has been crucial to whites' domination of visuality in Western culture.[28] And the domination of visuality—of the capacity to produce and reproduce visions and views *as* representations—has been critical to whites' domination of political and cultural media.

A Racial Construction

The degree to which the political structures of power in Western democracies actually require a differentiation between abstracted and particularized identities is unclear. Yet if whiteness functions as an expression of power by marking others' differences from whites, then otherness is necessary to the production, practice, and power of whiteness. Toni Morrison has proposed a model of racial differences in American literature written by whites according to which the differences between white and black persons are determined by and clearly necessary to the identity of white Americans. From the seventeenth through the twentieth centuries, Morrison argues in *Playing in the Dark*, the African population of the United States was used by European American writers to work through their own fears and insecurities and to "construct . . . the American as a new white man." Especially early on, European Americans experienced "the terror of human freedom," which included "Americans' fear of being outcast, of failing, of powerlessness; their fear of boundarylessness . . . ; their fear of loneliness, of aggression both external and internal."[29]

By projecting the fearful elements of their situation onto Africans,

Europeans were able to identify themselves in positive and ideal terms.

> Black slavery enriched the country's creative possibilities. For in that construction of blackness *and* enslavement could be found not only the not-free but also, with the dramatic polarity created by skin color, the projection of the not-me. The result was a playground for the imagination. What rose up out of collective needs to allay internal fears and to rationalize external exploitation was an American Africanism—a fabricated brew of darkness, otherness, alarm, and desire that is uniquely American.

With Africanism as a background or "playground," the white American is able to sort out his own conflicts by transferring the unwanted parts of himself onto a "blank darkness" of "rawness and savagery."[30] According to this redistribution, white men can be seen as enlightened, civilized, free, and individual because black people are seen as dark, savage, enslaved, and personally undifferentiated.

In the background that African Americanism provided for the distinction of autonomous white men, Morrison distinguishes figures made to constitute a ground by being massed together. The distinction of white figures depends, then, on rendering other figures invisible—refusing, that is, to see them. This spatial conception revises the relation of figure to ground. The ground is itself composed of figures, but with so little space between them as to appear undifferentiated. The figures that appear "against" such a background stand out because they keep their distance. The kind of distinction they acquire is a relief from the burden of their own undesirable characteristics that is achieved as an architectural relief. Whites "stand out" not because of any inherent difference from the background but because of distances they keep from it. According to this analysis, Morrison contends that African American people have never been absent from American literature or from public discourses on morality and politics. "Africanism is inextricable from the definition of Americanness—from its origins on through its integrated or disintegrating twentieth-century self."[31]

Morrison's model of whiteness is a visual model, and the degree to which white culture depends on imagery is important to her critique of its cultural media, particularly in the novel *Jazz*.[32] Morrison's imagery indicates that white identity is less abstract than the ideal of eighteenth-century political theory. In fact, she in some ways seems to reverse the terms of other critics' thinking, in that she identifies white persons as individually distinguished and black persons not as particularized but as massed together without differentiation in this model of racial difference. According to her analysis, it is the distinction of black persons that becomes invisible in whites' constructions of race.

Yet Morrison adds much to an understanding of white identity as an abstraction, because she identifies white representations of race in America with a kind of symbolic visual field. The white identity can be distinguished only against a ground of darkness and materiality. "Otherness" becomes a constituent of the abstract ideal rather than left out of it. African persons were put in the place of otherness by white writers and thereby seen to materialize not only qualities white people did not want to be identified with but also the difference between white people and those undesirable qualities.

Spaces of Whiteness

According to the construction Morrison theorizes, a collective white identity in the United States depended on an imaginative "projection of the not-me" beyond the bounds of the self, or the selfsame. The spatial dynamics of this racial economy indicate a reconception of collective, public identities that is crucial, I think, to a recognition of racism in the public spheres of Western democracies. If white persons project certain kinds of otherness beyond the bounds of whiteness, they also project a wide range of both similarities and differences into public exchange *as* parts of whiteness. Identities of whiteness are in circulation, one might say, in the space between any individual white person and the irremediably "other," massed identity of blackness.

In the public space of whiteness, which whites identify as open space with much room for distinction and for circulation, whiteness is experienced in extraordinary variety. One medium in which such variety has been experienced is public debate; an exclusive group of white males has represented their identity as nevertheless open to and inclusive of differences. Similarly, in the more visual terms of twentieth-century public life, there is a wide range of images of whiteness. White persons, therefore, can experience their identity not merely as selfsame but as diverse. They thus enter into exchanges of identity that seem open and inclusive of differences even as they are exclusive. The spatial character of these limits and exclusions is indicated by the production and reproduction of imagery in cultural media.

Habermas has argued that, by the twentieth century, participants in public political spheres were understood to be motivated not by common principles of reason but by economic interests. This meant that such participants behaved as consumers: "When the laws of the market governing the sphere of commodity exchange and of social labor also pervaded the sphere reserved for private people as a public, rational-critical debate had a tendency to be replaced by consumption, and the web of public communication unraveled into acts of individuated reception, however uniform in mode."[33] As consumers, citizens did not represent their own thoughts and opinions but instead became consumers of representations, produced in the media. Public political life became a matter of publicity, of advertising and "public relations." The "public figure" develops into a representation of political authority rather than a person who rationally represents and debates ideas in public life. "The public sphere becomes the court *before* whose public prestige can be displayed—rather than *in* which public critical debate is carried on."[34]

In James's and Faulkner's depictions of whiteness, however, individuals are not only consumers but also producers, and especially reproducers, of images and views that appear in the media. Yet such views and figures are, as Habermas suggests, primarily visual media. When Milly Theale plays the role of a dove, she causes others to "see" her as such. Her identity is iconic, moreover, in that the dove is a highly conventional image. In other novels, most emphatically in *The Golden Bowl,* the production of images and views has no specific content. Adam Verver's wide, empty view of things in *The Golden Bowl* is "a view that was 'big' even when restricted to the stars."[35] To produce a "view" can be equated with producing a painter's—or especially, perhaps, in James's case, a critic's—perspective. This perspective is mobile, allowing for the views of many particular images and even of many angles on many images. The mobility of such a point of view or the capacity to take various points of view means that perspective is abstracted from specific objects—or, indeed, any particular subject— and is therefore identifiable as highly changeable and diverse.

An individual's views, therefore, do not distinguish the individual by his or her particular opinions so much as by his or her position in space. In fact, it is primarily space that distinguishes such views from one another. "I see it this way" and "from my point of view" become visual metaphors for opinion in part because the relative character of opinion is understood to depend on location. The common medium of political opinion, which may once have been rational thought, is no longer within the individual. Nor does the individual distinguish his or her political position by means of ideas. Political position is merely position, a point of view.[36]

There is still a common medium, however, for the expression of political views—the cultural collection of views and roles available. This medium is something like a language but is more similar to a collection of landscape views in a museum or a repertoire of plays and roles in a theater company. People can "expand" their identities by adopting such views and roles; in so doing they express both differences and their likeness with other persons, because anyone can take the same positions or views. Verver identifies his expansive view of things with Keats's image of Cortez's view of the Pacific. These imaginative likenesses indicate a coherence among individuals, a unity that is spiritual but also social. The common accessibility of views and roles, which are not thought but reproduced—"taken"—as if they were visual views and spatial positions, allows for the equivalence of persons as well as the expression of differences. But every different view is reproducible, by means of "changes of position" that would let anyone see things as someone else sees them.

Individuals can see themselves, or parts of themselves, in these images and signs; others, at least in part, are also represented. This space of circulating signs and images is more important to the unity of a group than is any bounded structure, because the unity of the group lies not in containment but in the open expression of similarities and differences by the individuals in the group.[37] This representation of similarity and difference provides the group with cohesion and diversity. The communal or racial identity provided by these means is one that allows, even encourages, the expression of differences within the group.[38]

The convertibility of positions among such persons means that they are both subjects and objects of view. More recent critics have focused attention on the limited dimensions of female imagery in public spheres of Western cultures.[39] But if "woman's socially prescribed status as an image formulates an epistemological position defined by powers that overshadow her potential as an observer,"[40] male characters in Faulkner's *Light in August* both assume the status of an image in the eyes of other men and assume an epistemological position as active observers of men and women. The male's "status as an image" that is also produced by males marks a compatibility of identity as image with identity as an active producer of images. Such a compatibility is one feature of racial whiteness in Faulkner's fiction.

Unlike images of women that limit females' status to that of objects, the imagery practiced by white males in *Light in August* identifies males as likenesses. Males thereby assume the capacity to produce representations and to act as or *be* representative. In both cases, they are identified with meaning that exceeds not only that of any object but also that of any individual. Recognized as likenesses of other men, male appearance and behavior mark a group identity.

Open Exclusions

One other spatial model for a production of racial or cultural differences has been given by Edward W. Said. More discursive than figurative, Said's "imaginary geography" nevertheless helps clarify the spatial dimensions of racial whiteness. To some extent, Said adopts Gaston Bachelard's model of houses and other spaces that people occupy as spaces filled by emotional projections: "Space acquires emotional and even rational sense by a kind of poetic process, whereby the vacant or anonymous reaches of distance are converted into meaning for us here."[41] This meaningful understanding of what is spatially and temporally distant strengthens the sense of self too. "There is no doubt that imaginative geography and history help the mind to intensify its own sense of itself by dramatizing the distance and difference between what is close to it and what is far away."[42] In these readings, the self projects meaning into spaces and times beyond the experience of the self and thus demarcates differences as well as similarities so as to render self and other meaningful.

Such imaginative projections, into time as well as space, do not merely distinguish inside from outside or self from other.[43] Nor do they merely appropriate what is distant into familiar terms. Instead, Said argues, it is as if a middle space opens up, a space in which the media that negotiate differences circulate. There are, for example, particular "lenses through which the Orient is experienced" in Europe: "the journey, the history, the fable, the stereotype, the polemical confrontation." These lenses "shape the language, perception, and form of the encounter between East and West. What gives the immense number of encounters some unity, however, is the vacillation" that occurs when westerners look at the Orient.[44]

Seen, for example, as both an Eden to return to and a New World, the Orient becomes multiple "Orients" with "a capacity for entertaining and confusing the mind."

> Something patently foreign and distant acquires, for one reason or another, a status more rather than less familiar. One tends to stop judging things either as completely novel or as completely well known; a new median category emerges, a category that allows one to see new things, things seen for the first time, as versions of a previously known thing. . . . Islam thereafter is "handled": its novelty and its suggestiveness are brought under control so that relatively nuanced discriminations are now made that would have been impossible had the raw novelty of Islam been left unattended.[45]

In this medium of understanding or knowing Islam, Islam is represented by the same terms and structures of knowledge that Western scholars use for other experience. Once this representation occurs, the profound otherness of Islam—any elements of Islam that do not fit the terms of Western understanding—is eliminated from recognition.

Something like this medium occurs in the public spheres of white culture in James and Faulkner. Insofar as "others"—that is, persons not previously identified as white Americans—are included within this group, they must represent their identities in the common terms of whiteness, which means abstracted from history and particularity. The assimilation that occurs is an assimilation not simply of differences but also of an individual's identity into familiar and expansive terms of difference. All persons represented as white are translatable into media that abstract their identities into certain forms of likeness and difference. It is the allowance for difference that lets whiteness appear inclusive even as it excludes.

Theoretically, anyone could join. But one limit to inclusive participation is the very openness of insiders' identities. To enter into this open exchange of identity and difference, an individual must recognize his or her identity as a construction of relations between an impersonal self and an impersonal other. One has to be free of personal history, except insofar as that experience can be assimilated into the impersonal terms of, for example, a Freudian model of personal history. Those people who are bound to a specific past or to other particularities of experience are the ones excluded. Boundaries characterize the excluded, and expansiveness, the included.

When linguistic signs are replaced by visual images as the media of exchange, the abstraction of identity from particular and historical experience is reinforced. This is especially so to the extent that, in the twentieth century, images are seen as media rather than as representations of objects. As such, images can belong to multiple persons, as is true for images of advertising that are thought to be assimilable by many persons. The exchange of images within the visual media of culture also depends on the seeming suspension of images, as if within empty space. Such images are free of specific referents or histories and can be adapted or assigned to various people.

Late in *The Wings of the Dove*, Kate Croy looks at Milly Theale in her white dress and rare pearls and says, "I see myself."[46] Kate sees herself in Milly's image and in Milly's place because Milly has been displaced from her own history and has identified herself in the reproducible terms of cultural icons. Yet female characters in the novels of James and Faulkner that I consider here tend to mark a limit to the inclusiveness of a white American race. It is characteristic of gender distinctions in these works that the women in *The Wings of the Dove*, limited to reproductions of identity, are able to produce no "clear" difference between American and English persons. In *The Golden Bowl*, Maggie Verver learns from her father, Adam, to open up American identity to a multiplicity of views that so far exceeds any European identity as to constitute a distinct medium of racial production. But Maggie is an exception. Female characters in these novels are usually more "dense" than male characters—less open and less clear in their views of both self and other. Thus women often produce their identities as "covers" rather than clear views; this is true of Milly Theale and Kate Croy, as well as of Fanny Assingham in *The Golden Bowl*.

In Faulkner's works female characters acquire even more density. Despite her absence in *The Sound and the Fury*, Caddy Compson is not convincingly "white" in any abstract sense of the term; she is a disappointment to men, for example, in her lack of innocence. In this novel as in *Light in August*, whiteness is a male enterprise, because white women are incapable of representing any ideal. So much is this the case with Joanna Burden in the later novel that she is called "dark." Both Caddy and Joanna are identified in bodily terms, as is Dilsey, the only major character in either novel who is definitely black. But whereas the white female characters are morally deficient, Dilsey effectively embodies the goodness that white women lack. In this peculiar economy of female morality, women, as is true in *The Wings of the Dove,* have no effective means of racial distinction. Faulkner even more than James feminizes the threat of racial assimilation.

Recognition of such distinctions of gender in these novels emphasizes the importance of space in the production of a white race. Women usually fail where men succeed in the production of open space that is necessary to the theoretical or imaginary clarity and openness of racial whiteness. Moreover, the empty space that is imagined to surround images is what enables the mobility of subjects. Persons can adopt various views because they can imagine themselves moving through space and looking at things from various angles.

The spaces that seem to open up within the critical consciousness of James's characters in *The Golden Bowl* are blank spaces that consciousness can move through and negotiate. The emptiness of such spaces poses particular views as choices. The openness of choice, owing to the openness of the space perceived between various views, further demarcates the freedom of the individual to distinguish the self. Faulkner also emphasizes an openness to difference in the media of white identity. But it is not so much free choice as it is an open participation in conflict that allows for the liberal expression of individual identity in *The Sound and the Fury* and *Light in August*.

In both novels, conventional images and roles enable self-divided, dualistic individuals to represent themselves in conflict in a public space. Such conflicts are more often conflicts of games or war than of debate. But the representation of opposition implies, like public debate, a coverage of different positions. Moreover, because these images and roles can be taken by many if not all white males, they are experienced as parts of a shared symbolic order. Given this common order, roles of conflict do not appear merely as projections of conflicted selves but also as parts in a public repertory of plays. Their open representation further marks these conflicting parts as stable, even as a shared medium of community.

Productivity as Racial Difference

Morrison's analysis of racial whiteness stresses the production of racial differences. Such a focus is not unusual among critics of race.[47] Yet the production of racial and cultural identity and difference has been somewhat obscured by the attention critics have given to the individual consumption of representations of these phenomena in the media—by viewers of films, for example. James, Faulkner, and Morrison represent individuals as producers and reproducers of racial identities and differences. It is more exact to say that these authors represent individuals as media or means of such production and reproduction. According to these representations, individuals are means of aesthetic as well as rational production.

According to James and Faulkner, the participation of private individuals in the production of political views is an undertaking that depends on an imaginative projection of the self into cultural exchange. This undertaking also depends, at least to some extent, on a reproduction of views and roles that are seen and played by others. As the example of Milly Theale suggests, the production of images of likeness—not just of images but of images like other images—that I identify with white racial identity is a form of aesthetic production. Especially for James, the production of racial likeness is comparable to the production of works of art.

In *The Wings of the Dove* whiteness is an identity produced imaginatively and imitatively; Milly Theale compares herself to painters, specifically to the "lady copyists" who paint likenesses of museum pictures. In *The Golden Bowl,* the production of white American identity is likened to the Ververs' collection of works of art to be put on display in a museum in American City. In Faulkner's *The Sound and the Fury* and *Light in August,* white identity is also produced by individuals' imaginations. These productions and reproductions are not always specifically aesthetic, but one aesthetic mode of reproduction in *Light in August* is theatrical: characters both play roles and act as members of a theater audience.

It is perhaps the capacity of white characters to shift their identity into symbolic dimensions that most markedly distinguishes them from "black" characters in the novels by James and Faulkner that I consider here. Images of blackness in the fiction of the two authors also assume symbolic significance; the very terms "blackness" and "darkness" pick up moral and religious attributes as automatically and clearly as a white dove picks up those of innocence.[48] Yet "black" or "dark" persons in these novels are also associated with material attributes that resist transformation into symbolic terms. Moreover, these characters lack the capacity to produce such transformations. The Italian prince in *The Golden Bowl* who is identified with "darkness" and "blackness," for example, understands his racial identity as an inherited and inherent identity difficult, if not impossible, to change.

In their identification of racial whiteness with not only images of whiteness but the capacity to produce images, both James and Faulkner elaborate whiteness as an extraordinarily powerful phenomenon. The productive power depicted as characteristic of racial whiteness means that whiteness is a phenomenon of change and creativity, in the media and other cultural institutions. Moreover, the inclusiveness of "whiteness" extends to the capacity of any individual mentally to reproduce the likenesses that consolidate the race. If the images of white racial identity are produced by media, individual imaginations are among these media. One effect of this is greatly to increase the coherence and consistency of racial whiteness. In addition, the white individual experiences the reproduction of whiteness as an exercise of choice. Thus his or, less often, her power to choose and to express white identity locates the power of whiteness, at least theoretically, in each white individual.

Black Culture

Morrison does not depict white characters to any significant degree in either *Sula* or *Jazz*. In this sense—in the form of individuals—racial whiteness is absent. The effects of white views of black identity, however, are present in cultures and characters alike. In Morrison's characters, consciousness derives more from W. E. B. Du Bois's theory of African American double consciousness than from his white contemporaries, such as James or Freud. Du Bois's double consciousness may disallow the production of images and views that occurs in the consciousness of James's characters, because the black individual's double consciousness sees whites excluding the black self from view.[49] In *Playing in the Dark*, Morrison fills in such apparently blank spaces in visions of whiteness. The production of what is missing in such constructions—figures that are rendered invisible by distance and detachment—is a production Morrison identifies, too, within black cultures in both *Sula* and *Jazz*.

Other productions are also necessary to the resistance of black characters to white constructions of black identity. Although Morrison argues in *Playing in the Dark* that white Americans identify Africans as a mass, virtually a material mass of indistinct and undistinguished individuals, the experience of characters in *Sula* and *Jazz* is broken apart by whites. Lost in this fracturing are means of coherence, the forms and relations by which persons create and recognize consistency: of body, of individual identity, of group identity. The fractures that white culture introduces, or forces, into black experience appear as absences. There are empty spaces between persons and between parts of persons rather than relations of consistency among persons.

Characters respond to these constructions of absence by negotiating and renegotiating spatial distances in order to produce individual and black identity. Female characters in *Sula* engage in physical redistributions of space. Whether they keep house or keep their houses messy, producing order or disorder, they control their lives by clearing and filling in space. Such spacing techniques are also useful to constructions of identity. Sula is a character who repeatedly produces breaks in things, clearing a space for her own identity, at the cost of any and all consistency. What preoccupies black consciousness in this novel is a history of losses: not only lost persons and objects but lost opportunities and lost means of change as well. The emptiness left by these losses is what characters control with their spatial manipulations. The character Sula is used by the community to locate and thereby contain these losses. She herself, made to occupy a space of loss, thereby serves as a means of community.

In *Jazz*, black culture is produced and reproduced in the historical medium of music. In this novel characters experience themselves as means of reproducing traditional forms of African American music. They thereby identify themselves both as part of black cultural history and as means of creating and reproducing such history. Moreover, because variations and improvisations are traditional elements of black music, characters are able to produce individual differences without alienating themselves from racial identity.

Music creates and reproduces consistency among individuals, in forms of both repetition and variation, and African American music has a history of doing so. As Paul Gilroy argues:

> Art, particularly in the form of music and dance, was offered to slaves as a substitute for the formal political freedoms they were denied under the plantation regime. The expressive cultures developed in slavery continue to preserve in artistic form needs and desires which go far beyond the mere satisfaction of material wants. . . . The particular aesthetic which the continuity of expressive culture preserves derives not from dispassionate and rational evaluation of the artistic object but from an inescapably subjective contemplation of the mimetic functions of artistic performance in the processes of struggles towards emancipation, citizenship, and eventually autonomy.[50]

Gilroy identifies a comprehensiveness of aesthetic expression that historically served as a means of political self-representation as well as cultural identity. Given the political oppression of plantation life, political expression occurred through aesthetic means—that is, the mimetic expression of individual interests and the bodily expression of political as well as material needs.[51]

In these performances of political and aesthetic expression, it was not through critical debate but through exchanges of call-and-response that community was experienced.[52] Call-and-response is the "antiphonal back-and-forth pattern which exists in many African American oral traditional forms, from sermon to interjective folktale to blues, jazz and spirituals."[53] Coherence and consistency among persons are produced as the individual performer calls forth responses and so cultivates a group identity, even for the most particular variations improvised by the performer. The multiple dynamics of performer and audience, past and present, repetition and variation, contribute to a complex consistency of cultural and individual expression.[54]

A double or even multiple consciousness is important to such communal identifications. It is in the practical critical responses of reaction and revision—responses that occur among rather than within individuals, and responses that change persons and things rather than merely seeing them differently—that Morrison's black communities and cultures produce identity. Representations both of individuals and of characters' self-expression in *Sula* and *Jazz* are expansive, then, in ways different from the expansiveness attributable to whiteness.

These exchanges tend to limit the extent of individual self-expression and express instead identity among persons. Social disputes in these novels extend individual identity into exchanges that may, indeed, change rather than merely broaden or reproduce individual views.

In *Sula* and *Jazz*, music is only one medium of black cultural production. Yet part of the power of black musical culture in *Jazz* clearly lies in nonvisual means of transmission and production. In oral and instrumental performances of African American music, bodies are not imaged as likenesses that mark an abstract consistency among persons. The performing body, taking various shapes and forms, must be variable to act as a means of expression and must improvise forms of expression, which limits the importance of visual reproduction. The likenesses produced are not primarily visual but are sounds and patterns of sounds. The medium of black music, expressed through the media of black bodies and minds, which contribute both memory and imagination, produces consistency in repetitions as well as difference, in variations that are also part of the tradition of such music.

The increasing political and economic power of black persons in the United States since the 1950s may be due, as Houston A. Baker Jr. argues, to the "radically new forms of visibility, or black publicity," that were developed especially by Martin Luther King Jr.[55] But in her novels set in the early part of the twentieth century, Morrison identifies visual culture as a source of suffering and alienation for black people, for the desirable looks and images reproduced in American culture are white. Instead, Morrison cultivates media of reproduction that allow for more variation of representation and response. She identifies, particularly in *Jazz*, such media as crucial to the history of African American culture. The degree to which musical forms of exchange and expression are absorbed into the personal, social, and political experience of her characters makes evident an extraordinary consistency of black culture, a consistency that lies outside the bounds of visual imagery.

Black Identity as Response

In their sense of self and in their relations to one another, characters in *Jazz* make evident social processes of expression and community that have been historically characteristic of numerous black religious and aesthetic practices. The call-and-response structure of experience provides a medium of involvement and improvisation among persons. Images may circulate, but those images are subject to review. Images are not finished likenesses that people use as such but are altered and reformed from critical perspectives. Like the critical practices of black spectatorship that bell hooks has discussed as "the oppositional gaze," the ways Morrison's characters look at the world become critical responses.[56] It is in doublings of perspective that processes of call-and-response, like the double entendre of blues language, provide the most crucial component of racial and cultural identity in both *Sula* and *Jazz*.[57]

Characters in novels by James and Faulkner, in public and private exchanges, take roles and views and reproduce thereby the diversity and the consistency of white culture. In *Sula* and *Jazz*, characters engage in more critical exchanges. They produce not takes but double takes, as representations that are also responses to representations, of white and black culture. Faulkner's and James's white American cultures are identified with and in an illusion of expansive, open space that depends on closing out certain persons from view. Morrison's black American cultures struggle to claim the spaces of their existence, their culture, and their history that whites have seen as empty. To do so, black persons are forced to look at things twice. Given the constructions of meaning available in white culture, they can find their places only by refusing to use those constructions as given.

In the visual terms of white media, the double take produces something out of focus, with an excess of information. As takes on white culture, such critical responses are illicit, even outlaw behavior. But as takes on black culture, what I call double takes are necessary to productions of identity in *Sula* and *Jazz*. Critical relations in these novels reorder identity and difference in terms that make such oppositions as law / outlaw and visible / invisible inapplicable as means of inclusion or exclusion. Patrick O'Donnell has suggested that the works of Faulkner and Morrison, when considered in relation to each other, need to be understood in terms of "intertextual differential[s]."[58] What might be called intercultural differentials also need consideration when reading these works in relation to each other.

Sula Peace is the character in Morrison's work most intensely engaged in the processes of critical revision that are constitutive of her communities. Sula seems never to see things as others see them. She has the effect of providing more extensive views, opening up what Hortense Spillers calls "subperspectives or *angles onto* a larger seeing" because she breaks apart elements of meaning that other people connect.[59] What Sula produces are not images but splits in images as well as disconnections of other kinds. Moreover, although she is an outcast, she is kept within the community of the Bottom, belonging there as the necessary expression of losses that the community cannot openly admit without coming apart.

To keep the outlaw within the community is crucial to the African American experience in which persons have achieved individuality only outside the bounds of white constructions of meaning.[60] In *Jazz*, two characters who commit crimes remain in the community. Jazz itself is identified by conventional white culture as an illegitimate form of music; Alice Manfred "knew from sermons and editorials that it wasn't real music—just colored folks' stuff."[61] And Morrison's narrator and her characters in *Jazz* use the illicit double meanings of jazz and blues lyrics to make room in the language of white culture for black meaning.

Yet it is in personal exchanges among characters, in *Sula* and especially in *Jazz*, that a call-and-response pattern most clearly enables a critical review of experience to occur. In informal conversations and debates, particularly among women in domestic settings, individual views of situations are expressed, reviewed, reformed. Such exchanges are not always logical. Often responses are more emotional than rational, and the likenesses produced are emotional rather than either imaged or rational agreement. Nonetheless, these domestications of call-and-response exchanges, which also can be seen as privatizations of public political debate, place critical exchange at the center of private life. The informal relations of neighbors and friends that characterize Morrison's black communities change, or interchange, the boundaries of public and private spheres.

These are not exchanges of images whose reproducible likeness guarantees identity within a racial group but rather exchanges of responses. The crucial difference is that white views and images mediate racial likeness. Mediation is structured and occurs in the signs of representation, just as, in Lacanian theory, entry into language is what provides an identity for the self. In this model of identity, the self becomes self-as-other by means of language and thereby enters community. In Morrison's communities, double mediation is required by black persons, just as double alienation is imposed on black persons by the representations of the dominant culture. Here double consciousness is not understood as a universal process of structuring identity but as a specific historical effect.[62] Rather than finding identity in language, black persons, because of their history of alienation, find identity in response to language or in language as response. The historical need for response as the expression of political resistance is continued in the responsive structure of expression among black persons in the twentieth century: responses to each other and to white culture.

The importance of women to cultural productivity in *Sula* and *Jazz* is indicative of the informality and adaptability of behavior in their communities. By informality I mean that womens' behavior does not conform to fixed structures, in which persons have particular parts or roles. Certainly characters may act according to received forms of behavior, and they may reproduce roles and parts that others have played before them. But, as in the music of jazz, the cultural heritage of responsiveness emphasizes not only the reproduction of forms of behavior but also the reproduction of an adaptability that cannot simply repeat earlier forms of behavior if it is to work. The central roles that women play in the communities of the Bottom and the City are not, therefore, centralized according to prescribed distinctions of gender, nor are they definable according to the kind of structure of significance that requires female characters in *The Sound and the Fury* to be lacking significance. Women's roles in *Sula* and *Jazz,* and those of men too, seem instead to continue to be played improvisationally and pragmatically. They are historically determined, that is, both insofar as they are influenced by past experience and insofar as they remain, in the present, in process of determination: as responses to circumstances and as means of producing alternatives to those circumstances.[63]

Visible Differences

In his discussion of black music and its productions of historical, aesthetic, and political identity, Gilroy emphasizes that what is missing from such productions and necessary to the political power of whiteness is textuality. Textual reproduction allows the debates and discourses of whiteness to deliver cultural authority far more extensive than any conversation or performance can achieve. "We must enquire," Gilroy insists, "whether a definition of modern rationality such as that employed by Habermas leaves room for a liberatory, aesthetic moment which is emphatically anti- or even pre-discursive."[64]

In considering communities represented by James, Faulkner, and Morrison, one must qualify the distinction Gilroy indicates between productions of rational public debate and aesthetic productions. In novels by these authors, racial and cultural identity is produced and reproduced as an aesthetic enterprise. If, as Warner argues, white men in eighteenth-century America used printed media to consolidate a national identity, by the twentieth century the use of print for the reproduction of images changes the process of political discourse. The public sphere of political exchange extends to include nonrational exchanges of images. Whiteness is not, or is no longer, reproduced in forms so clearly distinguishable from aesthetic models.

Yet in this later process of reproduction, as in the exchanges of rational debate, a common identity is produced that is inclusive of and dependent on individual distinction. In James's and Faulkner's representations of white identity, white persons are distinguished from others, who are seen as dark or black, and much of white distinction depends on such contrasts. Moreover, white individuals are distinguished from one another. Assimilations of individuality are precluded by the abstract terms of racial likeness, by the apparent choice of such likeness, and by the choice of identities that also confer distinction: a character's identity as a dove, for example, or as a Civil War general. The crucial invisibility in this process is not white bodies; indeed, identity is often represented in images of bodies. Yet various phenomena that would obscure distinction remain invisible, such as the individuality of black persons or the repetitive character of the reproducible white individual. Producing white racial identity, then, depends on "seeing" whiteness—both understanding it and imaging it—in discursive terms that provide focus and obscurity sufficient to distinguish it from that of other groups of people.

In Morrison's novels the reproduction of racial identity is represented as a social and historical production that provides no such clear terms for vision or representation. For Morrison, the dynamics of individual, communal, and racial identification and differentiation remain not exactly invisible but not subject to clear representation either. The production of cultural identity in Morrison's African American communities is more inclusive than discursive models of whiteness because it depends on a doubling of discourse. Morrison "makes room" in her representations of public and private life in the United States for experience that, as Gilroy suggests, Habermas excludes from political validity. But it is not so much that her productions of black identity depend on "anti- or even pre-discursive" experience as that these cultural productions maintain a double and pragmatic political discourse.

Morrison thereby refuses the equivalence of discourse and vision that claims clarity and focus as necessary attributes of social meaning. She exposes the lenses through which whiteness is seen by whites as inadequate media for focusing on American races. Even if clear, or perhaps because they are clear, these lenses provide only exclusive representations. With less clarity, Morrison represents African American experience as doubled consciousness, doubled discourse, doubled or multiplied vision.

This interpretation of Morrison's African American cultures may seem to advocate the exclusion of African Americans from "view" in the symbolic field whose abstract visual terms govern American political identity. That is not my intention. I mean to identify productions of black culture in *Sula* and *Jazz* in critical relations to white culture, indicating reviews and revisions necessary to theoretically democratic political practices. Morrison's work calls attention, for example, to strategies of exclusion that may not appear at work in whiteness, and she questions the inclusiveness that is supposedly at work in whiteness. Her fiction represents historical limits to African American identity and, read in relation to works of James and Faulkner, also indicates historical limits to those authors' expansive conceptions of American whiteness and American culture. Taken together, novels of James, Faulkner, and Morrison suggest that racial differences are produced in American culture not only because democratic inclusiveness does not extend far enough but also because the very extensions available to democratic identity, in the abstract terms of whiteness, are limited and limiting.

In the readings that follow, I stress critical differences in productions of racial and cultural identity. Whereas in Morrison's work the nonvisual elements of racial identity are to a great extent assigned to history, James's and Faulkner's white characters cultivate an invisibility through more abstract representations of various kinds. Most important, I argue, their white characters produce abstract fields of visual representation that "comprehend" identity and difference. These comprehensive fields of "vision" allow for endless transformations of a clear white identity, but both comprehensiveness and transformability occur only with the abstraction of the field of representation from historical and social connections that threaten clarity. If the imagery produced within these fields is visual, the production of the fields of vision remains largely invisible.

Ruth Frankenberg is one critic who has argued that it is necessary to resist such abstractions of whiteness. "White women need," she insists, "to become conscious of the histories and specificities of our cultural positions, and of the political, economic, and creative fusions that form all cultures."[65] I contend that to account for the differences in the social and economic power of white and black identities in the United States, one must attend to histories of productivity in which "political, economic, and creative fusions" occur very differently. Frankenberg is uneasy with a white identity "emptied of any content other than that which is associated with racism or capitalism."[66] But I argue that a history of whiteness needs specifically to identify how racism and capitalism have benefited whiteness, and vice versa. To a great extent, I believe, it is because whiteness has been produced as an identity emptied of content that white people have exercised those benefits.

Visuality has played an important part in that emptying of content. It is not, therefore, by "seeing" both black and white identities that one can resist the historical differences in their power. Rather, one must think critically about visuality and the meaning of its dominance over other cultural media and identify, as Morrison does, the power of other media to produce very different identities.

Reproducing Whiteness

The Wings of the Dove

In *The Wings of the Dove* (1902), Milly Theale, a young, rich, white American woman visiting Europe, becomes ill and dies. This character, James says in his preface (1909) to the novel, was of a sort that had long interested him.

> I had from far back mentally projected a certain sort of young American as more the "heir of all the ages" than any other young person whatever . . . ; so that here was a chance to confer on some such figure a supremely touching value. To be the heir of all the ages only to know yourself, as that consciousness deepened, balked of your inheritance, would be to play the part, it struck me, or at least to arrive at the type, in the light on the whole the most becoming.[1]

The role James chooses for his "most becoming" American is one with "touching value." The pathos of the part depends on the American being both "the heir of all the ages" and "balked of your inheritance."

This particular conflation of power and powerlessness is one that I want to identify as a representation of racial whiteness. If "to be everything and nothing" characterizes whiteness,[2] to have everything and nothing is the condition of James's heroine in *The Wings of the Dove*. Milly Theale learns to represent her condition, moreover, in the comprehensive yet blank terms that define European and American whiteness in the novel.

It is in an iconic register that racial identity in this novel achieves both a completeness of significance and a void of particularity. The images adopted by characters may be identified with the visualization of individual identity that Habermas suggests became a primary means of political representation in twentieth-century democracies. What Robyn Wiegman calls "the ascendancy of technological corporealities" in this century means that "iconicity instead of corporeal abstraction" functions as the medium of public relations and that "commodified identities" become "the primary signifying form of the public sphere."[3]

Milly Theale becomes an icon in *The Wings of the Dove*, and she is something of a public figure. Yet even among iconic identities, as Wiegman emphasizes, racial difference has entailed distinctions between surfaces and depths of meaning.

> "Blackness" in particular becomes . . . not only more than skin deep, but epistemically linked to the articulation of other differences, most prominently gender. In this process, the possibilities of a kind of interior psychic complexity is overwritten by the determinations of the body's corporeal scripting, and the African (=American) is consigned to a psychological as well as a physical negativity of "being." At the same time, whiteness achieves its priority as a visible absence, signifying a dis-corporated, universal, and psychically complicated humanity.[4]

Here Wiegman discriminates between the bodily determination of black persons, as well as, to some extent, white women, and the symbolic indeterminacy of white male identity.

James also employs an economy of race, gender, surfaces, and depths of identity to produce differences between white Europeans and white Americans. According to this economy, only white male Americans distinguish themselves in terms of psychic complexity. White Europeans remain codified, identifying themselves in exchangeable and surface terms; these characters claim their own similarity, whereas white male Americans claim individual difference. In *The Wings of the Dove*, characters who participate in the public sphere of upper-middle-class social life in London are marked by a blankness. European codes of whiteness bring complexity to the surface of social exchange and blank out both "interior psychic complexity" and any bodily determination of identity. Milly Theale assumes iconic identity within this social sphere, James suggests, to avoid any moral responsibility for or bodily determination of her identity.

Both Milly's psychic complexity and her body are blanked out by representations that discount any particular or determinate identity.

The iconicity of whiteness in the novel, practiced primarily by female characters, depends on covering or screening identity so that neither particular material nor particular psychic qualities can be recognized as determinant. Milly's body is rendered indeterminate, as a body that may or may not be dying. Her material identity, once represented in these terms, has the effect of obscuring material determination. Milly's psyche is also obscured by representations, such as the dove, copied from a repertoire of likenesses available to multiple persons.

The American heiress in this novel thereby balks herself of her inheritance, James suggests, because she uses for herself the voided social code of Europeans. The white American male, whom James discusses in other words as well as in his preface to *The Wings of the Dove*, is to be identified by no void. He can be distinguished from Europeans, who cede responsibility for their identity to cultural codes, by his assumption of individual moral responsibility. His inner sense of responsibility, moreover, means that the white male American produces his meaning, whereas Europeans merely occupy established positions within their cultural codes of meaning. This distinction between productive Americans and merely reproductive Europeans becomes the most important mark of James's American whiteness.

Covers of Whiteness

The covers produced for Milly's individual identity do not hide it but reproduce it in comprehensive terms that allow for no hidden meaning. Thus the status of her body is suspended between the possibilities of life and death, which cover everything in the sense that their total opposition represents a complete range of possibilities; yet they determine nothing. Milly's inner character is similarly voided of the capacity to choose life or death when it is represented by an image of the Holy Spirit. Once Milly adopts the icon of the dove, her body as well as her character are discounted. As an iconic identity, the dove-like woman is nonparticular because many people could play the part. But the image also empties Milly of particularity because the Holy Spirit transcends both body and individual psyche.[5] An icon of transcendence, the dove is a cover of unlimited meaning that signifies no person in particular.

Milly Theale learns to assume the power of whiteness from English characters in the novel, whose icons she reproduces. In the role of the mere "American girl," Milly is able to provide a cover for her behavior. But in this role, her behavior is completely discounted; it is produced as marginal behavior for the sake of discountability. This occurs, for example, when Milly plays the part for Kate Croy and Merton Densher after unexpectedly meeting them at the National Gallery.

> Whatever the facts, their perfect manners, all round, saw them through. The finest part of Milly's own inspiration, it may further be mentioned, was the quick perception that what would be of most service was, so to speak, her own native wood-note. She had long been conscious with shame for her thin blood, or at least for her poor economy, of her unused margin as an American girl—closely indeed as in English air the text might appear to cover the page. She still had reserves of spontaneity, if not of comicality; so that all this cash in hand could now find employment. She became as spontaneous as possible and as American as it might conveniently appeal to Mr. Densher, after his travels, to find her. She said things in the air, and yet flattered herself that she struck him as saying them not in the tone of agitation but in the tone of New York. In the tone of New York agitation was beautifully discounted, and she had now a sufficient view of how much it might accordingly help her. (178–79)

Here Milly's agitation can be written off under cover of her marginality. The role of "the American girl" as margin depends on being abroad, and in Europe Milly is repeatedly able to empty situations of meaning because of her marginal status as an American. In Venice she will make use of "the national character that, in a woman still so young, made of the air breathed a virtual non-conductor" (323), precluding the development of meaning by emptying a situation of any manner of significance.

From the English, however, Milly learns to produce an effect of discountability that is covered by the text. This effect is available in iconic representations that both void persons of individual character and yet provide individuals with power. From the beginning of the novel, James's English characters identify themselves in roles of disinterestedness that, like the dove Milly will play, obscure qualities of individual character. But these characters acquire visibility and power in roles of self-denial because these roles are reproduced as parts of the construction of symbolic meaning.

The visibility and visuality of these representations is not only, or even always, a matter of their imagery. The public sphere of whiteness in *The Wings of the Dove* is a symbolic field that is theoretically inclusive and theoretically visualized as a complete range of points of view. The self-representations most powerful among the English characters are identifiable as views or aspects of a person: visual dimensions of identity that are each clearly only one of many. As a single view, any such representation is always inconclusive, and it is always, morever, a matter of position. As a political identity, a view, unlike the political opinions of Habermas's eighteenth-century democrats, is not produced by reason or any other internal element of an individual but by position, which accounts for the variety of views.

With subject and object identifiable by positions, they can be understood in absolutely impersonal terms, abstracted from particular individuals into a structure of relations that produces views. Among the English, then, is available an additional capacity to produce whiteness as "everything and nothing." With the identity of an individual viewed as and from a social position, a comprehensive range of identities is opened up, as all the various views that might be taken. Anyone can take any view, and anyone can be viewed from any angle, so that the same equivalence of persons is produced that allows multiple persons to play various parts from a repertoire of conventional roles. The likeness of individuals identified as views consists of the void of inner character and the full range of external views available. Thus no particular internal or external element of identity can be seen as being necessary to the individual's identity.

English Productions of Whiteness

The comprehensive blankness with which English characters in the novel represent themselves is evident in the opening scene, when Kate Croy pays a visit to her father, Lionel Croy, at his London rooming house. Since the death of her mother, Kate has been living with Maud Lowder, her rich aunt. But now she " 'wished to escape Aunt Maud' " (59). She offers to give up Maud's patronage and come live with her father, who has little money and who, owing to some never-specified scandal in the past, is socially "impossible" (56). Yet Kate's offer poses a dilemma for her father, who not only does not want his daughter with him but wants to have the credit for giving her up.

Thus it is that Mr. Croy, who has always "had indescribable arts, that quite turned the tables" (24), finds the tables turned on him.

> He wished her not to come to him, still less to settle with him, and had sent for her to give her up with some style and state; a part of the beauty of which, however, was to have been his sacrifice to her own detachment. There was no style, no state, unless she wished to forsake him. His idea had accordingly been to surrender her to her wish with all nobleness; it had by no means been to have positively to keep her off. (25)

Having counted on appearing to sacrifice his attachment to Kate's selfish detachment, for the sake of style and state, Croy finds himself put into the position he had planned to put Kate.

So begins the novel's consideration of sacrifice or "giving up," as characters compete to appear selfless. That such an appearance is a social position rather than an inner quality is indicated by the maneuvers that produce it. The representation of selflessness depends on the display of no internal characteristics but on jockeying for the position of self-sacrifice. These characters compete to assume a position of self-denial, moreover, through maneuvers that maintain identity as a non-particular, exchangeable attribute. Both self-denial and self-interest are produced as turns of the tables.

Croy manages to turn the tables on Kate when he points out that her appearance of sacrifice for his sake is a mere cover, since there is no gain for him: " 'You can describe yourself—*to* yourself—as, in a fine flight, giving up your aunt for me; but what good, I should like to know, would your fine flight do me?' " (28). In fact, he is correct: Kate has constructed a cover, with her "fine flight" of sacrifice for his sake that is also a flight of escape from Maud, for Kate's own sake. And it is this kind of cover that these characters are expert at reproducing. They cover themselves not by concealing their motives and interests but by constructing representations that, allowing for various views, cover everything.

By the end of the scene, neither character can hold on to the position of self-sacrifice, which has been exposed as self-interest. Each character is exposed from and by the other's perspective, which not only alters her and his apparent motives but identifies those motives as aspects of a situation. Thus there is little sense of exposing a hidden truth; what matters is on the surface. Characters are emptied of inner particularity insofar as their moral qualities become aspects and positions. Because each assumes the contrasting qualities of interest and disinterestedness with turns of the tables, neither position is experienced *as* a moral quality.

Signs of self-sacrifice and self-interest, if seen as opposite ends of a moral spectrum, might make possible a wide range of moral distinctions about a character. But these characters move suddenly from appearing as one to appearing as the other and seem concerned to use these characteristics as positions of power, which empties out the significance of self-sacrifice and self-interest as it rules out any subtle discriminations of character. With both characters occupying similar positions, they appear more alike than different. Little can be learned about Kate or Lionel Croy as individuals, except perhaps that each is less concerned with character than with position. Their "inner" lives are oriented outward, and they represent themselves in equivalent terms.

These exchanges reinforce the completeness of coverage that surfaces provide in the English social scene. The opening scene of the novel does not present depths of English character but a situation into which people fit. Nothing appears hidden—nothing is under the table—because the exposure of the attitude of sacrifice as a false position does not uncover any underlying reality. Neither her father's nor Kate's intended sacrifice is exposed as a cover for self-interest. Rather, sacrifice and self-interest are both exposed as two reversible aspects of a person, depending on which way she is turned. When turned one way, she looks good; from another aspect, she looks bad.

This is to effect a second kind of abstraction, not only of moral qualities from inner character but also of interest and desire from objects. Self-interest is no more aimed at an object than is self-sacrifice; both seek to get rid of objects. What might be seen as the hidden motive "beneath" the appearance of sacrifice is, in Kate's case, getting away from Maud and, in her father's case, getting away from Kate. Sacrifice becomes a false position, insofar as it is self-serving and others serve as pretexts for it. But it is not exactly a false appearance, because "giving up" is a real desire on both Kate's and her father's parts. Sacrifice is instead a *mere* appearance, a wholly nonreferential attitude, abstracted from subjects and objects alike, that is only surface, with both act and "underlying" motive aimed at getting rid of or turning away from things. If self-sacrifice does not work as a cover for self-interest in the opening scene, turning the tables does work as a cover, and it covers everything.

An American Race

The equivalence of characters who identify themselves in terms of such a cover poses difficulties for distinguishing white Americans from white Europeans. In *The Wings of the Dove*, however, Milly Theale prefers not to distinguish herself. She does so, in a sense, only when her American qualities discount her personal qualities. Increasingly, Milly models herself on what she sees and imagines in Kate Croy as she represents herself in and by reproductions of images and views. The appeal of pictures to Milly as means of self-representation lies in their surfaces, which limit meaning to visible dimensions and allow for ease of reproduction. When she visits the National Gallery, Milly recognizes that "she should have been a lady-copyist—it met so the case. The case was the case of escape, of living under water, of being at once impersonal and firm" (174). Nothing of the lady copyist is evident in the images she produces, and it is in this apparent vacuum of self that Milly finds "refuge" (174). She will go on to identify herself as a copy of Kate and find refuge in the apparent lack of self with which she will mimic Kate's capacity to cover herself.

As his preface to the novel makes clear, James himself was interested in distinguishing white Americans from Europeans. Yet this project is much more successful in *The Golden Bowl* than in *The Wings of the Dove*, in which Milly Theale produces an "impersonal" American identity highly assimilable to English identities. Michael Omi and Howard Winant explain that, according to the biological understanding of race that prevailed at the turn of the century, "race was equated with distinct hereditary characteristics. Differences in intelligence, temperament and sexuality (among other traits) were deemed to be racial in character."[6] Yet James followed conventional practice when he called "racial identities" what are now considered national identities. And it was in national terms that James's "American" race needed to be distinguished from European races, particularly because he is largely concerned with Americans of English descent, usually residents of New England. To distinguish the one group of white people from another, "ethnic" differences are used.

According to Omi and Winant, "the ethnicity-based paradigm arose in the 1920s and 1930s as an explicit challenge" to a biological understanding of race. Theories of ethnicity

> suggested that race was a *social* category. Race was but one of a number of determinants of ethnic group identity or ethnicity. Ethnicity itself was understood as the result of a group formation process based on culture and descent. "Culture" in this formulation included such diverse factors as religion, language, "customs," nationality and political identification. "Descent" involved heredity and a sense of group origins, thus suggesting that ethnicity was socially "primordial," if not biologically given, in character.[7]

With "descent" unavailable to distinguish James's white Americans from white Europeans, cultural differences remain paramount. Yet with racial distinctions located more in social than in biological identity, assimilation becomes a clearer theoretical possibility.[8]

Given the evident confusion about the basis and attributes of racial and national identities in debates at the turn of the century, Sara Blair convincingly argues that James's works "open a lens onto the instability of race—and particularly of whiteness—as a shifting structure of experience and feeling (and of commodification, violence, and repression)."[9] In both *The Wings of the Dove* and *The Golden Bowl*, characters cultivate and practice different forms and representations of racial whiteness. As an American "type," Milly Theale is unable, or unwilling, to distinguish herself from the English characters among whom she lives and dies. She is assimilated by means of reproductive techniques that both copy identity and empty identity of individual differences. Yet the Ververs of *The Golden Bowl* produce an American collective identity that resists processes of assimilation. In his later novel, James will identify a different form of whiteness, one that is cultivated as a specifically American identity.

The difficulty of distinguishing white cultures from one another is for James increased by the sense that American culture is blank and empty. Milly Theale is characterized, James writes in his preface to *The Wings of the Dove,* by "a strong and special implication of liberty, liberty of action, of choice, of appreciation, of contact—proceeding from sources that provide better for large independence, I think, than any other conditions in the world" (6). But if liberty is the particular characteristic of Americans, it is difficult to posit. Liberty may exist more as an absence than a presence, more as an openness than a construct. As such, it does little to define a person or a type.[10]

The difficulties involved in identifying white American character and white American culture are discussed by James in an earlier work, his 1878 book on Hawthorne. In Hawthorne's "American Notebooks," James sees "an extraordinary blankness—a curious paleness of colour and paucity of detail" (47).[11] For James, this metaphorical whiteness is caused by cultural absences, and he goes on to list some of them:

> No state, in the European sense of the word, and indeed barely a specific national name. No sovereign, no court, no personal loyalty, no aristocracy, no church, no clergy, no army, . . . no castles, . . . nor parsonages, nor thatched cottages . . . ; no great Universities nor public schools . . . ; no literature, no novels, no museums, no pictures, no political society, no sporting class—no Epsom nor Ascot! Some such list as that might be drawn up of the absent things in American life—especially in the American life of forty years ago. (48)

If to the English or French such absences would be "appalling," the American, James says, "knows that a good deal remains." But "what it is that remains—that is his secret, his joke, as one may say" (48).

Among the "fine compensations" (48) available to Americans for their lacks, humor is only one. Another is "the genuine democratic feeling" (51) that James finds in Hawthorne's diaries. Hawthorne identifies as gentlewomen and gentlemen various individuals who would not be called such in Europe, "the natural tendency in societies where the sense of equality prevails being to take for granted the high level rather than the low" (51). Another democratic characteristic of American feeling is evident in the attention Hawthorne pays to individuals. For "many Americans, and many New Englanders especially," James says,

> The individual counts for more, as it were, and, thanks to the absence of a variety of social types and of settled heads under which he may be easily and conveniently pigeon-holed, he is to a certain extent a wonder and a mystery. An Englishman, a Frenchman . . . has not that rather chilly and isolated sense of moral responsibility which is apt to visit a New Englander in such processes; and he has the advantage that his standards are fixed by the general consent of the society in which he lives. A Frenchman, in this respect, is particularly happy and comfortable. . . . The Englishman is not quite so well off, but he is better off than his poor interrogative and tentative cousin beyond the seas. He is blessed with a healthy mistrust of analysis, and hair-splitting is the occupation he most despises. . . . American intellectual standards are vague, and Hawthorne's countrymen are apt to hold the scales with a rather uncertain hand and a somewhat agitated conscience. (53)

Analytic, hair-splitting, conscientious—the American does not have the means of fixing "his" identity by such social codes as Europeans use. There is therefore an "absence of the off-hand element in the manner in which many Americans . . . make up their minds about people whom they meet" (52–53). And Americans remain, at least to some extent, "a wonder and a mystery" to one another.

This very different form of knowledge among Americans may also account for some of the blankness or emptiness that characterizes the culture of white Americans. In "that tendency to weigh moonbeams which in Hawthorne was almost as much a quality of race as of genius" (53), James does not see an absence of discriminations or an absence of details but an absence of substance. He is pointing to an excess of detail and discrimination, in that these are so individualized as to produce many more differences than similarities. But they lack weight; they do not produce knowledge. They provide a judgment that is vague both because it is inconclusive and because of the unwillingness of the judge to identify one individual in terms of others. Thus the judge must remain somewhat tentative and uncertain. The moral responsibility that the American feels, as an individual, when judging others causes too much consideration of those others as individuals for any conclusive identification.

If the white American is an unknown, then, this can be understood in terms of history, culture, and the conception of the individual in America. On the one hand, Americans lack much European culture. On the other hand, in their very lack of European culture can be identified their particular strengths. There is more individuality, more moral responsibility. In this comparison of two "white" cultures, the American character shifts from one kind of blankness to another. First seen as empty, it is then seen as full: so full of responsibility and discriminations as to produce no knowledge. Americans are more mysterious to one another than Europeans are to one another. Yet the European who identifies others by social code may know much less of persons as individuals. In European cultures, this suggests, individually discriminated identities are absent, whereas in American culture individuals have so much meaning as to be mysterious to one another.

As a revised conception of a white race, the American model, with much more scrutiny of individual character and much less certainty about individual identity, produces more variety as well as more mystery. The American model of whiteness becomes inclusive of variety and identifies respect for individual differences as a moral responsibility. If the white American is finally unknowable, that "blankness" is well on its way to being identifiable as the political power of racial whiteness, because it apparently includes and respects a great variety of individual differences.

Indefinite, unknowable, mysterious, not by reason of a lack of scrutiny but by virtue of scrutiny, the American mode of identifying persons produces both surveillance and freedom, knowledge and mystery; white American identity covers everything. In his essay on Hawthorne, the chief difference that James pinpoints between white individual identity in Europe and in America, then, is that in Europe social codes decide it, and in America it remains undecided. And this lack of decisive identity is cultivated: it is part of the culture of white Americans to be mysterious.

But though James begins here to identify the white American in positive terms, *The Wings of the Dove* suggests that he more fully develops a positive construction of a white American race by gendering it. Milly Theale elaborates a feminized American identity as a white American who evades responsibility and merely reproduces European codes and images of whiteness. She becomes a blank in the sense that European individuals are blank: identifiable only by her position in a social code, without internal individuality, originality, or moral responsibility for her position.

Identifying such lacks of responsibility and originality with females and with death, James is later free to envision a white American race in original and responsible rather than derivative and irresponsible terms. These latter Americans, like himself, are characterized by their creativity and originality rather than by imitation. They cultivate "blankness" for very different reasons: to expand their potential and enlarge their experience. Only capable of imitation, Milly lacks the means—not the money but the sense of responsibility and productivity—that for James should distinguish Americans.

Voids of Whiteness

In *The Wings of the Dove,* James develops a female model of racial whiteness in which the differences between "the American girl" (179) and "the London girl" (112) are voided of particularity. Milly Theale and Kate Croy appear as likenesses because Milly reproduces the form of identity used by the English in the novel. These people are known by positions they occupy and by categories into which they fit—like those "settled heads under which [they] may be easily and conveniently pigeon-holed"—rather than by any element of moral responsibility. According to this model of social position, people become interchangeable likenesses, in both their moral positions and their social positions.

In this visual model of identity, individual differences, made by positions, are limited to views. The views of an individual may be various, depending on the position of the individual and the position of the observer. Thus, in the opening scene of the novel, Kate Croy appears self-interested from one point of view and self-sacrificing from another. Moreover, these views are changeable because positions are changeable, and they are interchangeable too, for an individual may occupy multiple positions with equal claim to each. And all these variations contribute to the voiding of individual character.

What this system constructs for persons is no positive individual identity but individual identity as void and avoidance. The surfacing of identity provides "covers" for individual acts in the equivalence of multiple views of those acts. These practices are identifiable as necessary to the European construction of whiteness—as "everything and nothing"—in James's novel. Characters are individually absent from their representations of themselves. Yet their representations cover all possibilities of identity, so effectively screening identity as to rule out anything missing from the representation. Here the term "screening" means not obscuring but rather displaying a full range of possibilities of identity. In effect "cleared" by the blankness of representations that both cover everything and particularize nothing, characters reproduce covers for the purpose not of hiding but of clearing themselves. The emptying of motive allows for a clarity and openness of identity as well as for an impersonal identity, composed of sides that any of numerous persons can "take."

In *The Wings of the Dove,* James represents not only the reproduction of already-assimilated identities of equivalence but also processes of assimilation at work. As Kate and Milly practice the reproduction of whiteness, they bring to the surface and make evident both likeness and otherness. In their representations of each other, they produce an equivalence of hidden as well as visible character. Bringing the other's depths to the surface, each character also provides a cover for depths of her own character: her desire to take the place of the other. To detach the woman whose place she desires from that place, both Kate and Milly identify "other sides" to each other: some unseen aspect of the person, an aspect in shadow or partial darkness. Putting these other sides on view, Kate and Milly produce the other's otherness as an exchangeable view and thereby render it assimilable. Otherness is identified as "other sides" of a person and as such can be both viewed and occupied by multiple people.

Constructing Covers

The kind of coverage Kate Croy provides for her character in the opening scene of the novel is reproduced by her repeatedly. Making evident open views of her behavior while voiding herself of responsibility for any particular view, Kate returns from her father to Aunt Maud's house and provides herself with another cover, one that allows her to continue seeing Merton Densher, of whom Maud disapproves. Kate meets Densher in full view of her aunt's windows, where he habitually waits for her in Kensington Gardens.

> When, always, in due time, Kate Croy came out of her aunt's house, crossed the road and arrived by the nearest entrance, there was a general publicity in the proceeding which made it slightly anomalous. If their meeting was to be bold and free it might have taken place within-doors; if it was to be shy or secret it might have taken place almost anywhere better than under Mrs. Lowder's windows. They failed indeed to remain attached to that spot; they wandered and strolled. . . . But Kate had each time, at first, the air of wishing to expose herself to pursuit and capture if those things were in question. She made the point that she wasn't underhand, any more than she was vulgar. . . . The fact was that the relation between these young persons abounded in such oddities as were not inaptly symbolised by assignations that had a good deal more appearance than motive. (46–47)

Careful of appearances, Kate works to limit her meaning to looks, which afford complete coverage and keep her in the clear.

These assignations have more appearance than motive because there is no motive for them to occur as they do. If they were intended to be either "bold and free" or secret, they would take place elsewhere. But they can occur as they do for motives of neither boldness nor secrecy. Instead, Kate carries them off with "the air" of being open to capture if anyone wants to try it. She creates the impression of attempted pursuit and defies pursuit; there is no apparent reason to do so, for nobody is in pursuit.

Because the appearance she creates appears to have no motive, it allows no way "into" Kate; indeed, it suggests that there is nothing hidden within her, no interior motives or desires. She seems open about her own openness: careless and uncommitted. If she met Densher inside the house or in secret, she would seem to be taking a stand. But, from the beginning of the novel, Kate tends not to take stands. When faced, for example, with the need to decide whether to accept Aunt Maud's "intervention" in her life, she sees that such intervention is something "to be . . . either all put up with or all declined. Yet at the winter's end, nevertheless, she could scarce have said what stand she conceived she had taken. It wouldn't be the first time she had seen herself obliged to accept with smothered irony other peo-

ple's interpretation of her conduct" (34). Kate suspends decisive identification. She fits situations because she allows others to take her in
whatever way suits them.

Her "smothered irony" marks Kate's identity as distance: from
commitment, motive, desire, agency. Neither bold nor secret, under-
hand nor vulgar, she remains in the open, it seems, so as to remain
open to interpretation. As a model of whiteness, abstracted from inner
qualities, Kate's behavior produces an inclusive coverage of various
views that rules out individual particularity: the individual is always
detached from the aspects in which she appears and is never committed to or responsible for any particular aspect of her character.

A similar openness is displayed by Kate when she "confesses" the
self-interest of her own and her aunt's kindnesses to Milly Theale. As
in the park, she turns both her inside motive and her outside actions
to another's view. In this process, "she gave herself away . . . , and it
was naturally what most contributed to her candour" (168). Once
again characterizing herself by aversions—what she gets rid of or
gives away rather than what she wants—Kate turns aside knowledge.
And she precludes any other dimensions of knowledge, any depths
hidden beneath the surface, by emptying out interiors and covering a
complete range of character, from self-interest to self-sacrifice, on
the surface.

It is not surprising, therefore, that in Milly's eyes Kate Croy seems
extraordinarily able to "fit in." At a house party, where "she knew
people, and people knew her," Kate seems "a figure conditioned only
by the great facts of aspect, a figure to be waited for, named and fitted.
This was doubtless but a way of feeling that it was of her essence to be
peculiarly what the occasion, whatever it might be, demanded when
its demand was highest" (132). Milly identifies no basis within Kate
for the way she is seen by others. Her "aspect" depends on the occasion, and her "essence" is to fit the part the occasion demands.

What is going on inside Kate is and remains unknown. Her openness is her cover. Creating the illicit assignation open to detection,
Kate creates a crime without a motive and for which she is already
cleared. Unlike the unknown American individual that James discusses in his work on Hawthorne, Kate is unknown because she elimi-
nates individual character from knowledge. When James discusses
the difficulty of judging or knowing a morally responsible individual,
he argues that an American's judgment must be inconclusive. Be-

cause the means of knowledge—the terms, the types, the categories of representation and knowledge—are common, one must leave room for the ways that an individual differs from the shared or common terms of understanding. But if, for James, Hawthorne's inconclusive judgment of American individuals leaves knowledge open, Kate Croy is conclusively open. She puts an end to further possibilities of knowledge with a finished surface that is complete and inclusive in its representation of possibilities.

Kate's visualization of identity limits identity to views and aspects, surfaces whose multiple views compose character. There are no grounds for meaning here, or perhaps there are such "scattered" grounds as to rule out definition on the basis of grounds. This is suggested by the architectural figure James uses to represent Kate and Densher's relationship: "They had accepted their acquaintance as too short for an engagement, but they had treated it as long enough for almost anything else, and marriage was somehow before them like a temple without an avenue. They belonged to the temple and they met in the grounds; they were in the stage at which grounds in general offered much scattered refreshment" (52). Again locating her behavior somewhere outside definition, James suggests that Kate prefers to behave "openly" insofar as her relation to Densher can be taken "for almost anything else" but an engagement. "In the grounds" of the temple, they have grounds for a number of possible things. But "grounds in general" are grounds for nothing in particular. Because they desire to keep on such open grounds, Kate and Densher have no "avenue" to the temple, no way in.

Absenting Identity

Dependent for her own distinction on some distance between herself and others, Milly Theale not only travels in the novel but also absents herself from others who are present. She effects the latter kind of distance at her first dinner party in London, for example, when speaking to Lord Mark.

> She wished to get away from him, or indeed, much rather, away from herself so far as she was present to him. She saw already . . . that there would be a good deal more of him to come for her, and that the

special sign of their intercourse would be to keep herself out of the question. . . . This in fact might quite have begun, on the spot, with her returning again to the topic of the handsome girl. If she was to keep herself out she could naturally best do so by putting in somebody else. She accordingly put in Kate Croy. (107)

Here, Milly reproduces the move by which the English ancestors of white Americans initially distinguished themselves as Americans: she goes away. Desirous of a space between herself and the Englishman, she also reproduces the return to the English character that James, discussing Hawthorne, found necessary in order to distinguish the white American character. But James turned there to English and French characters to bring out American differences from them, as part of a process of discovery. Milly returns Lord Mark to the topic of Kate Croy so as to erase her own differences, to be "herself out of the question."

In her reproduction of the indeterminacy that effectively screens Kate Croy, Milly Theale adopts screens that obscure by their openness. Early in the novel, confronted with Lord Mark's interest, Milly uses Kate as a kind of screen. Milly eventually, though, represents herself as a screen. The most successful of the images and roles that she takes on effect a visible absence. One is the image of the dove. Another is the image of "a Veronese picture," probably *The Marriage Feast at Cana*,[12] which Milly reproduces in her palazzo in Venice and in which she appears "in a wonderful white dress," apparently as Christ (297, 301).

Both images identify Milly with the Holy Spirit; these white images of self-sacrifice also help to identify her self as absent. As a "dove," Milly positions herself according to a European code of meaning. Explanations for her behavior are then to be sought in the code, according to which she, an innocent and self-sacrificing person, is taken advantage of by others. Milly's body, which is possibly fatally ill, becomes the most effective screen for Milly's lacks because it seems to guarantee her inability to do anything about her condition. Like the grounds of Kate's temple, Milly's body serves only as "grounds in general," a material base for meaning that nevertheless determines nothing.

With her body and spirit emptied of any particular, determinate content, Milly's identity fully surfaces. Like lady copyists of Titians and Turners, Kate and Milly reproduce complete enough copies of other surfaces to obscure the inadequacy of the women capable only of reproduction; in fact, the merely reproductive woman remains completely unknown. Kate and Milly achieve this failure of recognition by producing themselves as open surfaces, without interior motives, and they try to keep out of interiors too. Or they may convert interiors into surfaces: When Milly remodels the interior of her palazzo in Venice so that it appears as a copy of a Veronese painting, she converts an enclosed domestic space into an open surface that, like a painting, has no inside and instead displays, as a cover, a complete representation. As when she "remodels" herself as a dove, the point is to provide coverage, in terms consistent and complete enough to explain or explain away anything in particular.

Employing images of whiteness with iconic significance, Milly may do no more than activate powers for which she is not responsible. It is not clear whether she means to exert power over others, given that her power accrues from the roles she plays. Milly's desire for power, one might say, is effectively whitewashed by her adoption of iconic imagery. James and Hawthorne produce the individual American identity as "a wonder and a mystery" by the moral responsibility with which they acknowledge his individuality. Milly Theale reproduces icons of wonder and mystery; individuality has nothing to do with them. They allow her to exercise enormous power over others but require the exercise of no moral responsibility. So Milly Theale becomes a cheap, female reproduction of the original American individual.

Reproducing Likenesses

Not only do they display covers, but Kate and Milly also reproduce the kind of occasion that allows for turning the tables. Thus they structure their relations to others in reversible terms, identifying "other sides" to situations and to people that limit difference to equivalent and exchangeable positions. As a result of this assimilation of otherness, Kate and Milly appear by the end of the novel peculiarly alike in their indeterminate, or "blank," moral status. It can be said equally of each of them that she appears innocent, seemingly having done nothing to hurt others, and that her innocence has contributed to the destruction of other people's lives. These two views of character span alternatives from innocence to responsibility, but the two views are merely alternative takes on the women, who remain in the clear because responsibility and innocence are mere aspects rather than internal qualities. The clear blankness of these white characters marks the kind of emptiness James identifies with racial and female assimilation.

The reproduction of likenesses that Milly effects as a copyist depends on the reconception of otherness as equivalence. When Milly visits Sir Luke Strett to learn his opinion of her medical condition, she is confronted with the particular problem of her life: that she "must make up [her] mind" to live and must "take the trouble" to do so (149, 151). When she leaves Sir Luke's office, she gradually reformulates her situation, which depends on her will, into one she shares with all the other people in Regent's Park.

> Here were wanderers anxious and tired like herself; here doubtless were hundreds of others just in the same box. Their box, their great common anxiety, what was it, in this grim breathing-space, but the practical question of life? They could live if they would; that is, like herself, they had been told so: she saw them all about her, on seats, digesting the information, recognising it again as something in a slightly different shape familiar enough, the blessed old truth that they would live if they could. (153)

Although assigned choice and will by others, these people find neither choice nor will inside themselves. Milly converts her options into a surface, a figure of speech in which the options are themselves convertible. The power of will to alter situation becomes a proposition simply reversible to the power of situation to alter will. For Milly, these then appear as "those two faces of the question between which there was so little to choose for inspiration" (156). Milly produces her likeness to other people by erasing will as a means of distinction. But will is not exactly erased so much as it is rendered no different from external situation.

Milly is inspired to take sides, one might say, only when she can thereby provide a cover that absolves her of any responsibility for doing so. The image of the dove, for example, provides a cover of innocence and self-sacrifice that blankets her with disinterestedness. Milly will use the wings of the dove, moreover, to provide a cover for others too. Merton Densher recognizes, at the party Milly gives at her palazzo in Venice, that she has provided comfort for all her friends.

> Milly was indeed a dove; this was the figure, though it most applied to her spirit. Yet he knew in a moment that Kate was just now, for reasons hidden from him, exceptionally under the impression of that element of wealth in her which was a power, which was a great power, and which was dove-like only so far as one remembered that doves have wings and wondrous flights, have them as well as tender tints and soft sounds. It even came to him dimly that such wings could in a given case—*had*, truly, in the case with which he was concerned—spread themselves for protection. Hadn't they, for that matter, lately taken an inordinate reach, and weren't Kate and Mrs. Lowder, weren't Susan Shepherd and he, wasn't *he* in particular, nestling under them to a great increase of immediate ease? (304)

Densher sees here that the wings of the dove make possible certain choices. One can ride on them or be under them. Such is also the case with the image of the "Eastern carpet" that occurs to Milly when she is feeling smothered by Maud Lowder.

Talking with Maud at a party, Milly becomes "really conscious of the enveloping flap of a protective mantle, a shelter with the weight of an Eastern carpet. An Eastern carpet, for wishing-purposes of one's own, was a thing to be on rather than under; still, however, if the girl should fail of breath it wouldn't be, she could feel, by Mrs. Lowder's fault" (134–35). Here Milly identifies two sides of a situation in which she is threatened with death but nobody is to blame. The image of the Eastern carpet, like that of the dove, is not identified as a means of flight but only as a means of cover, one that clears those on both sides of responsibility. The attraction of these images for Milly seems to lie in the potential turns of the tables they suggest. Viewed like the turning tables, the carpet and the wings are seen as surfaces that "make a difference" only insofar as people can position themselves on their opposite sides. Thus the value of the image is that it enables Milly to see her condition as a position and her position as reversible. Having felt stifled by Maud's carpet, Milly begins to turn the tables, not only on Maud but on other characters too.

With Kate first, Milly switches positions: "she would have something to supply, Kate something to take" (167). With Susie Stringham, after Sir Luke has visited, Milly decides "that she was going to be sorry for Susie, who, to all appearance, had been condemned . . . to be sorry for *her*. . . . She had . . . five minutes of exaltation in which she turned the tables on her friend" (240). And with Sir Luke soon afterward, Milly manages "almost to reverse for her their characters of patient and physician" (254).

Most emphatically, Milly turns the tables on Densher, who is sent to see her by Kate to " 'console her,' " as Kate says, " 'for all that, if she's stricken, she must see swept away' " (214). When Densher visits Milly, "extraordinarily, quite amazingly, he began to see that if his pity hadn't had to yield to still other things it would have had to yield quite definitely to her own. That was the way the case had turned round: he had made his visit to be sorry for her, but he would repeat it—if he did repeat it—in order that she might be sorry for him" (227). Yielding to pity, in what amounts to a pathetic neutralization of struggle, Densher becomes himself a pathetic person, even a hopeless case. If Milly "take[s] an interest" in him, she admits only to an interest in someone for whom "I'm afraid there's really nothing one can do" (257).

So Milly creates a situation about which nobody can do anything and for which nobody is at fault, putting Densher in the position she has previously occupied. She first identifies Densher as a hopeless case after meeting him with Kate in the National Gallery and inviting them to lunch. Kate spends this time obviously avoiding Densher; she speaks only to Susie Stringham. And this enables Milly to interpret Kate's relation to Densher as one of aversion.

> Little by little indeed, under the vividness of Kate's behaviour, the probabilities fell back into their order. Merton Densher was in love and Kate couldn't help it—could only be sorry and kind: wouldn't that, without wild flurries, cover everything? Milly at all events tried it as a cover, tried it hard, for the time; pulled it over her, in the front, the larger room, drew it up to her chin with energy. If it didn't, so treated, do everything for her, it did so much that she could herself supply the rest. (180)

The cover that Milly provides with her interpretation of Kate's behavior is, like the cover Kate and Mr. Croy produce in the opening scene of the novel, one of aversions. Kate appears to want to get rid of Densher, who appeals to Milly because she wants to avoid something too. She pays attention to Densher in this scene in order not to have to face Susie Stringham, who has been visited by Sir Luke and now knows about Milly's illness. Reproducing her avoidance and aversion in a representation of Kate's avoidance and aversion, Milly views Kate as a likeness of herself while also viewing Densher as another likeness of herself, from another view. Milly's ability to position people as likenesses of herself supplies the cover that voids them all of responsibility for how they are seen.

Identity as Avoidance

Milly and Kate represent not only likeness but also otherness in the reversible terms of two-sided surfaces. In particular, they identify an "other side" to each other so as to be able to see the self in the place of the other. Here again, otherness is assimilable once it is reconceived in reversible terms. When Milly meets Kate, she sees her as a type, "the London girl," which she has "conceived from the tales of travellers and the anecdotes of New York, from old porings over *Punch* and a liberal acquaintance with the fiction of the day" (112). Milly "placed this striking young person from the first in a story" (112). She breaks down the limits of type with stories of her own that concentrate on her lacks rather than articulating Kate's evident characteristics.

She imagines something missing, some hidden dimension of the other woman. "Milly expressed to Susan Shepherd more than once that Kate had some secret, some smothered trouble, besides all the rest of her history; and that if she had so good-naturedly helped Mrs. Lowder to meet them this was exactly to create a diversion, to give herself something else to think about" (112). Identifying herself as a diversion for Kate, Milly turns her own attention toward the part of Kate she imagines to be hidden from view.

Whereas the typing of persons depends on positive characteristics, it is by assigning absent elements to persons that the assimilation of types occurs here. As in a concept of whiteness that covers a variety of ethnic types, Milly's assimilation of Kate depends on absence. She must be able to imagine, that is, another heretofore hidden view of Kate that indicates likeness rather than difference. The likeness Milly produces lies not in a positive resemblance of persons but in their exchangeability. The other side of Kate that Milly imagines is not a particular aspect of Kate but a view of her in which she has no particular place.

Milly sees a shadow hanging over Kate. This "clear shadow of some probably eminent male interest, . . . from whatever source projected, hung at any rate over Milly's companion the whole week, and Kate Croy's handsome face smiled out of it" (113). When Milly learns that Kate knows Merton Densher, whom Milly has recently met in New York, the shadow over Kate becomes more distinct and more "exciting":

> Milly found herself seeing Kate, quite fixing her, in the light of the knowledge that it was a face on which Mr. Densher's eyes had more or less familiarly rested and which, by the same token, had looked, rather *more* beautifully than less, into his own. She pulled herself up indeed with the thought that it had inevitably looked, as beautifully as one would, into thousands of faces in which one might one's self never trace it; but just the odd result of the thought was to intensify for the girl that side of her friend which she had doubtless already been more prepared than she quite knew to think of as the "other," the not wholly calculable. It was fantastic, and Milly was aware of this; but the other side was what had, of a sudden, been turned straight toward her by the show of Mr. Densher's propinquity. She hadn't the excuse of knowing it for Kate's own, since nothing whatever as yet proved it particularly to be such. Never mind; it was with this other side now fully presented that Kate came and went, kissed her for greeting and for parting, talked, as usual, of everything but— as it had so abruptly become for Milly—*the* thing. (121–22)

Milly more or less consciously invents an "other side" for Kate, which is not hidden but "fully presented." Recognizing Kate at first as a sort of absent presence, Milly brings the absent view to light and even identifies whose view it is.

Milly will see this view repeatedly, even though she recognizes that she sees a "side" of Kate that may not be "Kate's own." In fact, she may be projecting her own otherness onto Kate.

> What happened was that afterwards, on separation, she wondered if the matter hadn't mainly been that she herself was so "other," so taken up with the unspoken; the strangest thing of all being, still subsequently, that when she asked herself how Kate could have

failed to feel it she became conscious of being here on the edge of a great darkness. She should never know how Kate truly felt about anything such a one as Milly Theale should give her to feel. Kate would never—and not from ill will nor from duplicity, but from a sort of failure of common terms—reduce it to such a one's comprehension or put it within her convenience. (122)

If on the one hand Milly identifies herself with Kate's "other side," she identifies only a superficial likeness. No depths of knowledge or feeling are entailed in her identification with Kate. Indeed, Milly seems to insist on the distance and "darkness" that separate them, and even to be offended by a failure of knowledge that she herself has intensified, if not created, in her imagination. Not only has Milly identified Kate as an averted presence, but she also sees the distance between them as owing neither to Kate nor to herself but as elements of their situation, in which there is merely a "failure of common terms."

Milly creates a mysterious side to Kate: not by producing an excess of scrupulous discriminations that the moral responsibility of a male American calls for, but by producing a void. Identified first as another side of Kate that Kate herself wants to avoid, the hidden aspect Milly imagines opens up a void as a dimension of Kate, a place Milly can then take. She claims Kate's "otherness" as her own, as she gradually puts herself in the position she sees Kate avoiding, as the object of Merton Densher's attention. Otherness becomes a turn of the tables, by which one can identify different views of a person. Though "not wholly calculable," that other side of Kate is an aspect Milly can see and, having seen, reproduce, because she has seen it as sheer aspect. As one view of many, this other side of Kate seems no particular part of her but merely a position; it is therefore reversible and exchangeable.

Milly will subsequently identify herself with such aspects of otherness as she first identifies in Kate. Thus when she confronts "the practical question of life," she can see personal responsibility ("I could if I would") as only one view of the situation. From the other side ("I would if I could"), which is also fully present, the first view is made indeterminate. She sees herself as she has seen Kate, as if in the shadow of some "otherness" that darkens what is present. And as she does with her image of Kate, Milly brings the shadow to light so that both views become apparent. This surfacing of otherness is crucial to the cover she is constructing for herself, because it identifies alternatives as parts, or exchangeable views, of a situation.

Kate Croy, meanwhile, has produced a similar construction of Milly. Kate represents Milly in shadow: " 'She doesn't see the future. It has opened out before her in these last weeks as a dark confused thing. . . . There's a shadow across it' " (213). This view of Milly, like the other side of Kate that Milly imagines, is a view to be avoided. But for Kate watching Milly, as for Milly watching Kate, this dark view is fully presented and becomes "*the* thing."

Having imagined this other side as void, Kate then clarifies it, using it as one definite alternative for Milly's existence. "She'll really live or she'll really not. She'll have it all or she'll miss it all. Now I don't think she'll have it all" (215). The incalculable consists of no positive identity but depends on the identification of a total opposition, everything or nothing. In effect assimilated by their identification as equivalent alternatives, everything and nothing, light and darkness, and life and death are voided of substantial differences. Having opened up another side, a void in which to position Milly, Kate is free to take the place she now occupies, and she works to become the rich heiress Milly now is.

By blanking out shadows, Kate, like Milly, "whitens" differences and effects a whitewash, too, of moral responsibility. Seeing everything in terms of two sides both opens up alternatives and renders alternatives reversible. Identity becomes indeterminate, suspended between two opposite ends of experience. Milly keeps reproducing such alternatives, but she is unable to produce any difference between them once she sees them as reversible. Their evident purpose is to provide not choice but a cover for the lack of responsibility that is the void of her own identity. Such reproductions of whiteness balk productive power; they empower nobody but reproduce persons in and as views whose power lies in their positions within a social structure.

A Masculine Model

In his preface to *The Wings of the Dove*, James works to distinguish his own productivity from that of Milly Theale. Negotiating a separation from Milly, once he sees her as dying, James also distinguishes the unassimilable from the assimilable white American by means of gendered differences. According to psychoanalytic models of psychic development, James effectively identifies assimilation as a female threat.

In James's preface, his own evasiveness about Milly's death marks a similarity between him and his evasive heroine that he works carefully to deny. He does so, in part, by arguing that his evasions and substitutions are required by his creativity. James remembers shifting his attention from the inevitability of Milly's death and his own "intimate relation to it" to "the interesting possibilities" that grew "roundabout" it (3), until he eventually recognized that a novelist cannot be concerned with dying.

> Why had one to look so straight in the face and so closely to cross-question that idea of making one's protagonist "sick"? . . . This circumstance, true enough, might disqualify it for many activities—even though we should have imputed to it the unsurpassable activity of passionate, of inspired resistance. This last fact was the real issue, for the way grew straight from the moment one recognised that the poet essentially *can't* be concerned with the act of dying. Let him deal with the sickest of the sick, it is still by the act of living that they appeal to him, and appeal the more as the conditions plot against them and prescribe the battle. (4)

When James averts his gaze from the dying Milly, however, he turns to look at someone else instead, someone whom he imagines on the other side of a medal.

> If one had seen that her stricken state was but half her case, the correlative half being the state of others as affected by her . . . then I was free to choose, as it were, the half with which I should begin. If, as I had fondly noted, the little world determined for her was to "bristle" . . . with meanings, so, by the same token, could I but make my medal hang free, its obverse and its reverse, its face and its back, would beautifully become optional for the spectator. (7)

Because of the "correlative" or what he also calls the "reflective" relation of his characters, James can start with Kate Croy rather than Milly. Having identified Milly and Kate as two sides of the same coin, they become optional, and James achieves freedom. "The medal *did* hang free—I felt this perfectly, I remember, from the moment I had comfortably laid the ground provided in my first Book, ground from which Milly is superficially so absent," and his own "free hand, in this connexion, was above all agreeable" (7–8).

It is understandably agreeable to James to exercise an option here, by which he enters into an exchange of one woman for another, the one being "half" of the other's "case." This exchange of parts makes possible, moreover, a series of displacements with which James "builds" his novel, thereby resembling the substitutions necessary, in Freudian theory, to the development of a healthy male ego. According to the terms of Freudian theory, the differences James indicates between his own behavior and that of Milly and the European characters of the novel identify him with substitutions necessary to language, law, and productivity; they identify the others with substitutions more characteristic of "balked" productivity, specifically with the perversions of fetishism. The norms of Freudian ego development, then, can be seen to buttress the racial / cultural distinctions that James denotes between his American self and European others.

In his preface, James recounts his writing of the novel and compares this process to the building of a bridge. With the metaphor of the bridge, James identifies his novel not only as an architectural construction but as one that did not go according to plan. The various characters who were to serve as "successive centres" of consciousness were planned, he says, to be "sufficiently solid *blocks* of wrought material . . . as to have weight and mass and carrying power. . . . Yet one's plan, alas, is one thing and one's result another" (8–9).

But if his novel did not meet his intent, James recognizes that the work of art seldom does fulfill its author's plan. Such cases as this are so "far from abnormal" as to suggest

> the "law" of the degree in which the artist's energy fairly depends on his fallibility. How much and how often . . . must he be a dupe, that of his prime object, to be at all measurably a master, that of his actual substitute for it—or in other words at all appreciably to exist? He places, after an earnest survey, the piers of his bridge . . . ; yet the bridge spans the stream, after the fact, in apparently complete independence of these properties, the principal grace of the original design. *They* were an illusion, for their necessary hour; but the span itself, whether of a single arch or of many, seems by the oddest chance in the world to be a reality; since, actually, the rueful builder, passing

under it, sees figures and hears sounds above; he makes out, with his heart in his throat, that it bears and is positively being "used." (9)

Linking mastery with substitution (of another object for the "prime object"), James identifies "the successive centres" that take the place of his central character as building blocks upon which his bridge is constructed. This bridge is actually built, however, on the illusion of supporting piers that carry the span of the bridge along a trajectory of successive displacements. The illusive "grounds" of this construction can be said to be a system of exchange that generates a line of substitutions, once James gives up his "prime object."

James depicts himself constructing a system of substitution that will carry him over the lacks—the death or castration—he first simply turned away from. Anika Lemaire provides a concise and useful summary of Jacques Lacan's theory of the [male] child's entry into symbolic exchange and acquisition of an ego.

> By assuming the Law of his father the child passes from the register of being (being the all-powerful phallus) to the register of having (having a limited and legitimate desire which can be formulated in an utterance) and enters into a quest for objects which are further and further removed from the initial object of his desire. Parallel to this, he follows a dialectic of identifications in which his Ego constitutes itself and in which the ideal of the self takes shape. We can see that it is in the transition from being to having that the subject's Spaltung is situated, the division between his conscious being and his unconscious being. The desire to be the phallus which is lacking in the mother, the desire for union with the mother, is repressed and replaced by a substitute which names it and at the same time transforms it: the symbol. If the Name-of-the-Father fulfills this function of symbolizing desire, if being "a" father henceforth replaces the desire for fusion, it is because the father reveals himself as he who *has* the desired phallus and as he who is able to use it in a socially normalized relationship.[13]

The possession of a means of representation and expression moves the child from being to having, from identification with objects to possession of objects.

If what the child acquires with the capacity for substitution and exchange is a capacity to distance himself from the mother, from parts of his own body, as well as from objects of desire, symbolic representation is a process of divisions in space that may be of as great importance as the inner splitting of conscious from unconscious experience. Possessing means of exchange, the male child is able to produce distances between what he is and what he has, between what he has and what females lack. Julia Kristeva theorizes that the primary fear that drives the child into symbolic substitution is not fear of castration but fear of abjection, a primary condition of undifferentiation from the mother. In this case, symbolic substitution would effect a separation from the mother, rejected or abjected by the child in fear not of castration but of "being swamped by the dual relationship, thereby risking the loss not of a part (castration) but of the totality of his living being."[14] In either case, the male child is enabled to change from a sense of being part of the mother to having something the mother lacks.

Unlike the two-sided figure of the medal, which is the figure James first uses to represent his aversion to Milly Theale, the figure of the bridge, also two-sided, does not function as a reversible surface but as a trajectory that can be used to carry weight over distances. A construction that enables movement from one side of something, such as a river, to another side, a bridge does not make the sides reversible but secures the distance between them while providing a medium that shifts the power of reversibility to those who use the bridge. The bridge is a means of changing sides, and the builder produces this means in order to control the difference between sides: by spanning them and by enabling a choice between them.

The female child, excluded from entering the symbolic, lacks that means of producing and securing distance from the mother. She is, moreover, as a female, coded *as* abject: lumped together with other women in cultural identifications. The male entity confronts the undifferentiated mother first with physical difference and then with symbolic mediation. The female entity confronts the undifferentiated mother with no means of distinction but the space between them. Identity remains a matter of location, as the gap between distinction and undifferentiation is experienced not as the gap between symbolic and real experience but as distance imposed between two substantially similar entities. The female, then, is more dependent for her own distinction on opening up space between self and other; she remains more dependent on open space for distinction than does the male, who has access to symbolic separations.

According to James's feminized depiction of whiteness in *The Wings of the Dove*, the London girl and the American girl are able to produce differences between them only as voids. James's bridge is a medium of symbolic construction that can be used to produce differences. Entered into on the assumption that he possesses that which is the "grounds" of exchange, the male's symbolic substitutions are a means of production grounded on the "capital" he possesses. For the female, whose body is identified as void, something exists in the space that the male economy identifies as empty. But she cannot build on or use the solidity of her body for exchange, because in the eyes of others it neither constitutes grounds nor has exchange value. The female characters of the novel, void of any means of production, reproduce only avoidance as the difference between self and other. Even when reproducing iconic identity, Kate and Milly do so as avoidance: using figures that denote emptiness or blankness rather than figures that denote positive constructs of identity. Feminine reproductivity yields no substantial difference, only voids, given that females are void of the means of constructing differences.

Female Fetishism

The peculiarly female character of the threat of assimilation and the specifically female concern with spatial distances from other females are indicated early in *The Wings of the Dove*. Both Kate and Milly make efforts to keep their distance from older women who act as guardians to them. In the opening scene, Kate offers to live with her father only because " 'I wished to escape Aunt Maud,' " and when her father refuses her, it is clear " 'that I don't escape' " (59). Living with Mrs. Lowder, Kate hides up in her own room, unwilling "to forsake her refuge" because to do so would mean "a surrender, though she couldn't yet have said exactly of what: a general surrender of everything—that was at moments the way it presented itself—to Aunt Maud's looming 'personality' "(36). Not only does Mrs. Lowder make Kate feel "that she might be devoured" like a kid by a lioness (37), but Kate's older sister, Marian, poses a similar threat. "Kate's most constant feeling about her was that she would make her, Kate, do things. . . . There were always people to snatch at you, and it would never occur to *them* that they were eating you up" (38–39). At this point in Kate's experience, she maintains her separate existence only by keeping within her room; otherwise, she feels that she risks being taken into these other women.

Unlike Kate, Milly Theale begins the novel out in the open. Free of the numerous limits put on Kate, who is burdened with poverty as well as a dependent father and sister, Milly, rich and without family, travels to Europe, goes walking in the Alps, then moves on to London. Her only companion is Mrs. Stringham, whom Milly had met the previous winter and who is more observant than Mrs. Lowder seems to be of a younger woman's need for "detachment" (86). Yet Mrs. Stringham's curiosity about Milly causes her, too, to appear a lioness after prey. "She had almost the sense of tracking her young friend as if at a given moment to pounce. . . . She struck herself as hovering like a spy, applying tests, laying traps, concealing signs" (83). Because Milly's perspective is not provided, it is unclear whether she feels from Mrs. Stringham the pressure Kate feels from Mrs. Lowder. But it is just after Mrs. Stringham follows Milly one afternoon in the Alps, when Milly goes for a walk wishing to be alone, that Milly suddenly declares that she wants to go to London and first suggests that she may be seriously ill (89–92).

Kate's and Milly's productions of distance between themselves and other women may extend to Milly identifying her own death as a means of resisting assimilation.[15] James thereby puts his "balked" American heroine into the theoretically peculiar position of a female fetishist. According to conventional psychoanalytic wisdom, women, because they have no castration to fear, do not practice the sexual fetishism that denies "female lack." But confronted with the threat of her own indistinction, a woman may fetishistically produce lacks to be able to see herself as a distinct entity.

Fetishism is a mechanism for visualizing what persons fear is missing. As Elisabeth Bronfen says,

> Above all the fetish is connected with sight, more precisely with the desire to deny that something is absent from sight. The trope central to androcentric culture for the threat of castration is the absence at the centre of feminine genitalia, its 'nothing', just as blindness, the fear of losing one's sight, and castration are conceptually associated with each other. Triumphing over this anxiety is always connected with making things present to sight.[16]

According to this model of visualizing something whose lack is frightening, the female may produce images *of* nothing so as to fend off not her own castration but her own assimilation. If the female fears not the other woman's apparent lack of genitalia but the other woman's apparent lack of difference from herself, what she makes present to sight is that difference, as empty space.

The woman confronted with the threat of assimilation may, according to James's depiction, construct a screen to mark a space between them: a screen that avoids assimilation.[17] Such screens work, as I have argued is true in the novel, not to cover up anything but to mark distances. They effectively empty the differences between persons as they represent difference as void; individual entities are distinguished by what is between them. Externally distinguished as either aspects or views, individuals can be turned, reversed, replaced; but, because they are mere positions, the differences between self and other cannot be bridged or closed. What James suggests is that such a screening of identity, if it maintains the distance between persons, works only by reproducing individuals in similar, empty, exterior terms, as apparent likenesses and equivalents. Thus, although assimilation cannot occur in space, it takes place in the reproduction of identities recognizable as no different from one another.

Symbolically equivalent, such individuals become, in the abstract terms of representation, indistinguishable from one another. Using iconic reproduction to represent assimilation, Milly avoids the responsibility and productivity that distinguish Hawthorne and James. She reproduces her whiteness as a whitewash and reproduces American character as a void.

Collective Whiteness in

The Golden Bowl

In *The Golden Bowl,* James is again concerned with the relations of Americans and Europeans. Adam Verver is a rich, middle-aged, white American, an art collector on such a grand scale that he is having built a museum, back in "American City," to house his works of art. At the beginning of the novel, his daughter, Maggie, marries an Italian prince, Amerigo, who has little money. Soon afterward, Adam, a widower, marries Charlotte Stant, a young American who was a school friend of his daughter and who, also short of money, has lived most of her life in Europe. Charlotte and the prince were lovers in the past, apparently unable to marry because of too little money; they become lovers again after they marry the Ververs. A fifth character, Fanny Assingham, an American married to an Englishman, is a friend and observer of the four principal characters.

I will argue that Adam Verver's art collection, a museum collection, functions as a model for an American "race" in *The Golden Bowl.* The museum collection is only one of several modes of Americanization in the novel that I will consider. But the Ververs' collectivity includes persons from a variety of places, with a variety of histories and with different experiences, too, of Americanization. This collectivity of persons is not, therefore, exactly identifiable as a race. It is a grouping that shares with other conceptions of the dominant, white population of the United States the sense that only "others," only persons not fully Americanized, are members of races. The racial and ethnic nonparticularity of this collection of persons can be identified as the blankness of racial whiteness, which does not appear to be a racial category.[1]

The "whiteness" of the collective American identity in *The Golden*

Bowl is the result of more complete abstractions of persons than occur in *The Wings of the Dove.* The Ververs' Americanization is a production of critical consciousness.[2] Rather than iconicizing identity, a process that fits persons into impersonal, conventional positions, the Ververs view individuals as media of identity. More abstracted from material identity than any image or representation, the recognition of persons as means of producing identity marks an increased abstraction of American consciousness and American nonrace.

Abstracted from their particular histories, individuals are subject, as in the earlier novel, to various views and seen in a variety of likenesses, but these views and likenesses, identified by individual consciousness, are seen, or imagined, at the same time. The result is not a complete identity; there is no definite "fit." Adam Verver, for example, sees in his daughter images of both "nymphs and nuns," two inconsistent types.[3] Because she fits both types, Maggie's identity is suspended between them; in part she appears a nymph, and in part, a nun. She also is thereby seen as some kind of relation between nymph and nun, for her identity has referents in both types. Identified as mediate relation as well as likeness, Maggie becomes in her father's eyes an image with multiple referents that is also, therefore, a link between types. Rather than assimilating types, such a view of Maggie increases the diversity of her identities by suspending her between types. She approximates the bridge with which James identifies the work of fiction in his preface to *The Wings of the Dove,* but she bridges more than two sides, or views, of identity.

Suspended between conventional positions and types and subject, moreover, to additional likenesses, as when her father recognizes her mother in her, Maggie is the potential means of connecting, in part, numerous images and types. Mr. Verver's consciousness is the medium in which this abstraction of Maggie occurs, and in *The Golden Bowl* the individual consciousness, as is true of the Americans James discussed in his 1878 work on Hawthorne, is a means of producing identity. Not only is the individual consciousness responsible for the indeterminate identity of other persons, but other persons, once identified as media, also produce different perspectives on other individuals. Thus Maggie, part nymph, part nun, part mother, provides a new angle on all these, as well as, potentially, a new angle on everything seen in relation to her.

According to the Ververs' experience, "Americans" are reconceived as parts of a new collective through a critical perspective that detaches them from their past cultures and identifies them instead in relation to other Americans. In a sense, "background" and history come out of the depths; the relations that constitute identity are located on surfaces, as persons remodel themselves by adopting parts of various models available. This diversification of identity is dependent on the groundlessness, the changeability, and the productive capacity of any particular view of any person.[4] Whereas the adoption of iconic identities in *The Wings of the Dove* enables individuals to exercise the cultural power of the icon, the Ververs' power in *The Golden Bowl* surpasses that of any icon to become the power of media: the power of means that include money but also ways of imagining, imaging, and otherwise producing cultural identity as cultural diversity.

Collections and Collectives

Resemblances between the Ververs' process of Americanization and a museum collection occur, first, in the detachment of individual "pieces" of a collection from their origins and cultural pasts. The abstraction of such works of art proceeds, Philip Fisher argues, in three stages. Objects are "silenced" as images of a culture when they are "stripped from their context (when the crucifix is taken out of the cathedral, the cathedral is taken out of the crucifix)." Then objects from other cultures, already mute because their cultural functions are alien or unknown, are joined to the collections. Finally, to these collections are added " 'modern' abstract objects, progressively 'absent' of images."[5]

This progressive abstraction of objects from their cultural and historical contexts does not aim at their individualization. Instead, objects become pieces of a collection, identified in relation to its other pieces. Fisher argues, more specifically, that works of art enter into relations of art history.

> It is essential to see that the "subject" of the museum is not the individual work of art but relations between works of art, both what they have in common (styles, schools, periods) and what in the sharpest way clashes in their juxtaposition. The single scroll in a Japanese temple, seen alone in the act of meditation, seen *at rest*, is an object, as

far as any can be, in itself. That we walk through a museum, walk past the art, recapitulates in our act the motion of art history itself, its restlessness, its forward motion, its power to link.[6]

Such a mobilizing of observation locates works of art on a trajectory, according to which they have no singular identity in space or time but are always projected for meaning toward other pieces.

Yet more processes of abstraction revise museum pieces into relations or media of art history. Not only are works of art pieces of a collection, but they also come to be constructed of pieces of other works. Thus many modern works of art are assemblages, or reassemblages, of pieces, Fisher argues, and their status as objects is further "weakened."

> Picasso's sculpture of a bull's head made from the seat and handlebars of a bicycle reassembles what had been up to that moment the assembly called bicycle into one called work of art, image of a bull. In the same act he admits that this assembly itself is one possibility and that the disassembly and future permutation of the parts exists as an element of the nature of the present work. The objects become restless and weak, imposing themselves on the stock of parts only feebly and at a felt distance from the matter. At first there is, in effect, a feeling of object loss, as though the world of actual things had ceased to exist but memories of things (like the bull in the case of Picasso) could be evoked out of combinations of scrap. But at the price of weakening the reality of any single precise object what we have done through the part system is to transfer the reality to the system as a whole and to the play of transformations and possibilities that it invites.[7]

It is the transformability or convertibility of parts and pieces of objects, in changing relations with one another, that becomes the most important component of such works of art.[8]

If the relations between works of art assume paramount importance, as they allow pieces to be, in part, transformed into one another, the visitor to the museum is encouraged to recognize parts of pieces in other pieces. To do so, the critical perspective of the viewer must remain abstracted from the object status of various "pieces" and able to consider them in detachment even from their own parts. For James, such an abstraction of consciousness from objects opens up various lines of reference for works of art, of which a historical trajectory is only one. Removed from their original cultural and geographical places, put together with pieces from other cultures and places, and subject, moreover, to rearrangement of position when on display, artworks in a collection have no fixed meaning, no depth of meaning, but also no single line linking them together and directing them toward a future. They can be rearranged and reinterpreted to mean different things by different people, and as various pieces are put on display and put into storage, relations within the exhibit change. In a sense, these pieces are also rearranged as people walk around them and look at them from different angles, seeing a number of artworks in different relations to one another.[9]

The "museum mentality" in *The Golden Bowl* is one of getting around—of moving around rather than moving only forward.[10] Mobility makes possible different views, which increases the transformability of works viewed, in that from different angles different parts may assume more or less importance. In his emphasis on "getting around," James suggests another modernist conception of the museum, which Beatriz Colomina discusses in her work on the architect Le Corbusier. For Le Corbusier, the museum is "obsolete as a nineteenth-century accumulative institution" because of mass media, which reproduce and publish images and descriptions of works of art. The museum, therefore, cannot contain even the artworks it owns and displays. Great art, dependent for recognition not on "mere documentation but [on] the classification of information," is located more appropriately in a filing cabinet.[11]

This displacement of a collection of objects to a collection of sheets of paper on file transforms all objects into surfaces and media.

> Le Corbusier's displacement of the museum into the filing cabinet, and of the filing cabinet into the mass media, is not just a displacement of one architecture, one kind of object for another, but a displacement of the whole institution of architecture, a displacement of all objects.
>
> What is at stake is the displacement of *interiority*. When Le Corbusier takes on the actual physical problem of the museum, he precisely undermines the traditional sense of enclosure, the boundary between inside and outside.[12]

Fisher points to a similar surfacing of art in the museum when he discusses the museum as choosing "pure path" over "rooms," with, for example, "portable walls that break and turn the path but never complete the archaic rectangles."[13] Colomina emphasizes less a trajectory or path of images in space than the multiplicity of views that open up. Both because works of art are reproduced by mass media and because their aesthetic value depends on classification in relation to other works more than on documentation of origin, museum pieces are subject to various, possibly a limitless variety of, views.

Classification places things in groups, and identity of type occurs in the relations identifiable among parts of a group. Racial classification can take place in ways parallel to arrangements of art exhibits. But in a museum, classes are subject to rearrangement, both when pieces are moved around into different groups and when individual pieces are looked at from different angles.

James's American Ververs depend on a parallel surfacing in their identification of persons as views. And they produce views as parts of persons, as of artworks. These views, collected together, produce no single type but various provisional types, as the viewer, or the mind of the viewer, moves on to different views. Identity becomes improvisational, made up of views as parts or pieces, but never a final or complete phenomenon. The "American" interests in *The Golden Bowl* identify the museum display with the production of relations and projections in space. It is possible to argue, following Colomina, that James identifies American productivity with media productivity: not with the production of objects but with the production and reproduction of views of objects, from variable angles.

But the Ververs' production of views and relations has other effects, crucial to a collectivity of Americans as well as to a museum collection. They collect both persons and pieces of art as they move around. Their ability to get around also enables them to get around certain obstacles that stand in the way of their collectivity. In a sense, it is the status of *objects* that is the primary obstacle, for objects must be reconceived as more unstable media to effect collective relations. The process of collection that composes an American "race" as nonrace in *The Golden Bowl* reforms persons so that they lose status as objects and become identified as the pieces, parts, and relations—the media—of a collection. These aspects of whiteness are visible, but not as material whiteness. They are the visibility that modernity has abstracted from material history and material bodies and reproduced as a comprehensive field of representation.

Getting Around

The central issue of the novel's plot is whether Maggie Verver can successfully separate her husband and Charlotte, who share a history as lovers. She finally does so, rearranging the lives of the two married couples accordingly. One inspiration or "model" for this rearrangement might be the golden bowl itself. The damaged bowl, glass rather than gold, is not of "museum quality" but nevertheless achieves a certain museum quality when it is smashed into pieces. Once broken apart, the pieces of the bowl have no identity as a useful object; specifically, they have no identity as a container that might hold anything. The disintegration of the interior occurs with the appearance of four pieces that, in form, have only outsides. These pieces are still displayed, though; Maggie picks them up from the floor and sets them on the mantel (451). Lacking contents, no longer holding meaning or anything else, the pieces can be moved around and rearranged. With much more surface area as pieces, the bowl is subject to a virtually endless range of forms, depending on how one chooses to arrange the pieces and where in relation to them one chooses to stand.

For Maggie to circumvent the obstacle that her husband's affair with Charlotte poses to her marriage and her happiness, she not only must separate the two individuals joined in the affair but also must convert them from objects defined by interiors into objects defined by their exterior surfaces. Maggie's recognition of interiority as the obstacle she faces occurs at the beginning of the fourth book of the novel, when she considers "the situation" of the life she shares with her father, her husband, and her father's wife, Charlotte.

This recognition occurs before Maggie knows that her husband and stepmother are lovers but seems to be an early stage of knowledge.

> This situation had been occupying for months and months the very centre of the garden of her life, but it had reared itself there like some strange tall tower of ivory, or perhaps rather some wonderful beautiful but outlandish pagoda, a structure plated with hard bright porcelain, coloured and figured and adorned at the overhanging eaves with silver bells. . . . She had walked round and round it—that was what she felt; she had carried on her existence in the space left her for circulation, a space that sometimes seemed ample and sometimes narrow: looking up all the while at the fair structure that spread itself

so amply and rose so high, but never quite making out as yet where she might have entered had she wished. . . . The great decorated surface had remained consistently impenetrable and inscrutable. At present however, . . . she had caught herself distinctly in the act . . . of stepping unprecedentedly near. (327–28)

Maggie's situation seems to "rear itself" as a "strange" structure when it appears to be not simply an arrangement of persons but an arrangement with an interior as well: a part from which she is excluded. The interior and the exterior estrange her, as Maggie identifies the structure with an ivory tower, an Eastern pagoda, and then, "by the distance at which it kept her, a Mahometan mosque, with which no base heretic could take a liberty" (328). Becoming increasingly specific in her identification of this object, Maggie also becomes increasingly specific about her estrangement.

Until now, Maggie has treated the imaginary structure like a museum piece, walking around it, enjoying its beauty. But here it is as if the museum piece is being returned to cultural origins, as it increases its distance and unfamiliarity. If in a museum, the insides of the structure would either be emptied or displayed; its surface would be identifiable in relation to other works of art. Both these surfacings of knowledge occur when the more experienced collector Adam thinks of a work of art. And Adam's way of seeing people *as* works of art in a collection is what Maggie will learn in the course of the novel.

As Maggie sees herself walking around the structure in the garden, her father imagines her as a figure walking around the outside of a vase. But the vase is for Adam a piece of art history. With no significant inside, its exterior is also subject to the classifications that allow a viewer to know it. In Maggie's figure, Adam recognizes

the appearance of some slight slim draped "antique" of Vatican or Capitoline halls, late and refined, rare as a note and immortal as a link, set in motion by the miraculous infusion of a modern impulse and yet, for all the sudden freedom of folds and footsteps forsaken after centuries by their pedestal, keeping still the quality, the perfect felicity, of the statue; the blurred absent eyes, the smoothed elegant nameless head, the impersonal flit of a creature lost in an alien age and passing as an image in worn relief round and round a precious vase. (172)

Displaced, blurred, absent, nameless, this impersonal image of Maggie places her in a kind of static motion, like the figures on Keats's Grecian urn: stuck in place and time even as she passes on, endlessly moving but getting nowhere. On the other hand, Adam's perspective here is that of not only an observer of the work of art but also a critic who identifies the figure in relation to pieces of art that came before and after the vase around which she walks.

As a critic, Adam's sense is comparative and is "kept sharp, year after year, by the collation of types and signs, the comparison of fine object with fine object, of one degree of finish, of one form of the exquisite with another" (172). From this perspective, the figure on the vase is set in a motion that gets somewhere, extending Maggie's meaning in relation to other figures. Seen as a link, as Fisher suggests happens in the museum, the figure is both infused by "modern impulse," freed from the pedestal so that her clothing and her feet appear to move, yet nevertheless like an ancient statue, "lost in an alien age," as she passes around the vase. A link between ancient and modern, in a "line" of development in which one thing leads to another, she moves forward rather than merely "round and round."

According to the detachment of the museum viewer, various relations among works of art take precedence over historical and cultural relations. This process of reorientation, moreover, makes connections that open up possibilities of meaning rather than narrowing down identity once various predecessors and types of representation are recognized.

> She had always had odd moments of striking him, daughter of his very own though she was, as a figure thus simplified, "generalised" in its grace, a figure with which his human connexion was fairly interrupted by some vague analogy of turn and attitude, something shyly mythological and nymph-like. The trick, he wasn't uncomplacently aware, was mainly of his own mind. . . . And what was more to the point still, it often operated while he was quite at the same time conscious that Maggie had been described, even in her prettiness, as "prim" . . . ; while he remembered that when once she had been told before him familiarly that she resembled a nun she had replied that she was delighted to hear it and would certainly try to; while also, finally, it was present to him that . . . she brought her hair down very straight and flat over her temples, in the constant manner of her

mother, who hadn't been a bit mythological. Nymphs and nuns were certainly separate types, but Mr. Verver, when he really amused himself, let consistency go. (172)

The "generalization" that occurs here allows Maggie to be likened not only to nymphs but to nuns as well as to her own mother. In this process of discrimination and classification, she enters not a line but an expanse of meanings.

Maggie herself becomes a collection or "collation of types and signs" which do not fit together with any consistency but which engage the viewer with several referents for the figure viewed. The types of "nymph" and "nun" are two referents for her image, and her likeness to them opens up an ambiguity about Maggie, moreover, that might generate more ideas and likenesses. Nymph, nun, and daughter of her mother, whom she both does and does not resemble, Maggie is seen here to take on not only a "wealth" of meaning but a means of producing more meaning still, because the comparisons of her with certain predecessors open up differences and likenesses. This wealth is produced in the medium of critical consciousness, then. It is subject to reproduction, and Adam reproduces many of the views he sees: from works of art such as Keats's poems, for example. Yet Adam produces means as well as images; the medium of his consciousness produces views of his daughter as herself a way of revising views of other things and persons.

Patchwork Race

Fanny Assingham is another American collector in *The Golden Bowl*, though of pieces less valuable than those Adam Verver collects. Like other characters, too, Fanny can be identified as a kind of museum piece. As Maggie is nymph and nun, Fanny appears to belong to various types, but she lacks internal depth or historical backing for her appearance.

Type was there, at the worst, in Mrs. Assingham's dark neat head, on which the crisp black hair made waves so fine and so numerous that she looked even more in the fashion of the hour than she desired. Full of discriminations against the obvious, she had yet to accept a flagrant appearance and to make the best of misleading signs. Her richness of hue, her generous nose, her eyebrows marked like those of an actress—these things, with an added amplitude of person on which middle age had set its seal, seemed to present her insistently as a daughter of the South, or still more of the East, a creature formed by hammocks and divans. . . . She was in fact however neither a pampered Jewess nor a lazy Creole; New York had been recordedly her birthplace and "Europe" punctually her discipline. (64)

Given this "disparity between her aspect and her character," Mrs. Assingham chooses to accentuate it. "It was her theory that nature itself had overdressed her and that her only course was to drown, as it was hopeless to try to chasten, the over-dressing" (64). With the apparent intention of increasing the disparity between aspect and character so that the two cannot be assumed equivalent, she treats the signs of type as effects she herself can reproduce.

The "type" that is evident in Mrs. Assingham's body is racial type, which is identifiable according to a process of abstraction similar to that of museum pieces. But racial type depends on abstracting from individual bodies a number of particular characteristics held in common by members of a race. According to this process of abstraction, "type" is a collection of attributes that defines a group. Nymphs and nuns are types, too, characterized by certain traits shared in common. For a person's body to be racially typed, one type must prevail in her or his physical appearance. But in Fanny's case such prevalence tells nothing about her origins or her character; her typical traits are instead "misleading signs." "Type," then, is present only as a construction of signs that refer to no background, origin, or "depth." It is a matter of arrangement and subject to rearrangement, cutting out and piecing, like dressmaking or, in this case, the construction of a patchwork quilt.

Mrs. Assingham does not overdress only her excesses; she also fills in certain holes—her lacks hardly show because they too have been "done over." But these "holes" do perhaps share with her appearance and her name a certain redundancy.

She had in her life two great holes to fill, and she described herself as dropping social scraps into them as she had known old ladies, in her early American time, drop morsels of silk into the baskets in which they collected the material for some eventual patchwork quilt. One of these gaps in Mrs. Assingham's completeness was her want of children; the other was her want of wealth. It was wonderful how little either, in the fulness of time, came to show; sympathy and curiosity could render their objects practically filial, just as an English husband who in his military years had "run" everything in his regiment could make economy blossom like the rose. (65)

Fanny Assingham makes do with substitute objects of filial concern and with economy instead of wealth. These "practically," over the "fulness of time," fill in the holes in her life. James does not suggest that Fanny actually pieces together a quilt but that she collects the scraps with which to do so. As a quilt these pieces would provide a cover: a patchwork of art—and an American form of art—that collects and arranges pieces of refuse. Both processes obscure the holes and are improvisations, making do with bits of leftover material. But so far Fanny has made do with merely collecting her scraps.

The "cover" Fanny puts on her "holes," therefore, is not quite that of a fetish object, a screen concealing a void. Her collection is a potential screen, but with "holes" still showing some, there is only partial coverage. Unlike the covers constructed by female characters in *The Wings of the Dove*, Fanny's collection of pieces does not cover the ground; it is always in process. If, ideally, a collection should be complete, with pieces representing all types and periods of art, this is never actually the case in a museum. As Fisher points out:

> Each museum is a fragment of one ideal museum. . . . [A]ll museums have gaps, the history each displays is a history with holes, and the public must fill those gaps with memories of other collections. The ideal museum would be at last the complete history in which the path would go from horizon to horizon, each picture answering the questions asked by its neighbors, each intelligible in the visible society of styles and periods.[14]

Fanny's collection of scraps and pieces, then, is like a museum collection; theoretically the pieces could eventually be put together into the complete cover a quilt provides, but, as it is, holes are still apparent.

If Fanny does not produce a cover, she, like the Ververs, produces an American identity *as* productivity. Rather than fitting together her excesses and lacks, Fanny's overdressing opens up more gaps— between aspect and character—after which her collection of "scraps" adds more accumulation to the picture, also without filling in gaps.

Working with "natural" excesses and lacks, she "regroups" her attributes so that they signal variety rather than type. This is a female form of American business, as busyness, and it is collection as decoration. Like a "busy" room, Fanny's body is decorated with lots of stuff. And she seems to accumulate only more: waves in her hair, weight on her body, "multitudinous" things and details.

> So she was covered and surrounded with "things," which were frankly toys and shams, a part of the amusement with which she rejoiced to supply her friends. These friends were in the game—that of playing with the disparity between her aspect and her character. Her character was attested by the second movement of her face, which convinced the beholder that her vision of the humours of the world was not supine, not passive. She enjoyed, she needed the warm air of friendship, but the eyes of the American city looked out, somehow, for the opportunity of it, from under the lids of Jerusalem. With her false indolence, in short, her false leisure, her false pearls and palms and courts and fountains, she was a person for whom life was multitudinous detail, detail that left her, as it at any moment found her, unappalled and unwearied. (64)

With all these falsities, Fanny does not cover up but produces more "misleading signs," as well as a wealth of details.

What marks Fanny as an American, however, are not these signs but her eyes. Their opportunistic interest in "multitudinous detail" contributes to the variety of her appearance, but they are not themselves a sign. Vision, as the most peculiarly American quality of Fanny and the Ververs, is a means of producing signs. But as a "view," Fanny's lookout has no particular contents. She sees many things, but the way she sees them—her means of rearranging and reproducing them as misleading signs—is not represented. Here James indicates what will become clearer in the case of Adam: that the quintessential American character is not visible or readable but blank, itself a medium of views and representations.

With her excesses, Fanny defeats type and demands to be identified in pieces. Both typing and discriminating—grouping together and distinguishing between—become matters of production and reproduction, resulting in numerous different possibilities. Like Adam Verver, a collector who "cared that a work of art of price should 'look like' the master to whom it might perhaps be deceitfully attributed" (144),

Fanny brings to the surface her collection of pieces, cuts them off from any historical or cultural depths, and identifies them as sheer image.

She thereby becomes, in effect, raceless. The opportunistic, energetic, Anglo-Saxon, Protestant New Yorker that she is but that her appearance belies is not identified as type or race. These characteristics are represented as invisible, for one thing. Sunk beneath the surface of her body, apparent only in the outlook of her eyes, Fanny's racial identity is replaced by a representation of race that allows it to appear as altogether a construction of signs. Like her "race," moreover, her "history" as it appears is a product of misrepresentations. With this identity, too, Fanny makes do. And she therefore indicates that American history is also produced as misleading signs.

According to the history reported in English society, the Assinghams' marriage was among the earliest matches between "American girls" and Englishmen.

> The pleasant pair had been, as to the risk taken on either side, bold and original, honourably marked, for the evening of life, as discoverers of a kind of hymeneal Northwest Passage. Mrs. Assingham knew better, knew there had been no historic hour, from that of Pocahontas down, when some young Englishman hadn't precipitately believed and some American girl hadn't, with a few more gradations, availed herself to the full of her incapacity to doubt; but she accepted resignedly the laurel of the founder, since she was in fact pretty well the *doyenne,* above ground, of her transplanted tribe, and since, above all, she *had* invented combinations, though she hadn't invented Bob's own. (65)

This laurel joins the other false things Fanny wears ("false indolence" as well as "false pearls"). Their "honourable marking" as explorers of a Northwest Passage, like the marking of her body as racial type, is misleading. But Fanny has "invented combinations" that give her some right to the title; she has been partially responsible for the prince meeting Maggie Verver. So the laurel fits to a degree.

Fanny's model of Americanism is patchwork improvisation. She makes do with what is available, as bits and pieces subject to rearrangement. According to a more conventional economy, what Fanny has to work with is "scrap." Like the "wretched refuse" welcomed to New York's harbor by Emma Lazarus's lines on the Statue of Liberty, the refuse Fanny takes up can be converted into a collective of "pieces" whose marginality or abjection is irrelevant to their new grouping. The legend of her past and her "race" are made up, as are the quilts, of bits and pieces fitted together, with the holes partly filled in with more combinations of scraps.

As with an American "nonrace," type is defeated here by the collection and abstraction of "scraps" from their origins. Because only marginal, either excess or lack, in those original cultures, the population of "wretched refuse" presents itself as atypical. Then, moreover, these scraps are pieced together with those of other cultures. If, in this arrangement of pieces, types appear, they are wholly unreliable as signs of any depths of meaning. Both types and histories become misleading signs: made up of bits and pieces that signal racial or historical origin no more surely than do works in a museum.

Race Effaced

As scrap and refuse, the material Fanny has to work with in her representation of her identity is more easily rearranged into new combinations because it is marginal to begin with. More "effaced" than museum pieces,[15] the "typical" American immigrant is identifiable as belonging nowhere; he or she is in a position of abjection regardless of country of origin. For James, however, abjection is not simply a nonplace of origin but also a condition of America, which remains, especially from an upper-class European perspective, "nowhere." Each of the five central characters of *The Golden Bowl* is identified as abject at some point in the novel. The images of Charlotte as an animal on a lead (523–24) and as an animal or prisoner in a cage (484) are the most memorable of these descriptions. But the most actively "self-effacing" characters are the Ververs: Adam, who always appears insignificant, and Maggie, who chooses to play the scapegoat.

Maggie is also effaced insofar as she is nymph and nun in her father's eyes; her individual history and character are wiped out not only by the types but by the ambivalent suspension of her identity between types. Both Fanny and Maggie, moreover, enact effacement as they assume humble positions in relation to others. For Fanny, the model for her own humility is the scrap used in the quilt. Maggie also uses a sort of junk—images taken from forms of literary "trash." Without a place in any museum or the equivalent collectivity of canonical literature, the literary types with whom Maggie compares herself, including gunslingers, settlers, frontier traders, and "Indians" (540, 549), are American images pulled out of their cultural habitats to be reproduced, in part, in the domestic relations of an American family living abroad.

In *The Wings of the Dove*, Milly Theale's marginality serves her as a cover. When she exploits others' tendency to discount her as "the American girl," she obscures her identity within a screen of actions that others can dismiss as familiar and as insignificant. The marginality of Fanny and the Ververs allows them instead to exploit the discounted images they reproduce. Whereas Milly uses icons already invested with enormous cultural value to serve her as cover, Maggie uses only bits of iconic imagery, bits often from trashy works in the first place. Dealing in iconic junk, Maggie exploits her freedom to do what she likes with material that has little value to anyone else. She reproduces these images and roles in pieces and new combinations that make them still less valuable in any existing market. But they enable her to explore and exploit ways of rearranging and reassembling persons in relation to one another.

Like the golden bowl, "stories of the wild west" (540) that Maggie draws on for aspects of her self offer means of "getting around." The situation that Maggie identifies as a pagoda or mosque is one that she can finally get around, perhaps, only when it is disassembled. Made of painted porcelain tiles, the structure in "the very centre of the garden of her life" (327) might be more valuable in pieces, such as the "extraordinary set of oriental tiles" (179), museum pieces that were once, or were made to be, pieces of something else, bought by Adam Verver in his only purchase of art in the novel (190–92). In the form of tiles, a medium of building rather than a building, the pagoda would become museum pieces without the interior that puzzles Maggie in the larger form, as well as without the surface or face of that larger form.

Such a surfacing and effacement of an object makes it subject to improvisation rather than knowledge, providing means of identity but no single structure or type of identity. Like the "misleading signs" of a quilt's pieces, such a medium is not a typing mechanism. Any grouping together of such signs is piecemeal, arbitrary, and subject to rearrangement. The improvisational character of combinations identifies typing as simply one possible arrangement. Unlike imperialist

improvisations that Stephen Greenblatt has analyzed in colonial ex-
pansions, whereby a culture's forms are maintained while their contents are replaced, with the effect of tricking persons into accepting
the imperialists, James's American improvisations have no content.[16]
Improvisation in a sense *is* meaning here; its mobility matters, but not
the particular meanings that are rendered mobile. Thus the expansiveness of the Ververs' American identity is identified by James as an
expanse of representation.[17] And the combinations produced by improvisation are highly abstract, like many of the patterns of American
quilts. Even if a particular "piece" has contents—as when later in the
novel Maggie holds up a book and feels like characters "in stories of
the wild west . . . who threw up their hands on certain occasions for a
sign they weren't carrying revolvers" (540)—those contents have extremely limited meaning and context.

It is only in Adam Verver that the purest, emptiest form of the
abstract American vision appears. Unlike Fanny or Maggie, Adam's
own figure is nondescript. He makes it so, James suggests, by calling
no attention to his body and always wearing the same style of black
and white clothing. Adam is identified as a view or an aspect not
because of his figure but insofar as the only marked characteristic of
his body is his eyes.

James describes the face as an empty room.

> His neat colourless face, provided with the merely indispensable
> features, suggested immediately, for a description, that it was *clear,*
> and in this manner somewhat resembled a small decent room, clean-
> swept and unencumbered with furniture, but drawing a particular
> advantage . . . from the outlook of a pair of ample and uncurtained
> windows. There was something in Adam Verver's eyes that both
> admitted the morning and the evening in unusual quantities and
> gave the modest area the outward extension of a view that was "big"
> even when restricted to the stars. (161)

According to this description, Adam's clear face is effectively effaced
as his eyes open it up into an empty room. With this "outward extension," the difference between inside and outside fairly disappears,
because the "interior" contains nothing and yet is all on his face.

The "clarity" of both surface and depths in this image erases any
difference between them, and both become, in effect, open spaces, a

pure expanse of view. In addition, Adam's eyes suggest the "ambiguity of your scarce knowing if they most carried their possessor's vision out or most opened themselves to your own" (161), so that the openings in Adam that his eyes represent allow for no containment but only movement. The direction in which movement occurs is less important than the openness to movement in multiple directions, and movement of a kind that translates part of the self into the outer world or allows part of the outer world entry.

Colomina's discussion of windows in Le Corbusier's museums and other modern interiors, in which distinctions between outside and inside disappear, emphasizes that windows become only views. "The house is not simply constructed as a material object from which certain views then become possible. The house is no more than a series of views choreographed by the visitor."[18] According to this reconfiguration, windows make possible various angles and views, but these views are all equally "flat" and reproducible, like pictures on a wall. They allow for the representation and classification of the outside world, as with a series of photographs, but not for any projection into it. In Le Corbusier's model, any view out a window is like a painting or a reproduction of a painting. Although James identifies a different convertibility between windows and views, he sees in Adam Verver that his eyes, as windows, are media of production.

James figures Adam's face and eyes as openings into expanses.[19] His vision is a view, like a painting, but it has no particular contents. It is as a medium that his view is represented, a means of entry and exit that enables light to be admitted and the view to extend outward. The view is a representation, then, but rather than the reproducibility of images, it is the mobility of spatial limits and the changeability of view that are evident. This view of Adam is image as sheer view. As sheer view, he is also sheer means of production. Unlike Fanny, whose opportunistic eyes focus on various things and produce a various cover, Adam's vision is a power with no particular objects—he produces means.[20] Making room for the collection and arrangement of pieces of experience, new "angles" on them and views of them, Adam's consciousness extends space, as in a museum, so that mobility can produce more views.

The clarity of Adam's Americanness is not a matter of whiteness, James suggests. Whiteness has content, from Adam's point of view, for he views whiteness as a faded collation of many colors.[21] Like Fanny, Adam finds a various and "numerous array" of objects, as well as persons, "appealing." Even when alone,

> he always figured other persons—such was the law of his nature—as a numerous array. . . . [I]t had never for many minutes together been his portion not to feel himself surrounded and committed, never quite been his refreshment to make out where the many-coloured human appeal, represented by gradations of tint, diminishing concentric zones of intensity, of importunity, really faded to the impersonal whiteness for which his vision sometimes ached. It shaded off, the appeal—he would have admitted that; but he had as yet noted no point at which it positively stopped. (129–30)

Insofar as Adam "figures other persons" as "numerous array," they not only appeal to him but also importune him. He wishes for the refreshment or relief of an "impersonal whiteness," while recognizing such whiteness as composed only of many, if faint and faded, shades of color. Whiteness becomes simply a view of colored persons, produced by detachment and distance. It is in his ability to produce the medium of such a view, the space between subject and object, that James locates Adam's own American character and his American power.

The Prince's Collection

Looking at Charlotte when, at the beginning of the novel, he meets her again in London, the prince sees the parts of her body as items in a collection of "relics" that he keeps in a cabinet. And as his eyes scan this collection, he first sees her body as, like Fanny Assingham's, excessive.

> Making use then of clumsy terms of excess, the face was too narrow and too long, the eyes not large, and the mouth on the other hand by no means small. . . . But it was, strangely, as a cluster of possessions of his own that these things in Charlotte Stant now affected him; items in a full list, items recognised, each of them, as if, for the long interval [since he saw her last], they had been 'stored'—wrapped up, numbered, put away in a cabinet. . . . He saw the sleeves of her jacket drawn to her wrists, but he again made out the free arms within them

to be of the completely rounded, the polished slimness that Florentine sculptors in the great time had loved and of which the apparent firmness is expressed in their old silver and old bronze. He knew her narrow hands, he knew her long fingers and the shape and colour of her finger-nails, he knew her special beauty of movement and line when she turned her back, and the perfect working of all her main attachments, that of some wonderful finished instrument, something intently made for exhibition, for a prize. He knew above all the extraordinary fineness of her flexible waist, the stem of an expanded flower, which gave her a likeness also to some long loose silk purse, well filled with gold-pieces, but having been passed empty through a finger-ring that held it together. It was as if, before she turned to him, he had weighed the whole thing in his open palm and even heard a little the chink of the metal. (72–73)

Here the prince identifies Charlotte in terms very different from those used by Americans in the novel. The initial terms of excess, for example, are simply put aside. Fanny Assingham emphasizes the difference between herself and standard types—the racial type of the East, the type of the Jew, the female type of the mother, the type of American who marries an Englishman; she uses standards and types to produce her difference. The prince has no desire to produce anything different when he considers Charlotte Stant's body. He is in this passage dealing wholly with "the already known" (72).

Therefore he simply asserts Charlotte's identity with certain "models": the beautiful workings of finely made, "prize" instruments; the beautiful bodies worked by Florentine sculptors. When Adam Verver sees Maggie as a nymph, such recognition opens up various possibilities because of the differences he also recognizes in her: the qualities of a nun, for example. When the prince sees Charlotte as various aesthetic objects, these are added to his list, which is both full and familiar. The pieces into which he divides her body are put back together and always add up to the same thing, like money in a purse, contained in his hand, then put back in a cabinet.

The prince's attitude toward the "pieces" he looks at, which he represents in terms of feel as well as usage, effectively reverses the trajectory of the Ververs' art into a museum. The prince's collection here is private, contained, and composed of "tools" with particular historical and personal usage. From the Ververs' perspective, the prince is a pure reactionary. He returns to history, particularity, and interiority the pieces of his collection.

Charlotte is studied in parts here, but she is also a "whole thing." As an object of the prince's gaze and his possession, she becomes, unlike the "weakened" objects that Fisher identifies with the modern arts of transformation and assembly, strengthened as an object. Her strength consists, however, not exactly in her wholeness but in the fact that she is only broken down into, on the one hand, "workings" and, on the other hand, pieces of money. She herself is not seen as transformable, but she is translatable, as a "whole thing," into a market commodity. Charlotte's body has market value as well as use value. Both dimensions of value depend on stronger objects than does the Ververs' critical reconception of objects as means of producing value. As an older type of object in the history of art, a tool with specific uses, or as an object with high market value, Charlotte is seen by the prince in terms that it became part of the museum's role to erase from collections.

The Prince's Interior

Prince Amerigo feels like a similar object when he is about to marry Maggie Verver.

> It was as if he had been some old embossed coin, of a purity of gold no longer used, stamped with glorious arms, mediaeval, wonderful, of which the "worth" in mere modern change, sovereigns and half-crowns, would be great enough, but as to which, since there were finer ways of using it, such taking to pieces was superfluous. That was the image for the security in which it was open to him to rest; he was to constitute a possession, yet was to escape being reduced to his component parts. (56)

One problem for the prince is that, as such a coin, his value lies only in his face and the "glorious arms" that are no more than a sign of his past. His value seems all on the surface. Presumably, the arms and face, as bodily signs, are "misleading"—that is, unlike Charlotte, he is not desirable because of the parts of his body. The prince here is not effaced, nor is he divided up into parts. But once taken out of the exchanges with which he is familiar, the prince is no longer sure how he is valued by others.

"All that *was* before him was that he was invested with attributes. He was taken seriously. Lost there in the white mist was the seriousness in *them* that made them so take him" (57). It is the Ververs' investment, not the object invested in, that is blank. What the prince feels from them is "not so much an expectation of anything in particular as a large bland blank assumption of merits almost beyond notation" (56). For the prince the Ververs' whiteness is not clear at all. "Who but a billionaire could say what was fair exchange for a billion? That measure was the shrouded object" (57). The loss of knowledge of, as well as the power to declare, his own worth leaves the prince not exactly in the dark but in a white blankness he identifies with death.

American whiteness is here again imagined as "everything and nothing." If on the one hand the prince is beyond valuation, on the other hand that blankness is terrifying. As if confronted with his own entry into a museum, the prince sees that his value is high but also speculative: as if a projection into relations that have not yet developed. For the prince, as is evident in the measure he takes of Charlotte, value lies in depths and interiors.

Moreover, he has a history. Like the Assinghams' legendary identity as "discoverers of a kind of hymeneal Northwest Passage" (65), the prince is a descendant of a "make-believe discoverer," Amerigo Vespucci, who "got himself honoured as if he had" discovered America, though he came after Columbus (95). Yet the prince's history is a serious matter of records and archives, "known, root and branch, at every moment of its course" (96). By no means understood as "misleading signs" by the prince, this historical record is as inherent in his identity as is his race. The prince's body does not signal his race; he looks "no more sharply 'foreign' to an English view" than "a 'refined' Irishman" (44). But his race is within him. Unlike the American characters of the novel, the prince contains his history, his race, and his "personal" self.

When he is about to marry Maggie Verver, the prince looks forward not only to her money but to the "vast modern machineries and facilities" involved in the production of her wealth (51). It is "his view of *that* furniture that mainly constituted our young man's 'romance,'" according to which he will obtain means of production and get rid of the superstitious sense of futility that is now in the air, an "exhalation" of the family archives (52). But because the prince's interiorization of his history and race is not merely a sense that they are within him but also a sense that they permeate him, as would a smell, they are not easy to get rid of or to cover up.

> He was intelligent enough to feel quite humble, . . . to warn himself in short against arrogance and greed. Odd enough, of a truth, was his sense of this last danger—which may illustrate moreover his general attitude toward dangers from within. Personally, he considered, he hadn't the vices in question—and that was so much to the good. His race, on the other hand, had had them handsomely enough, and he was somehow full of his race. Its presence in him was like the consciousness of some inexpugnable scent in which his clothes, his whole person, his hands and the hair of his head, might have been steeped as in some chemical bath; the effect was nowhere in particular, yet he constantly felt himself at the mercy of the cause. He knew his antenatal history, knew it in every detail, and it was a thing to keep causes well before him. (51–52)

Here race lies in the parts of a person, but inseparably so, as an infusion. Fanny Assingham's body gives multiple racial "effects." The "effect" of the prince's race, however, is "nowhere in particular," and he is "placed" by something unlocatable, "like the consciousness of some inexpugnable scent." Not subject to rearrangement or redecoration with new furniture, as these would not affect the quality of the air, the prince's interior is not open to change.

Amerigo's sense not only of essences within him but also of interiors in general is the most marked characteristic of his thinking. He speaks of " 'two parts of me' ": " 'One is made up of the history, the doings, the marriages, the crimes, the follies, the boundless *bêtises* of other people . . . as public as they're abominable,' " and the other is " 'my single self,' " a " 'personal quantity' " (47). This latter part of him seems to the prince repeatedly unappreciated or unrecognized by those around him. His experience of English society is unsatisfactory because he feels "left out," but what is left out is an inner self.

There is only one person with whom the prince feels "a congruous whole" rather than "cut in two," and this is Charlotte, now Mrs. Verver (270). It is not only that Charlotte knows him from the past, has lived in Italy, and speaks Italian as if it were "in her blood" (79), but also that she herself is something whose parts the prince takes pleasure *in*. For the prince, parts of Charlotte are enclosed within other parts—parts of her body in her clothes, like money inside a purse, and all also pieces he can hold in his hands. His knowledge of her is based on control over entrance and egress, into and out of her body as well as the purse and the cabinet. Like the "part of his mind" he retreats into when weekending with the English upper class (270), Charlotte's body is something he can return into and keep back in an enclosed space that is his own.

American History

Unlike the Ververs, the prince conceives of Americanization in historical terms. The difficulties that confront him in his romantic quest for a new history include his old history as well as the Americans on whom his new history will depend. His difficulties are also internal: the prince does not understand "the motives of such people" (55–56); he neither sees the causes of the Ververs' behavior nor is clear about what they want from him.

Identifying their impenetrability with a blank whiteness, the prince recalls another American romance that suggests an image for his experience.

> He remembered to have read as a boy a wonderful tale by Allan Poe, his prospective wife's countryman . . . : the story of the shipwrecked Gordon Pym, who, drifting in a small boat further toward the North Pole—or was it the South?—than any one had ever done, found at a given moment before him a thickness of white air that was like a dazzling curtain of light, concealing as darkness conceals, yet of the colour of milk or of snow. There were moments when he felt his own boat move upon some such mystery. The state of mind of his new friends, including Mrs. Assingham herself, had resemblances to a great white curtain. He had never known curtains but as purple even to blackness—but as producing where they hung a darkness intended and ominous. (56)

Poe's white curtain is for the prince an image of the obscurity of the Ververs' behavior and their understanding, particularly the "large bland blank assumption of merits almost beyond notation" (56) that characterizes their treatment of him.

Later in the novel, the prince will sharpen this image and see the Ververs' white, impenetrable blankness as innocence, both the innocence of children and that of Eden. By doing so, he is also able to define more sharply his own identity, although because this process of definition is one of contrast he must resume the darkness of his previous history. To clarify the romantic dimensions of this reversion, I want to look at the scene in which the prince justifies his adultery with Charlotte, now married to Adam Verver, by viewing himself as having been not cuckolded but in effect castrated by his wife.

Having traveled with Charlotte for a weekend visit to Matcham, the prince feels "ridiculous." But "it had taken poor Maggie to invent a way so extremely unusual" to make her husband ridiculous. Because she has repeatedly "thrust" him together with Charlotte while clearly assuming their relationship to be innocent, Maggie, the prince thinks, has "seemed to publish one as idiotic or incapable": "as if a galantuomo [gentleman], as *he* at least constitutionally conceived galantuomini, could do anything *but* blush to 'go about' at such a rate with such a person as Mrs. Verver in a state of childlike innocence, the state of our primitive parents before the Fall" (275). Identifying "poor Maggie" as abject in her very "innocence," the prince shifts shame from knowledge to innocence and identifies knowledge as what he cannot afford to lose.

His adultery is thus where the prince locates his distinction, as an item excluded from the Ververs' big, blank assumption of merit. And he thereby consigns Maggie, instead of himself, to blankness. Having resumed the role of Prince of Darkness, Amerigo seems to have ruined his romantic chances for a new history, yet he nevertheless offers the Americans of the novel a revised romance in which they become innocent. As Toni Morrison has argued in *Playing in the Dark,* nineteenth-century white Americans could imagine themselves as new and innocent by means of reproducing, in literature such as Poe's story of Gordon Pym, a haunting darkness that was both Gothic and Africanist in character: "The slave population, it could be and was assumed, offered itself up as surrogate selves for meditation on problems of human freedom, its lure and its elusiveness. This black population was available for meditations on terror—the terror of European outcasts, their dread of failure, powerlessness, Nature without limits, natal loneliness, internal aggression, evil, sin, greed." With its capacity to absorb displaced internal conflicts, the "construction of blackness *and* enslavement" became the locus of "not only the not-free but also, with the dramatic polarity created by skin color, the projection of the not-me."[22] Such a transference is not quite what happens once James's prince, having jettisoned his history and feeling "terribly afraid" (58), begins his romance with America. But something similar occurs.

Settling in England rather than North America, the prince thinks himself unappreciated by both the Americans among whom he has married and the English among whom he lives. Feeling "cut in two" by English society and castrated by Maggie, the prince retrieves a sense of wholeness only by recovering the "darkness" he wished earlier to leave behind—the arrogance and greed that were the vices of his ancestors. Playing the part of the wicked, reactionary, Catholic, and southern aristocrat in a Gothic romance, the prince recovers dark-ness to achieve definition against the blank whiteness of the Ververs. By so doing, he causes the Ververs to recover that "blank whiteness," the innocence that seems much more evident against a European background than on home ground.

Such a romance effectively reverses the racial dynamics that con-stitute Morrison's American Africanism but provides the same kind of relief for those who practice it. If Poe's story of Gordon Pym dis-covers a blank whiteness only in contrast to blackness, Prince Ame-rigo's Gothic romance discovers a blank innocence for white Ameri-cans in his own need for definition. In both cases, a polarized, "black and white" set of distinctions is employed for the sake of clear defini-tion. Certain people are thrown out into a heap of abject forms, suffi-ciently indistinct as to provide a blank ground, against which the forms of the remaining persons stand out. The sharp distinctions can be gained not only by distinctions of color but also by distinctions of form, depending on the distances between persons in the background and persons in the foreground of any "view" of a group. The prince is thereby relieved of the threat of assimilation, as well as the castration and death that he associates with assimilation.[23]

The Ververs, however, do not see themselves as innocent, nor do they consider whiteness to be a blank or colorless phenomenon. The prince does not see himself as ever being assimilated into American whiteness.[24] From Maggie's vantage point, however, he may be, al-though she does not view assimilation into whiteness as what oc-curs in the process of Americanization. Amerigo's understanding of Americanization as an experience of loss is countered by the Ververs' experience of Americanization as constant productivity.

The abjection feared by the prince occurs, as Maggie sees it. Once she has told him that she knows about his affair with Charlotte, Maggie approves of the "polished . . . surface" the prince wears as the "one way in which a proud man reduced to abjection could hold himself" (483). From the prince's point of view, his good form functions as a cover, hiding his abjection within a beautiful exterior. But for Maggie, it is the relation of pride and abjection that is valuable; she sees both in him, as her father sees nymph and nun in her. "To make sure of it—to make sure of the beauty shining out of the humility and of the humility lurking in all the pride of his presence—she would have gone the length of paying more yet" (483). According to this description, the prince may retain a sense of his interior and exterior while Maggie sees both together, in ambiguous, inseparable relation. This is suggested again, I think, at the end of the novel, when she feels "pity and dread" when left alone with him (580). Rather than love fixed on an object, Maggie's feelings are suspended, traveling in two directions, in what may be considered a richer "collective" of feeling and potential feeling.

Assimilating Jews

In *The Golden Bowl* it is not only the "dark" prince but also Jewish characters who seem to resist the transcendent transformations of American whiteness. Fanny Assingham produces "misleading signs" that she is Jewish, with "[eye]lids of Jerusalem" marking her piecemeal and self-produced racial nonidentity. But Jewish characters in this novel are limited to conventional reproductions and exchanges of objects. They therefore seem able to reproduce only conventional and bodily signs of racial identity.

Both Sara Blair and Jonathan Freedman have discussed James's identification of Jewish characters with forms of representation and reproduction that he deemed threatening. Blair suggests that Jewish Americans in *The American Scene* produce "the very 'convertibility' of cultural identity" that James "fantasizes for his own performances." James differentiates himself from them by marking Jewish reproduction as excessive.[25] Freedman considers the position of Jews in *The Golden Bowl* in the context of late-nineteenth-century discussions of racial degeneracy and regeneracy.[26] He also argues that James identi-

fies Jews with excesses, particularly with "unchecked sexual reproduction" and "cultural reproduction." The "circulation of cultural
artifacts" in the novel is "subtended by and wrought through the
relentless power of capitalist exchange that it is the Jew's role here (as
throughout history) to embody and that it is Adam's role here to
harness and exploit."[27]

It is in the family of Mr. Gutermann-Seuss, the Jewish art dealer
from whom Adam Verver buys the Damascene tiles, that James most
clearly "embodies" reproduction. The effect is an obvious sameness;
all the family members look alike. In the eleven children, with "eleven
little brown clear faces, yet with such impersonal old eyes astride of
such impersonal old noses," and in "the fat ear-ringed aunts and the
glossy cockneyfied, familiar uncles, inimitable of accent and assumption" (190), is evident no particularity except of family or type: with
faces, eyes, and noses, for example, shared by all of them. Only some
of their features are physical, but it is the culturally reproduced characteristics—"accent and assumption"—that James insists are "inimitable." If these people are "inimitable" as a group, it would seem that
only those within the group can reproduce its characteristics. The
term suggests not that such features cannot be reproduced but that no
one would choose to do so. Both bodily and cultural characteristics
here are limited to "familiar" relations, those primarily of sameness.

The nameless shopkeeper in Bloomsbury, on the other hand, among
whose goods is the golden bowl, apparently has no noticeable physical features. The way he looks at Charlotte and Amerigo, with "an
extraordinary pair of eyes," is his most marked characteristic (113). As
a "type," this man interests Charlotte "partly because he cared so for
his things, and partly because he cared—well, so for *them*" (114). Maggie, too, will later say that " 'he took an interest in me' "; she " 'can
only think of him as kind' " (460). It is Prince Amerigo who does not
see anything interesting in the man. In fact, the prince does not notice
him at all: "Below a certain social plane, he never *saw*. One kind of
shopman was just like another to him" (114).

If to the prince "they all look alike," this is at first not a matter of
race but class; "he imaged them no more than if his eyes acted only for
the level of his own high head" (114). Later he types the man by moral
and racial slurs, dismissing him more actively: " 'that rascal,' " " 'a
horrid little beast,' " and " 'the little swindling Jew' " (122, 460, 292).
As when the prince dismisses the Ververs by typing them as innocent

children, he seems to feel pressures of assimilation from the shopkeeper. This accords with the way the shopkeeper, Charlotte says, has watched his customers: "that way of saying nothing with his lips when he's all the while pressing you so with his face, which shows how he knows you feel it" (114–15). This intensification of pressure threatens with knowledge as well as demand.

Freedman argues that the shopkeeper "serve[s] as the benchmark against which the assimilation of Amerigo [by Anglo-Saxons] is measured." The dealer redeems himself by confessing to Maggie that the golden bowl, which she has bought, is damaged and by offering to take it back. His "repentance" and confession thus serve as a model of conversion for her husband, who has also sold her damaged goods.[28] Yet the threat of assimilation, I think, does not extend to the American Ververs or to Fanny Assingham, all of whom exercise choice as a means of producing differentiation. Assimilation is a possibility that James limits to characters who do not choose to produce their differences from others.

When he returns to see Maggie, the shopkeeper exposes not only himself but also her husband as a cheat. His implicit conversion is made dubious by the fact that as he redeems himself, he betrays someone else. Given the prince's treatment of the shopkeeper, this is no more than a just return. But the principle of an eye for an eye is as much in evidence as is redemption. Yet if the shopkeeper's betrayal of the prince to Maggie appears to be age-old cultural practice, he reproduces this return only with the same consistency as does the prince. The very betrayal, that is, is another mark of similarity between these men.

Not knowing how the Ververs measure his worth, the prince from the beginning of the novel wishes to distinguish himself from their "large bland blank assumption of merit." In the face of Maggie's assumption that he can be trusted not to commit adultery, the prince claims adultery as his means of fending off castration. The shopkeeper also seems to take the prince's measure: when, in his shop, he suddenly speaks Italian, he threatens Amerigo with his knowledge of Amerigo's relationship with Charlotte, for Amerigo and Charlotte, speaking in Italian, have assumed that "their foreign tongue covered what they said" (116). Speaking the language of their cover, the shopkeeper threatens a kind of assimilation through his familiarity. His manner is otherwise somewhat familiar too, as he makes assumptions about Charlotte and the prince: for example, that they are married. The shopman's familiarity, unlike that of the Gutermann-Seuss family, is not biological or material; it is less contained, therefore, as it extends into exchanges of goods. It may, however, be a cultural reproduction, according to a stereotype that James corroborates by identifying both the Gutermann-Seuss uncles and the shopkeeper as "assuming" in their manners. Indeed, as a stereotype this familiarity may be reproduced in them, or it may be reproduced only in the eyes of those who observe them. James does not represent how the Jewish characters view themselves.

This threat of familiarity felt by the prince can do nothing but increase if he recognizes that, particularly because of his renewed and secret relationship with Charlotte, he is offering himself to the Ververs as damaged goods at a high price. The shopkeeper, in his discussion with Charlotte about whether the golden bowl can be given in good faith or is simply a bad bargain, brings into open discussion issues that the prince keeps to himself. And in doing so the shopkeeper threatens to expose still other covers.

Prince Amerigo is himself like the aesthetic objects in the novel that Freedman identifies as spoils of empire. Valued as signs of empire, such "spoils" are leftovers, cut off from the cultural context of their production and identified as signs of a past otherwise lost. Such commodities, like antiques, are at least supposed to be inimitable. The prince, however, reproducing the arrogance, greed, and, more self-consciously, the betrayals characteristic of his ancestors, experiences these attributes as imitable. Indeed, they are *only* imitable, in that they are no longer reproduced as part of any culture but are adopted by the Prince to mark his value.

In the market of rare antique objects, imitation spoils value. This double bind is one the prince never overcomes, and it is a double bind that James identifies for any American immigrant who attempts to retain a past cultural identity by means of reproduction. To reproduce the "inimitable" characteristics of race is to identify race as a matter of choice without taking responsibility for the choice. Moreover, the prince's reproduction of ancestral attributes denotes him as a reproducible likeness, and he is thereby liable to constant threats of assimilation. These he fends off by means of racism and other typings of persons. He produces an assimilation among others that allows him, by contrast, to appear distinct.

Racial identity and type begin to appear as representations of persons that assimilate persons. They do so insofar as they preclude choice. Once the prince claims his identity with his family and race, he can believe he has no choice in his actions but is determined by his history. The Jewish characters in the novel are also assimilated by the ways in which they appear to preclude choice. The relatives of Mr. Gutermann-Seuss are seen to be both similar and beyond choice in two senses. Their bodily reproduction of signs, which are not in their case misleading, and their cultural reproduction of attributes that others deem "inimitable" limit them to familiar likenesses. Whether the aunts and uncles copy their attributes consciously or unconsciously is never indicated, which only reinforces the sense that among these characters choice cannot be discerned. The shopkeeper whose "coercive" gaze (113) pressures his customers is assimilated, like the Gutermann-Seuss family, to stereotype, just as his coercive manner is aimed at assimilating others to his demands.

These characters are both assimilated and assimilating. Given James's representations, they can be seen as inimitable—that is, identified as a race—only by the exercise of choice, just as they can be seen as imitable only by the exercise of choice. Choice is necessary both to racial identity and to the identification of personal attributes that individuals choose. Here James reproduces what he depicts Maggie reproducing in her victory over Charlotte late in the novel: "The great thing was to allow her, was fairly to produce in her, the sense of highly choosing" (539). Coerced yet chosen, James's American identity as choice appears to suspend the differences between assimilation and difference, coercion and choice.

Americans

According to James's 1878 discussion of the morally responsible American character, a character, I believe, he continues to produce in *The Golden Bowl*, self-conscious and responsible Americans identify each other by conscientious discriminations that, though certainly subject to reproduction, arrive at no definite identification. To some extent identity remains blank, and although blanks can be repeatedly reproduced, their contents cannot be equated, and they cannot be reproduced as determinate.

This openness of identity is emphatic in *The Golden Bowl* because Adam produces space as the most crucial means of identity. Adam's image of the prince, therefore, is an architectural exterior that allows Adam room to maneuver, just as his image of his relationship with Maggie is an open space. "At first, . . . their decent little old-time union, Maggie's and his own, had resembled a good deal some pleasant public square, in the heart of an old city, into which a great Palladian church, say—something with a grand architectural front—had suddenly been dropped; so that the rest of the place, the space in front, the way round, . . . had been temporarily compromised" (135). Eventually, however, "the sky had lifted, the horizon receded, the very foreground itself expanded" (135). "The limit stood off, the way round was easy," and "the Prince, for his father-in-law, while remaining solidly a feature, ceased to be at all ominously a block" (136).

What Adam produces here, in his view of the prince, is space, "air that had cleared and lightened," with "wider perspectives and large waiting spaces" (135). Space is the medium of views, and this description indicates the circulation in space that provides Adam with both room to maneuver and more views. He is able to produce his means of circulation, open space, because of the distance with which his critical consciousness views things.

Adam Verver is no innocent. He has made it his business, as a collector of art, "to rifle the Golden Isles" (140). Whereas the prince feels like Poe's Pym, Adam compares his experience, again using a piece of Keats's poetry, with that of "stout Cortez in the presence of the Pacific."

> [Keats's sonnet] consorted so with Mr. Verver's consciousness of the way in which at a given moment he had stared at *his* Pacific that a couple of perusals of the immortal lines had sufficed to stamp them in his memory. His "peak in Darien" was the sudden hour that had transformed his life, the hour of his perceiving with a mute inward gasp akin to the low moan of apprehensive passion that a world was left him to conquer and that he might conquer it if he tried. (139)

Putting himself in the place of the European explorer and exploiter, Adam Verver is a conqueror in his views. Adam remembers Keats's poem for its vision, whereas the prince remembers Poe's story for its obscurity. The two characters' different capacities for perception are due to the very different demands they make on the objects they look at.

It is as an expanse, like the expanse of the Pacific or of the American frontier, that Adam repeatedly looks at things. According to this "outlook," he recognizes the world around him as potential for movement. Both expanses suggest distance more than any particular form of expansion. The ocean is an image that does not suggest an expanse of anything—ground, wealth, possessions—so much as one over which greatly extended motion can occur. These expanses always signal something other than pure distance: another side to the ocean, another world beyond the frontier. But they remain pure exterior, pure outside, signaling room to maneuver—room to get around—more than any object or objective.

The Ververs' productivity ranges beyond the reproduction and circulation of objects to become a circulation that produces views. Though they collect objects, it is they, not their objects, that circulate. In Maggie this is evident near the end of the novel. The most effective assemblage of iconic junk that she imagines is her idea of her place more as a post: "a post of the kind spoken of as advanced—with which she was to have found herself connected in the fashion of a settler or a trader in a new country; in the likeness even of some Indian squaw with a papoose on her back and barbarous beadwork to sell. Maggie's own, in short, would have been sought in vain in the most rudimentary map of the social relations as such" (549). These images are unlike the icons sold by European dealers that Freedman identifies as "detritus of empire."[29] They are not objects, for one thing. Moreover, imagined as parts of the social relations on a frontier, these likenesses mark the border at which empire "advances."

At the border, Maggie imagines not only the traders but also the settlers and the "Indian squaw" trading. Though reproduced, probably from literature or prints, these images are collected with an effect of perpetual displacement and exchange, from various views.[30] Maggie's views suggest, then, that she deals in novel productions rather than with what empire leaves behind. As a vision of American "whiteness," this imagery depicts figures who get around, who explore and exploit and exchange—at a "post" that marks both lookout and outlook and at which all figures are on the lookout, in multiple senses.

In James's vision of American identity, Fanny, Maggie, and Adam signal various shades of whiteness. Fanny's consciousness pieces together from scraps an assemblage of identity that is the least abstract and the most reproductive. She is the densest of these whites; she produces the identity closest to a cover. Maggie's consciousness both reproduces bits and pieces of identity and produces space. Moreover, these elements serve her as media for producing additional views of identity. Adam Verver's is the most abstract consciousness in the novel. He is seen as open space, and he also sees, in his most inspired productions of identity, open space as sheer view.

Clear rather than white, Adam is identified, in terms beyond whiteness, as capable of everything and yet as nothing. Less committed to reproduction than American women, in accord with stereotypes of gender, Adam conforms to James's American type only in the abstraction and productivity of a consciousness that is collective of views. Without particularity in any of his crucial American characteristics, Adam conforms to type, James suggests, only insofar as type is an immaterial and diverse collective.

It is only in the abstract, however, that James's critical intelligence provides a common medium of cultural identity for persons from various places, histories, and "races." As the Jewish characters of the novel indicate, the exercise of choice is not equally available to various persons. Unlike English Americans or Italian Americans, Jewish Americans as well as African Americans have been identified as groups on the basis of signs: signs, supposedly provided by the inimitable body, that are assumed not to mislead. Thus the critical consciousness that allows characters to choose American identity in *The Golden Bowl* seems to have only limited choices in the experience of certain Americans.

It is not clear, for example, that Africans captured and forced to live in America as slaves could exercise free choice about their displacement. If the prince is the darkest character in *The Golden Bowl*, his identification with darkness, as a wholly metaphorical attribute, fails to represent the experience of African Americans. An Italian who looks Irish, the prince has in his body, as in his knowledge of several languages, alternative possible identities. Though he ends up "fixed" in a "place . . . made for him beforehand by innumerable facts" of history (548–49), the prince's fixity appears to result from the way he chooses to see things. And he looks at things in a way that identifies "darkness" with European knowledge, sophistication, and aristocracy: marks of his distinction.

In *The Golden Bowl,* James identifies a critical modernist consciousness, with its power of choice, as a mark of American character and of an American "nonrace." Consciousness appears as a means of transcending racial distinctions and opening identity to diverse views. Nevertheless, the novel shows how modernist self-consciousness and even the exercise of individual choice limit identity. Evident in the openness of choice and the clarity of American consciousness are less clear signs and means of exclusion. In later twentieth-century American literature, self-consciousness and choice will more distinctly become characteristics of racial whiteness.

chapter three

Self-Division as Racial Divide

The Sound and the Fury

In *The Sound and the Fury* Faulkner identifies "white" male characters in terms of a modernist consciousness. The modernist alienation of the individual psyche becomes the inalienable property of the white man.[1] Largely because of the self-division that is characteristic of the Compson men, these white characters are seen as a cohesive group. In a sense, such a person cannot be considered "like" another person; having internalized otherness, the self-divided individuals contain both likeness and difference and thereby resist assimilation within any group. Yet because of their self-division, those characterized by such a consciousness are, as a group, rendered unassimilable. This unassimilable status, one they as individuals have in common, is marked off in the novel by the extreme assimilability of black characters, who, without the self-division characteristic of a modernist consciousness, are depicted as capable of merging individual with group identity.

Much recent criticism of Faulkner's work has focused on his depiction of women, particularly on their absent status.[2] It seems to me that white female characters in *The Sound and the Fury* both are understood by white male characters to be absent and represent themselves as absent when they are present. In his discriminations among white male and white female characters, then, Faulkner can be said to distribute the identities and differences of symbolic value. By virtue of this distribution, white men in their self-consciousness are both present and absent, both alike and different. White women do not seem to experience such self-division: they are either missing altogether or understand themselves to be absent. But in their absence these women play a part in the symbolic distributions that structure meaning for white characters.[3] According to these distributions, white men produce many likenesses—in images, role-playing, memory, and other forms of reproduction—and white women produce mostly differences.

Black characters, however, both male and female, appear to be left out of this differential distribution of presence and absence. Black characters are present during most of the novel, but because they are merely present—simply *there*—their presence is without symbolic value. Rendered wholly assimilable, these characters are both present to white characters and presented to readers like the background or "staging ground" that Toni Morrison has theorized was necessary to "the elaboration of the quintessential American identity" in nineteenth-century white American literature.[4] In *The Sound and the Fury*, published in 1929, Faulkner identifies both individual and cultural differences between white and black characters. And one effect of these differences is that only black characteristics seem assimilable. The novel works against possibilities of black persons becoming, like whites, unassimilable modernist characters.

White Likeness

The culture with which the Compson family is identified is a particular white, male, southern culture marked by extraordinary likenesses in individual psychology and group behavior. As John Irwin emphasizes in his study of Faulkner, *Doubling and Incest/Repetition and Revenge*, historical repetition structures both the individual psyche and the family likeness of the Compson men.

> It is only when we see in the murder of Bon by Henry [in *Absalom, Absalom*] what Quentin saw in it—that Quentin's own situation appears to be a repetition of the earlier story—that we begin to understand the reason for Quentin's suicide [in *The Sound and the Fury*]. And this whole repetitive structure is made even more problematic by the fact that the explanation which Quentin gives for Bon's murder (that Bon is black, i.e., the shadow self) may well be simply the return of the repressed—simply an unconscious projection of Quentin's own psychic history. Quentin's situation becomes endlessly repetitive insofar as he constantly creates the predecessors of that situation in his narration of past events.

Not only is this repetitive history that of family and individual psyche; it is that of the South. "For Faulkner, doubling and incest are both images of the self-enclosed—the inability of the ego to break out of the circle of the self and of the individual to break out of the ring of the family—and as such, both appear in his novels as symbols of the state of the South after the Civil War, symbols of a region turned in upon itself."[5]

If southern, family, and individual identity share the same structure, all are alienated, moreover, according to the terms of Freud's depiction of the male ego in Western culture. This ego is divided between repressed and conscious experience, between "primitive" desires and learned laws that control such desires. Part of the self is gratified by and part of the self is opposed to his "primitive" desires; similarly, part of the self is identified with and part of the self is repressed by the laws that prohibit satisfaction of narcissistic desires. The inability of a southern white male to accept defeat in the Civil War is paralleled to the inability of an individual to accept constraints on his ego. The pattern of individual alienation that Irwin traces is thus a cultural as much as a personal self-division. Both the individual's personal history and the family history could provide an adequate history for what is also a cultural production.[6]

The agreement of personal, family, regional, and cultural histories is partly what proves the validity or authenticity of the Compsons' individual experiences. Moreover, these histories agree to a peculiarly inclusive experience of identity—one that includes self and "other" as parts of self, family, region, and culture. To equate being black with being the shadow of a white man's self is not only to include black persons within the identity of white persons but also to make black persons necessary to that identity, which depends on an internalized division or opposition.[7]

If this European American identity is inclusive, however, it remains highly resistant to assimilation. For one thing, persons who are identifiable as shadows of the self cannot be united with the self; the alienation of self and shadow is the most necessary characteristic of such a self. Insofar as alienation is the internal structure of the individual psyche, the family, and the region of the South, assimilation of those outside individual, family, or region cannot occur. A likeness may be recognized among insiders, but the likeness lies in their repetition of the same alienation. The Compson men are most alike, perhaps, in their repeated inability to "break out," as Irwin says, of the circle that includes them. Their likeness includes, therefore, both the representation and the negation of difference. For anyone aiming to break into that circle, no position is really available. It is a comprehensive as well as an exclusive identity.

In his discussion of cultural and racial identities in "Race into Culture," Walter Benn Michaels argues that an American past, an African American past, or any other cultural past must be conceived not as a past of personal experience (a person's "*actual* past") but as a "people's past" in order to function as a basis for cultural identity. Given this distinction, Michaels suggests that "the real question . . . is not *which* past should count as ours but why *any* past should count as ours. Virtually all the events and actions that we study did not happen to us and were not done by us."[8] One answer to the question Michaels poses, an answer indicated by *The Sound and the Fury*, is that modernist conceptions of the individual self depend on the involuntary repetition of a past that cannot voluntarily be jettisoned from identity. Memory causes individuals to reproduce elements of the past, and imagination may reproduce elements even of a past not actually one's own but learned from others' representations. The political region of the South shares, or is understood to share, characteristics of familial and psychological history, and because individual memory and imagination reproduce these characteristics, the "actual past" of each of the Compson men is not recognizable as a past separable from southern or familial history.

Black Difference

This is not the case with black characters in the novel. Unlike Faulkner's characterization of the Compsons, his depiction of African American characters is dehistoricized and anti-individualistic. Dilsey is the most individualized African American character in the novel, and she seems virtually selfless, expressing no needs and making no demands for herself. Her presence is undivided by self-consciousness. And Dilsey's ability to take the part of white persons as well as black persons indicates that she can assimilate divisions of race, as she can divisions of history: "I've seed de first en de last," she repeats after the

Easter service, as if her consciousness can see beyond the experience of time that tears apart the white men of the novel.[9]

The assimilability of Faulkner's black characters is clearest in the church service, during which they enter into an identity with one another and with a mythic rather than a historical past. Their shared belief in Christianity allows for a communal experience of unity apparently unavailable to white characters. To the question, Why should any past count as ours? the experience of Faulkner's black characters offers a very different answer from that dictated by his white characters' self-consciousness.

In their church service on Easter Sunday, the African Americans of *The Sound and the Fury* experience an extraordinary "recollection" when the Reverend Shegog speaks.

> "I got the recollection and the blood of the Lamb!" . . . And the congregation seemed to watch with its own eyes while the voice consumed him, until he was nothing and they were nothing and there was not even a voice but instead their hearts were speaking to one another in chanting measures beyond the need for words, so that when he came to rest against the reading desk, his monkey face lifted and his whole attitude that of a serene, tortured crucifix that transcended its shabbiness and insignificance and made it of no moment, a long moaning expulsion of breath rose from them, and a woman's single soprano: "Yes, Jesus!" (367–68)

In their shared recollection of Jesus and the Bible, this group of persons is also collected together so intensely that they communicate without words. "Consumed" by his voice, Shegog transcends the "insignificance" of his own face and body to appear as a "serene, tortured crucifix."[10] This collective and recollective experience is one in which individuals are submerged in a shared consciousness that seems to transcend history as well as individuality. The "actual pasts" and bodies of these individuals are lost sight of, whereas what is "seen" transcends time.

Evident in this scene are several elements of "black expressive cultures" that Paul Gilroy has identified as crucial to the political experience of black persons and to the distinguishing of that experience from European Enlightenment models of a public sphere. Gilroy argues that "the extreme patterns of communication defined by the institution of plantation slavery dictate that we recognize the anti-discursive and extra-linguistic ramifications of power at work in shaping communicative acts." Shegog's performance in the church, then, might be analyzed in terms of "the specific dynamics of performance" that have been important to black cultural experience and whose significance can be missed by "approaches to black culture that have been premised exclusively on textuality and narrative rather than dramaturgy, enunciation, and gesture—the pre- and anti-discursive constituents of black metacommunication."[11]

Representing the performative medium through which Shegog recollects communal identity, Faulkner indicates that black characters have depths of emotional ties among themselves of which the white characters are clearly incapable. Yet the experience in the black church, because it is one in which the Compson men clearly have no place whatever, marks the assimilability of black characters at the same time that it emphasizes the alienated status of white characters. The communal experience of Faulkner's black characters is characterized by what could be seen as an ideal capacity for unity and selflessness. But that ideal capacity is not enacted as an ideal; it seems to require none of the struggle entailed in the Compsons' thinking.[12] Nor does the collective identity of Faulkner's black characters make evident any capacity for political representation or resistance.

White males in *The Sound and the Fury* are identified according to an economy of similarity and difference that is marked out on a symbolic field inclusive of both. Black characters are not represented on this field. And this distinction is not simply a mark of gender and racial difference in the novel. It is a distinction with great political weight, insofar as a democratic public sphere is made up of the rational debate of differing individuals. The field of democratic debate is one in which the identification and expression of differences marks individuals as "equal." The internal struggles of the modernist consciousness are publicized as democratic exchange. According to this economy, Faulkner's white male Americans claim both depths and surfaces of identity, both private and public dimensions of experience, as complex, highly differentiated and articulated spheres of identity. White male identity in the novel is relentlessly discursive, both externally and internally differentiated within a symbolic field. Not only does this identity include surfaces as well as depths, but it includes both self and other.

Western democracy entails a history, Joan W. Scott has argued, of debate about the characteristics—of race, gender, and individuals—that are said to belong to the concept of the democratic individual.[13] But if the white male ego, and only the white male ego, experiences struggle as an internal psychological identity, the white male belongs at the center of such debates in a way others do not. White women and "others" can take part in debate and represent different attributes of individuality. White men contain debate by expressing multiple differences among and within themselves. And they do so not by reason of rights or of political power that any person could assume but by reason of a deep self-division that marks their distinction from persons of other races and genders.

The field of symbolic white male identity in *The Sound and the Fury* produces distinctions of gender and race, but in different ways. Within this field, white men can occupy positions interchangeably; they take multiple points of view within their psyche, and they can "see" the points of view of other white men too. White women in the novel are excluded from any position within this symbolic field, I argue, because they do not see men as men see themselves. Refusing to recognize men in the terms men use to represent themselves, these women seem to be missing from their proper places or to occupy some position that has no place within the symbolic field of white identity. Yet unlike these white females, who are without exchangeable points of view, black characters in the novel appear so undifferentiated as to be incapable of assuming distinct positions. They remain as if a mass, as if indistinguishable from the field on which white men take positions.

A Lacanian Model of Gender

In her discussion of feminist psychoanalytic approaches to Faulkner's work, Carolyn Porter argues for a revision of polarized distinctions between female and male identity in his novels. Using Lacanian theory, Porter insists that both female and male identities are formed in relation to a lack, and both are effected by substitution. Thus female as well as male charactes participate in doubling and repetition:

> If, on the one hand, in the Imaginary—the field of representation—the mother is fated to be displaced by the "woman" who becomes her

substitute, and is already effaced by the Name of the Father to whom she must give her child, Faulkner brings into view, and accords speaking privileges to that mother, as someone herself trapped by and in a male Imaginary. At the same time, if the Father in the social Imaginary must represent the discourse of the Other, must occupy the position of authority designated by the "paternal metaphor," he is also trapped, compelled to an imposture which dictates that he conceal not merely his weaknesses, but that very imposture—something that, as we know, Mr. Compson fails to do. In this register, that is, "male lack" is the effect, in the Imaginary, of a more fundamental lack in Being itself, one that opens with the birth of the subject as subject, that is represented in the (always missing) phallus, and that finally closes only in death.

If both mother and father are compelled to conceal lacks, they work with different degrees of lack.

> [Woman's] function is to bear the burden of a double lack—she must conceal her own as well as the man's, that is. But, at the same time, the father's function in the Imaginary—as representative of Law, authority—depends upon his ability to conceal his lack—indeed not only his lack of the phallus, but as well, what that lack implies, viz., that his paternal identity is an imposture.

According to this argument, Porter does not distinguish the concept of "mother" in Faulkner's work as either plenitude or lack. " 'Mother,' in short, is a word, as Addie Bundren [in *As I Lay Dying*] will say, 'a shape to fill a lack,' the lack that opens at birth, and is only later, retrospectively, seen as a vacuum to be filled.' "[14]

Fathers, then, have a role to fill; mothers, as shapes to fill a lack, have a gap to fill. Various distinctions might be made between these functions, but one important difference is that between a player and a shape, only one of which denotes a subject. Yet the mother does not only fill and conceal lacks. She is initially supposed to recognize the child's lack. The infant's initial demand, Porter argues, following Lacan, is "not for an object that will *complete* a lack, it is a demand for the Other's recognition *of* that lack. By responding to the child's need, the mother does not erase it, she recognizes it."[15]

Thus in *The Sound and the Fury* according to Porter's rereading, Caddy, the absent sister and the woman whose lack is most important to the Compson brothers, is, in retrospect, neither a presence nor an absence. The men remember her as present and then absent, but it is not she that is missed by her brothers. Rather, they miss recognition of their lack, or recognition that they are lacking. I will take some liberties with this line of interpretation, particularly in that the Compson brothers seem to me to desire, even as adults, some recognition from women of internal division and struggle. If they do, it cannot be for the lack experienced at birth but may be for what the child misses on accession to language and, with language, entry into history.

White Men's Struggles

Quentin and Jason Compson play a number of roles, and in doing so they replay obsessively the doubleness that marks the alienated modern self-consciousness. Both characters imagine and imaginatively participate in various conflicts, in which they confront and try to get even with their opponents. These plays and replays occur on a particular field, which may be likened to the Lacanian Imaginary as a "field of representation." It is a playing field or a battlefield, one identified by Mr. Compson, when he gives Quentin his watch, as the location of man's infinite frustration.

> It was Grandfather's and when Father gave it to me he said, Quentin, I give you the mausoleum of all hope and desire; it's rather excruciatingly apt that you will use it to gain the reducto absurdum of all human experience which can fit your individual needs no better than it fitted his or his father's. I give it to you not that you may remember time, but that you might forget it now and then for a moment and not spend all your breath trying to conquer it. Because no battle is ever won he said. They are not even fought. The field only reveals to man his own folly and despair, and victory is an illusion of philosophers and fools. (93)

Mr. Compson suggests that time has the identity of a "primal" lack. According to Lacan's theory of the individual self, language can be identified with history. History is entered when the self recognizes itself as other, and time passes as the increasing division of self that structures alienation and self-consciousness.[16] According to this Freudian model of consciousness as history, Mr. Compson is right to insist that the individual can never confront or contest time. Time cannot be opposed to this self because in a sense this self is composed of time. Time is present as the force that constitutes the inner division which structures selfhood; time is present to the self, then, as an absence within the self, as the part of the self that the self, once represented in language, is missing.

To identify, as Faulkner does here, a missing battle as the crucial lack in men's experience is to indicate that the deepest need of the Compson men is for opposition. If the male is responsible, as Porter argues, for playing the role of the father in Faulkner's novels, men who play that role also are players in a contest taking place on this field. Throughout the novel, the Compson men obsessively reproduce various oppositions that give meaning and stability to their experience. Men are identified in struggles that replay the battle with time that cannot be won or even fought. The desire to fight time is a desire for revenge, to get back what has been lost in time and to get back at time for having lost it. But time does not appear; it is present only as an absence, only in signs but not directly apprehensible. And for that reason, the Compsons' struggles and conflicts are shams, though they are nevertheless these men's only means of identity.

The men in the Compson family reproduce likenesses in the roles they assume and, more generally, in the reflections that make up their consciousness. Except for Benjy, the brothers seem to recognize each opposition they produce and take part in as an illusion. But what goes through Benjy's mind also seems for the most part a re-presentation or reflection of something else. When his sensations, such as the sound of the word "Caddy," cause him to shift from the present to the past, he makes what Olga Vickery calls a "mechanical identification" to produce "the exact replica of the incident."[17] Benjy's "self-reflective" experience is objective rather than subjective, produced by such objects as mirrors. Caddy herself often comforts Benjy by acting as a kind of mirror.[18] When he cries or moans, she produces, or reproduces, an object or sensation that pleased him in the past. She stops wearing perfume when she realizes that it upsets him, thereby keeping his experience as repetitive as possible (48–51). And Benjy thinks of Caddy as a likeness—"*She smelled like trees*" (51).

The reproduction of likenesses such as a mirror reflects is necessary to Quentin and Jason too. When they imagine the conflicts they need to fight, they equate the opposing "sides" with reflections and reversals that represent both sides as evenly matched and all situations as reversible. Evened out, the opponents do not actually fight, as Mr. Compson says. But insofar as the opponents represent the enemy, time, the men can feel that they stay even with time.

What Benjy has that his brothers are incapable of having is the experience of pure repetition, an ability to get back to past experience with no awareness that it is past. Quentin's reflections on the past always include a sense of loss, because he wants absolute, one-of-a-kind experience, as if to get back to some state before time and representation. As his mind produces likenesses, therefore, he is always missing something, and this sense of lack is inescapable, he recognizes, because it is built into language.

For a time, at least, Quentin believes that one misses things because one has had and then lost them. But as his father points out to him, what Quentin misses is something he has never had and never can have. "Father said it's because you are a virgin; dont you see? Women are never virgins. Purity is a negative state and therefore contrary to nature. It's nature is hurting you not Caddy and I said That's just words and he said So is virginity and I said you dont know. You cant know and he said Yes. On the instant when we come to realize that tragedy is second-hand" (143–44). Because purity is a negative state, an abstract ideal imagined as a contradiction to nature, it can never be realized except in words, as a representation. For Quentin, the fact that his father recognizes purity only as a word means that he does not know anything about it—he does not know what Quentin is missing. But Mr. Compson agrees that "you can't know" what you are missing, only that you are missing something. This is the secondhand character of lack itself. All tragedy is secondhand because all loss is secondhand; the object desired and lacked is only an imagined object—a likeness or representation of lack.

When Quentin rips the hands off his watch, he attempts to destroy the means of representation that both differentiates firsthand from secondhand experience and makes the two equally repeatable. But getting rid of the hands that tell the difference between moments of time does not get rid of secondhandedness. Just as Quentin cannot get outside language even as he imagines experience outside it, he realizes that he has made no difference to his watch, which goes on marking the passage of time: "There were about a dozen watches in the window, a dozen different hours and each with the same assertive and contradictory assurance that mine had, without any hands at all. Contradicting one another. I could hear mine, ticking away inside my pocket, even though nobody could see it, even though it could tell nothing if anyone could" (104). The fact that his watch can tell nothing does not affect the assurance with which it ticks. That the watch does not show time and that the other watches all show different times indicates that what shows is irrelevant to time. The assurance and contradiction of what shows are like the dynamics of male role-playing, with various assertive individuals contradicting one another. With such awareness of time, Quentin and, later, Jason "see" that they cannot win.

Because the very representations they produce to fight time are using it up, time clearly continues to pass even in the very shows they put on to withstand it. They can be defeated by an opponent who does not even show up to fight. The underlying problem is not evident on the field; it does not lie in the oppositions represented there but in the fact that time can prevail without being represented.

Jason and Quentin put on a show of fighting; the roles they play and replay are roles of combat. But like Quentin tricking his shadow and getting the better of it, they deal only with evidences of time, not time itself. What is happening, all along and out of sight, is the passing of time. And the men's awareness of what is missing from the field of battle means they see that their struggles are mere show.[19]

Missing Mothers

Jason's narrative, like Quentin's, begins with a parent passing on to a son an "object" that represents the parent's failure. But what Jason takes off his mother's hands is not a maternal heirloom but the girl Quentin, Caddy's daughter, passed from Caddy to her mother and now to Jason. Whereas the grandfather's watch is recognized by father and son as "the mausoleum of all hope and desire," the girl Quentin still inspires hope and desire in mother and son, who are determined to control her. "If you want me to control her," Jason says to Mrs. Compson, "just say so and keep your hands off" (225). That Jason wants his mother's hands off suggests, in its reflection of Quentin tearing the hands off his watch, that women are identified by Jason as *similar to* time. Like time, the girl Quentin is unaffected by the removal of the mother's hands. And like time, Quentin, on the run and still running at the end of the novel, continues to elude Jason.

And like his brother Quentin, Jason is always running out of time. But unlike Quentin, he insists that he can get even. In Jason's mind, battles are fought all the time. He represents his own fighting as a reversal, an attempt to get even or get back for something done to him. And this form of reflection, which turns back a former enemy and turns a past situation around, also seems capable of canceling out time.

It is all a matter of show, with Jason determined to "show them": " 'You do a thing like that again and I'll make you sorry you ever drew breath,' I says" (233); "These damned little slick haired squirts, thinking they are raising so much hell, I'll show them something about hell I says, and you too" (301); " 'I'll show him about jobs' " (382). Each of these projections of a showdown, at which Jason will demonstrate something decisively, promises that he will get the better of other people. As showdowns that never happen, these projections become yet more experiences of missing "things" that never were: battles are never fought, let alone won, as Mr. Compson has predicted. And this occurs in part because the conflicts are always ways of getting back at or even with others; the reason to fight is past and can never be gotten back. Partly Jason's battles can be neither fought nor won because what he desires to show and have recognized is lack itself.

When the last of his showdowns-that-never-happen is about to be recognized as a lost cause, Jason is running after his niece Quentin, hoping to recover the money she has taken from his room. It is Easter Sunday, and he needs help.

> He thought of how he'd find a church at last and take a team and of the owner coming out, shouting at him and of himself striking the man down. "I'm Jason Compson. See if you can stop me. See if you can elect a man to office that can stop me," he said, thinking of himself entering the courthouse with a file of soldiers and dragging the sheriff out. "Thinks he can sit with his hands folded and see me lose my job. I'll show him about jobs." Of his niece he did not think at all, nor of the arbitrary valuation of the money. Neither of them had had entity or individuality for him for ten years; together they merely symbolized the job in the bank of which he had been deprived before he ever got it. (381–82)

Planning to get even with others who will "see," Jason imagines himself overpowering other men, forcing them to do what he wants. But everything Jason has to show is missing. The scenes in which he gets the better of others occur only in his imagination. Missing conflicts over a missing object, neither the conflicts nor the object of the conflicts ever existed in the first place.

This experience of representation may be driven, as Porter suggests, by the fact that the mother never recognized his lack. If the self passing in time is the missing self—if the self past in time is the lack that requires recognition when it enters language and history—these men keep replaying the experience of time as lack in order to show time and to show it up, but they achieve no recognition for missing time. In the novel, neither the mother of the brothers nor their sister, Caddy—the mother of the girl Quentin—recognizes the men's lack of what they have never had. Caddy knows what is bothering Jason but dismisses its significance: "'Oh,' she says, 'that job'" (252).

Mrs. Compson also fails to recognize her sons' lacks. The most explicit of the exchanges in which Mrs. Compson accepts Jason's role-playing with no sense of anything missing is the repeated routine in which he gives her copies of Caddy's checks. Jason cashes the checks for himself but reproduces them so that his mother can burn them up. Replaying this routine, Mrs. Compson accepts the likenesses Jason provides, but only to destroy them. She does not recognize what is missing—the real checks—nor does she see any value in the representations Jason provides.

That Mrs. Compson demonstrates no awareness of others' role-playing may be due to her understanding of herself as fully absent from the roles she plays. One can say that she plays the martyr. To Dilsey she complains, "'Am I never to have one minute's peace,'" and predicts, "'I'll be gone soon, and you and Jason will both get along better'" (73). And she assures Jason, "'I know you dont intend to make it more difficult for me. But it's my place to suffer for my children,'" and "'I try to please you all, . . . I try to make things as easy as I can'" (274, 275). In these assertions, Mrs. Compson projects a negation of her present existence: she is dead, she is never at peace, she is in a condition unintended by others, or she is not in the condition she intended. When she insists that Caddy and her name be banished from the house, "'It's not myself. . . . It's for Quentin's sake,'" she insists (274), repeating her constant self-negation at the same time that she lays down the law. The role Mrs. Compson plays, then, is a role of nonexistence within the law. She always represents herself as missing.

The recognition Mrs. Compson gives Jason is not of his lack but of her lack. And she not only represents herself as missing but also insists that no one is able to recognize her and everybody misunderstands her. Thus she represents herself as different from the person and the actions that show to others. Jason occasionally challenges the obvious discrepancy between what she does and what she says she does. At one point, when his mother insists, " 'I dont mean to worry you,' " Jason responds, " 'I'm glad to hear that. . . . I wasn't sure. I thought I might have been mistaken' " (296). Mrs. Compson's refusal to identify herself with the self others see evokes an appropriate response from her son: a show of agreement that disclaims, by means of irony, the agreement shown. This perverse exchange certainly involves recognition of lack, on both sides. Indeed, the mother's mirror reflection of lack, as if she always experiences what the child experiences when entering language, allows for no recognition of the child's particularity.

For Mrs. Compson, the most important lack exists within the symbolic register; it is the failure of the patriarchal order to recognize her as significant. She therefore uses language to remove herself from that order: to insist that she is never present to representations. If she fails to provide the recognition her sons need, this may be because she knows no difference between what shows and what is lacking: for her, what shows *is* lacking.

The third of the Compson women who fails to recognize what men are missing is the girl Quentin. And she also seems not to recognize what is missing in her uncle's shows. Quentin actually does what Jason only threatens to do: she fills the gap between show and act. She threatens to rip off her dress if it has been bought with Jason's money. " 'See if I wouldn't,' " she says. And then Jason realizes "that she really was trying to tear it, to tear it right off of her. . . . It made me so mad for a minute it kind of blinded me" (233). For Quentin to threaten is not posture, and the effect is not that Jason sees but that he is blind with rage. She shows him what is missing from his show—by actually doing what she says she'll do—and he cannot see what she is doing because for him show is imposture: it cannot be realized. Finally, she really "shows" Jason again by getting back the money he has taken from her and getting away with it. And then she is again, like her mother, really what white men say white women are: missing.

The identification of white women with time occurs because they run; particularly, they run out on men. It also occurs as women appear to prevail, without struggle, by simply doing what men only realize in imagination. It is difficult to identify these women's realization of absence as a desirable quality, but it may be necessary prior to the experience of desire. Insofar as the self's lack of self needs recognition, the white women of the novel have something men need. They reflect back to men the lack men experience; for the man, then, these women are likenesses of his missing self. The women, however, experience lack without apparently being divided by it, as if what a woman lacks is not merely a matter of representation but *is* her self.

If the mother never recognized the lack that constituted and constitutes the male self, then the male has to keep replaying his lack to make it show and so be recognizable. But all he can show is the representation, not the lacking self behind the representation, which is the self in time. The lacking of self and the passing of time both happen beneath the surfaces of experience. Therefore all the sons see in their reflections are images in reverse. They see as if in mirrors because they themselves must take the place of the reflective other that the mother cannot fill. What each misses is the one who would look at him and recognize if not a self behind the image (since there is no such subject) then a lack behind the image: the distance of separation that has constituted the self. What is missed by them all is a reflection of what they are missing.

It is difficult to see how any woman could provide this recognition without remaining in the realm of missing experience. One might argue that the Compson women "fulfill" these men's needs by presenting themselves as missing; as such, they can only be shapes to fill a lack. But the Compson women are also unable to provide any recognition of the lacking self of Compson men because they themselves seem to be unaware of the difference between what shows and what is missing. It appears, at least, that these women do not experience the internal struggle of present and missing male consciousness.

Missing in Action

The field on which the battle with time is never fought, like the field of the Lacanian Imaginary, may be "seen" only vaguely, lying as it does behind, in time and space, symbolic representations. It is a sort of shadow field, apparent not in the reflections of double consciousness but in the reflection of consciousness by the unconscious. In *The Sound and the Fury*, this field is still available to the imaginations and representations of white men, I think, because of the way they see black people.[20] Black people make up the field on which substitutes for time appear and figure as adversaries. To do so, they are conceived as timeless and as persons existing outside the terms of language that divide white men from themselves and from one another.

Functioning as a field against which white figures are distinguished, black characters, unlike white women, are not shapes to fill a lack. They are usually seen as shapeless or without any distinct figure. As indistinct figures they cannot be represented as individuals. Moreover, they appear to perceive only dimly the distinctions most critical to white self-consciousness: those of self and other and of past and present. In the church service particularly, during which the "figure" of Shegog is rendered insignificant and people see "the beginning and the ending," individual and temporal distinctions are assimilated in both individual and collective consciousness.

Experiencing without conflict differences polarized within the white man's psyche, African American characters are apparently not self-divided. They are contradictory, Quentin insists, but they do not seem to mind. Quentin "remembers" these characteristics of black persons when he returns home from college and sees, from the train, a black man on a mule.

> They passed smoothly from sight that way, with that quality about them of shabby and timeless patience, of static serenity: that blending of childlike and ready incompetence and paradoxical reliability that tends and protects them it loves out of all reason and robs them steadily and evades responsibility and obligations by means too barefaced to be called subterfuge even and is taken in theft or evasion with only that frank and spontaneous admiration for the victor which a gentleman feels for anyone who beats him in a fair contest, and withal a fond and unflagging tolerance for whitefolks' vagaries like that of a grandparent for unpredictable and troublesome children, which I had forgotten. (107–8)

Here black people are identified with conflicting qualities, especially in their "blending of childlike and ready incompetence and paradoxical reliability" but also in their likeness to both children and grand-parents and in their protection and robbery of those they love. There is no apparent structure of self-division to account for these qualities, which appear to be assimilated within individuals and within a group of individuals for no reason and with no order. It also appears that these individuals are assimilable to animals, for "they" at the beginning of the passage refers to the man and his mule, though, presumably, in the rest of passage "they" refers to black people in general. Representing Shegog with a "monkey face" and Dilsey as a cow, Faulkner repeatedly encourages this assimilation.

The figure of the black man on the mule is undistinguished *as* a figure both because man merges with mule and because he is seen to represent all black people in the South. It is interesting that the only other black male figure described in the novel, Reverend Shegog in the church, is also seen as shabby and serene. Not only the figure but also the identity of these black people is for Quentin undistinguished and unmemorable. "I didn't know that I really had missed Roskus and Dilsey and them until that morning," when he sees the man and the mule (106). The unconscious level at which Quentin misses these people again marks their indistinction on any field of representation. The oppositions that the Compson brothers imagine and replay occur in an imaginary or symbolic realm of consciousness. The contrast provided by the field of undifferentiated black figures for the distinguished white characters is not a contrast of opponents or of distinct and equivalent forms but one of field and form. Those in the background do not "figure" in this relationship. They are identified as material rather than form; moreover, they materialize or realize in action experience that white people only represent.

These characteristics are most evident in Dilsey. Though she does contradict Jason and Mrs. Compson at various times, especially about the way they treat Quentin and Benjy, Dilsey never objects to their treatment of her. In fact, she seldom represents herself or her own interests as if they are distinct from those of others. On Easter morning, for example, Mrs. Compson causes Dilsey unnecessary additional work and reprimands her for not doing her work.

> "Haven't you started breakfast yet?"
> "I'll tend to dat too," Dilsey said. "You better git back in bed twell Luster make yo fire. Hit cold dis mawnin."

"I know it," Mrs Compson said. "My feet are like ice. . . . " She watched Dilsey mount the stairs. It took her a long while. "You know how it frets Jason when breakfast is late," Mrs Compson said.

"I can't do but one thing at a time," Dilsey said. "You git on back to bed, fo I has you on my hands dis mawnin too."

Dilsey, who is old and has difficulty climbing stairs, is coming up to dress Benjy because Mrs. Compson has complained that Luster had not yet done so. Mrs. Compson allows Dilsey to get to the top of the stairs before letting her know that Benjy is not even awake.

Dilsey stopped. With her foot lifted to the next step she stood there, her hand against the wall and the grey splash of the window behind her, motionless and shapeless she loomed.

"He aint awake den?" she said.

"He wasn't when I looked in," Mrs Compson said. . . .

Dilsey said nothing. She made no further move, but though she could not see her save as a blobby shape without depth, Mrs Compson knew that she had lowered her face a little and that she stood now like a cow in the rain, as she held the empty water bottle by its neck.

"You're not the one who has to bear it," Mrs. Compson said. "It's not your responsibility. You can go away. You dont have to bear the brunt of it day in and day out. . . . "

Dilsey said nothing. She turned slowly and descended, lowering her body from step to step, as a small child does, her hand against the wall. "You go on and let him alone," she said. "Dont go in dar no mo, now. I'll send Luster up soon as I find him. Let him alone, now."
(338–39)

In this passage there are several images of Dilsey. She appears as a shapeless blob, then a "blobby shape," a cow, and a child. Mrs. Compson also represents her like a child when she claims Dilsey bears no responsibility.

Dilsey does not represent herself in any way to contradict these representations. It is characteristic of her to produce no defense of herself when she is attacked or criticized by white people. She seems to ignore them or, "like a cow in the rain," simply to withstand them. But she does so while indicating that she will go on with what she has to do and will not be interfered with, as if she can cope with anything. This determined activity seldom distinguishes her. She acts, in a sense, as the white woman's reverse, for she is and does what Mrs. Compson is not and does not do. Mrs. Compson claims to pay for everything, to suffer for the sake of the family, to bear all the responsibility. But it is Dilsey who actually does these things. Mrs. Compson is the mother, but Dilsey raises the children, again actualizing what Mrs. Compson claims in name only. And Mrs. Compson lies in bed most of the time, but according to the evidence of her movements Dilsey is the one in pain.

Dilsey's insistence that she can cope with anything that happens is indication of her endurance and her ability to withstand what seem to the Compsons catastrophic events. In this sense she is stronger than the Compsons, which she insists is so. " 'Now, now,' she says [to the girl Quentin], 'He aint gwine so much as lay his hand on you while Ise here' " (230). And to Mrs. Compson, frightened at Jason's anger when his money has been stolen, " 'Now, now, . . . Whut kin happen? I right here' " (351). Dilsey's repeated refrain of "now, now" asserts a temporal presence that none of the Compsons recognizes, and her own presence, without internal "otherness," is apparently sufficient to withstand others' attacks.

But if Dilsey's capacity to take on a great deal of work, to take on Jason when he threatens to hurt Quentin, to take on responsibilities that the Compsons will not bear, marks her strength, this strength is not depicted in terms of heroism. When Dilsey "takes on" responsibility, what occurs is similar to what happens to her body in the kitchen when she begins work on Easter morning.

> She sang, to herself at first, something without particular tune or words, repetitive, mournful and plaintive, austere, as she ground a faint, steady snowing of flour onto the bread board. The stove had begun to heat the room . . . and presently she was singing louder, as if her voice too had been thawed out by the growing warmth. (336)

> The room grew warmer. Soon Dilsey's skin had taken on a rich, lustrous quality as compared with that as of a faint dusting of wood ashes which both it and Luster's had worn, as she moved about the kitchen, gathering about her the raw materials of food, coordinating the meal. (341)

In descriptions that repeatedly note her lack of particularity—in the tune as well as the words she sings, in the skin like Luster's—Dilsey's body also absorbs the characteristics of her environment. With a body that takes on heat and color, Dilsey is assimilated to or by the heat of the fire. And the steadiness of her work here reflects the indistinctness of her body. She appears unthinking, receptive, and increasingly comfortable as she takes on the extraordinary labors of her housework.

Unresistant in many ways, Dilsey does stand up to white people, especially Jason when he tries to hurt the girl Quentin. She also attempts to protect Luster from being hurt when Jason pretends he will sell him a ticket to the "show" that has come to town.

> "Gimme one of um, Mr. Jason," he says. "You aint gwine need um bofe."
> . . . "I came in here to burn them up. But if you want to buy one for a nickel?" I says, looking at him and opening the stove lid.
> . . . "Go on," she says, "Drop hit in. Go on. Git hit over with."
> "You can have it for a nickel," I says.
> "Go on," Dilsey says. "He aint got no nickel. Go on. Drop hit in."
> "All right," I says. I dropped it in and Dilsey shut the stove. (318–19)

Dilsey watches Jason's performance but provides no recognition of any self behind it. Although she insists he should be ashamed (318), she also seems to egg him on in his cruelty. But in this encouragement Dilsey allows Jason no choice or power in his actions, which she hurries up to get them over with. Treating Jason as yet something else to be put up with and gotten through, Dilsey gives him no recognition as an actor with any power over the role he plays. Rather than recognizing him as lacking in time, Dilsey places him in time, as something that will pass away if she just waits.

In such scenes, Dilsey is identified with Bergsonian endurance, as she is in the last line of the novel: "Dilsey. They endured" (427). As the pronoun here indicates, Dilsey's absorption in time seems inseparable from her assimilation in and by other people. Yet the underlying experience of duration is, for Henri Bergson, a highly desirable level of consciousness.

> There are finally two different selves, one of which is, as it were, the external projection of the other, its spatial and, so to speak, social representation. We reach the former by deep introspection, which leads us to grasp our inner states as living things, constantly *becoming*, as states not amenable to measure, which permeate one another

and of which the succession in duration has nothing in common with juxtaposition in homogeneous space. But the moments at which we thus grasp ourselves are rare, and that is just why we are rarely free.[21]

For Bergson, to be in time is to be free of social representation by language, which stabilizes, in its consistency, experience that is unstable and inconsistent. Dilsey's endurance is thereby linked to her refusal to represent herself. Unlike "the word with well-defined outlines" that "overwhelms or at least covers over the delicate and fugitive impressions of our individual consciousness,"[22] Dilsey is recognized as a shapeless figure, a blob.

But if Dilsey can experience a "freedom" in Bergson's terms, she does not seem to experience the doubleness that constitutes a full self. On the surface and in social groups, she experiences the duration that for Bergson is a buried and unsocial part of experience. For Bergson, what is desirable, presumably, is having it both ways: having the social and political representation yet also being able to experience the inner state that is absent to social representation. In African American culture the continuity of Bergsonian duration may be neither buried nor asocial. But according to Faulkner's depiction of individual consciousness, the realization of such continuity marks persons as outside civil society and history both.

Dilsey is identified within a wholly private realm of domestic experience, one in which white women too have been traditionally excluded from political power. But another kind of continuity marks the exclusion of the larger black community in the novel from political significance. The scene in the church on Easter Sunday, the only scene in the novel that depicts a public meeting, indicates that political disenfranchisement characterizes the representation of black persons in the novel.

In Reverend Shegog's sermon he recalls scriptural history as he moves through time to the end of time:

> "Dey passed away in Egypt, de swingin chariots; de generations passed away. Wus a rich man: whar he now, O breddren? Wus a po man: whar he now, O sistuhn?" . . .
>
> "I sees hit, breddren! I sees hit! Sees de blastin, blindin sight! . . . I hears de boasting en de braggin: Ef you be Jesus, lif up yo tree en walk! . . .
>
> " . . . I sees de doom crack en hears de golden horns shoutin down

de glory, en de arisen dead whus got de blood en de ricklickshun of de Lamb!" (369–70)

What Shegog sees here is somewhere beyond time, because it is both a representation of the past and it moves representation beyond the end of the world. As he passes through time, Shegog insists that time passes away: the past disappears in the "now" and in the future. But all these moments in time are recollected here, to be reproduced as scenes for public show.

Shegog, whom the congregation watches "as they would a man on a tight rope" (366), also speaks various parts in this show. But unlike Lacanian imposture, the roles Shegog plays are not for purposes of individual distinction or distinction of the law but for purposes of recollection by the group of its common, transcendent identity and belief. Shegog takes parts remembered and imagined by all the congregation in order to call forth a unity, not only among themselves but also between their present and the future in which they will be called to account for the way they have lived. To collect together these various parts is not to realize them as parts to be performed in individual alienation but as parts of the group experience to be performed in communion.

Nevertheless, the very lack of alienated consciousness evident in this scene of collective identity can be recognized as a reason for excluding these persons from the public sphere of political power, insofar as that political sphere is associated with struggle, debate, and individual differences. White males in *The Sound and the Fury* elaborate in their experiences of self-division the alienation that marks their political currency. Their "common" experience is abstract—that is, they are commonly seen to be a particular type of distinct individual, and their common experience of this abstract structure of individuality is what unites them. Black characters, on the other hand, have a common experience of their very commonness. They do not require representation to experience this undivided identity, which is not an abstraction. It is experienced most intensely "in chanting measures beyond the need for words" (367), and it is apparently capable of assimilating them into complete agreement.

According to the novel's white male model of significance, which depends on various oppositions, black people as they are depicted both in public and private cannot be identified as either equals or opponents of white people. If, as I have suggested, Dilsey can be seen as Mrs. Compson's reverse, their positions cannot be reversed; Mrs. Compson does not function as Dilsey's opposite. Whereas Mrs. Compson is all talk, Dilsey is all action; she materializes Mrs. Compson's representations. And in her materialized and unrepresented status, she appears as a background that sets off Mrs. Compson's distinction. I have argued that white women enact the absence that white men identify with women, but Dilsey's activation of Mrs. Compson's claims is a different matter. White women's active confirmation of their symbolic status, or lack of status, confirms also the symbolic register in which they are represented as lack. And although they occupy the place of lack, white women occupy a place that is absolutely necessary to this structure of representation and this concept of male psyche.

Mrs. Compson needs Dilsey, and she needs Dilsey's labor. But the material register in which these needs are identifiable has no significance within the symbolic and psychic abstractions that structure significance in the novel. Nor does the collective experience of African American characters, which is not an abstract common identity and which is characterized by assimilations of various kinds, have any place in a political sphere that theoretically depends on the expression of individual differences.

chapter four

Playing White Men in

Light in August

If *The Sound and the Fury* focuses attention on the white individual consciousness, *Light in August* is a novel in which Faulkner attends more closely to a white community. Not one of the central characters—Joe Christmas, Byron Bunch, or Gail Hightower—is a native of Jefferson, Mississippi, where the novel takes place, but all play parts in the public life of this community. The public life of Jefferson is not composed of "native" elements but of elements abstracted from any historical setting and reproduced by white men, who take parts belonging to no single individual. Public life occurs as a process similar to a theatrical production or a sports event, in which men take positions and engage in acts, reproduced from an established repertoire of plays, that are easily recognized by onlookers.

A similar community exists in the town near which Joe Christmas lives while growing up, the adopted son of the McEacherns.

> The town was a railroad division point. Even in midweek there were many men about the streets. The whole air of the place was masculine, transient: a population even whose husbands were at home only at intervals and on holiday—a population of men who led esoteric lives whose actual scenes were removed and whose intermittent presence was pandered to like that of patrons in a theatre.[1]

The transience of this place, a transience Faulkner identifies with masculinity, means that many men move through its streets; their scenery also moves. As if in a theater, the "actual scenes" of these men's lives "were removed," and they are viewed against other removable backdrops. Only intermittently present, both at home and in public, these men appear as the actors and the audience in a theater.

Theaters of Whiteness

In the restaurant they go into on a back street of this town, Joe and McEachern confront such an audience.

> What [Joe] saw was . . . a big, blonde woman behind a cigar case near the front and a clump of men at the far end of the counter, not eating, who all turned as one and looked at him and McEachern when they entered, through the smoke of cigarettes. Nobody said anything at all. They just looked at McEachern and Joe. . . . The men were not in overalls and they all wore hats, and their faces were all alike: not young and not old; not farmers and not townsmen either. They looked like people who had just got off a train and who would be gone tomorrow and who did not have any address. (151–52)

Here the men that watch the entrance of Joe and McEachern look "all alike" and are there only temporarily. The likenesses of these men, to one another and to other people who "just got off a train," are characteristic of the way white men create identity among themselves in this novel. Even when not personally known, white men are recognized as likenesses that identify them in familiar terms. All alike but unspecific, the men at the counter nonetheless remain difficult to pin down by means of appearance or address.

At this restaurant several kinds of pandering occur, for Bobbie the waitress is also a prostitute, brought from Memphis to work for Max, who runs the restaurant. Joe and Bobbie become lovers; for Max, even this somewhat anomalous action can be converted into parts of a familiar show: " 'She says maybe she likes him best. It's Romeo and Juliet. For sweet Jesus! . . . Max Confrey presenting Miss Bobbie Allen, the youth's companion' " (167).

In *Light in August* it is white men who do the looking that constitutes public meaning, and it is also mostly white men whose meaning is limited to their looks. Lena Grove, who is the first character to appear in the novel, is identified immediately by the men who watch her, but what they see in her is a story: her particular history, which is accurately read into her looks. When Joe Christmas and then Lucas

Burch/Brown appear as strangers looking for work at the mill in Jefferson, they are seen *as* looks.

> [Joe Christmas appeared] one Friday morning three years ago. And the group of men at work in the planer shed looked up, and saw the stranger standing there, watching them. . . . He looked like a tramp, yet not like a tramp either. . . . He did not look like a professional hobo in his professional rags, but there was something definitely rootless about him, as though no town nor city was his, no street, no walls, no square of earth his home. And that he carried his knowledge with him always as though it were a banner, with a quality ruthless, lonely, and almost proud. . . .
>
> They did not know who he was. None of them had ever seen him before. "Except that's a pretty risky look for a man to wear on his face in public," one said: "He might forget and use it somewhere where somebody wont like it." (27–28)

Joe's "looks" are not only his physical appearance, how he looks to others, but also the ways in which he actively looks *at* others. In this visual economy of looks, looks are both read and exchanged, and rather than appearing as insufficient signs, they are used as means of knowledge.

The sufficiency of looks to meaningful readings of white men is even clearer when Brown, who has changed his name from Lucas Burch sometime after leaving Lena Grove pregnant, appears at the mill two years after Christmas had arrived.

> He was young too, tall, already in overalls which looked as though he had been in them constantly for some time, and he looked as though he had been travelling light also. He had an alert, weakly handsome face with a small white scar beside the mouth that looked as if it had been contemplated a great deal in the mirror, and a way of jerking his head quickly and glancing over his shoulder like a mule does in front of an automobile in the road, Byron thought. . . .
>
> . . . "He puts me in mind of one of these cars running along the street with a radio in it. You can't make out what it is saying and the car aint going anywhere in particular and when you look at it close you see that there aint even anybody in it."
>
> "Yes," Mooney said. "He puts me in mind of a horse. Not a mean horse. Just a worthless horse. . . . Runs fast, all right, but it's always got a sore hoof when hitching-up time comes." (31–32)

Brown's looks are both the surface and depths of his identity, indicating to others the way he looks at himself in the mirror and the way he looks over his shoulder. The sufficiency of looks to identity is also indicated by the fact that what the men see in Brown's and Joe's looks is accurate. That is, Joe and Brown live up to their looks as interpreted by the men at the mill. Yet these readings are nonspecific, indicating more what is absent than present in the figures seen. Their looks provide a presence with no particular history, background, or action. Both men are "travelling light," and their looks are interpreted so as not to tie them to any place or time. It is their very lack of historical particularity that enables them to fit the public likenesses of other men.

If these figures can be transposed into other scenes, their parts can also be taken by other men. Brown already has two identities, as Brown and as Burch; Christmas and he appear to be two of a kind; and Lena Grove has come to Jefferson having heard that "Bunch" is at the mill and thinking that Bunch is Burch. Byron Bunch, moreover, takes the part of Burch/Brown: " 'I took care of his woman for him and I borned his child for him' " (373).

When Lena appears, however, what white men see ties her to a particular past. Faulkner gives Lena's history before anyone sees her; men watching then identify her on the basis of her appearance but in terms of her history. That history is evident to them, with no communication from her.

> While Armstid and Winterbottom were squatting against the shady wall of Winterbottom's stable, they saw her pass in the road. They saw at once that she was young, pregnant, and a stranger. "I wonder where she got that belly," Winterbottom said.
>
> . . . "I reckon she knows where she is going," Winterbottom said. "She walks like it."
>
> "She'll have company, before she goes much further," Armstid said. The woman had now gone on, slowly, with her swelling and unmistakable burden. . . . "She aint come from nowhere close," Armstid said. "She's hitting that lick like she's been at it for a right smart while and had a right smart piece to go yet." (8)

All the likenesses and looks identify particular historical facts about the person watched. Her looks are unmistakable, and so, apparently, is her history.

Not only these men but also those who watch her the next morning on the porch at the store know all about her. "She sits quietly on the top step. . . . The squatting men along the wall look at her still and placid face and they think as Armstid thought and as Varner thinks: that she is thinking of a scoundrel who deserted her in trouble and who they believe that she will never see again, save his coattails perhaps already boardflat with running" (22). When white men look at a man, they see him looking back and they read his looks, both what he looks like and how he is looking at them. It is a visual exchange that produces likenesses and more looks. When these men look at a woman, they barely do look at her; neither of the men who give Lena rides looks directly at her (10–11, 24–25). Nor do they need to look at her to know all about her. Lena's looks allow them to recognize likenesses, but the likenesses narrow down rather than opening up identities for her. She looks like she has done just what she has done.

By confining their reading of male looks to surfaces, men are able to produce a collection of images that represent the common experience of white men. In analyses of men watching women, particularly in movies, feminist critics have suggested that images of women's bodies are seen as objects or fetishes. Limited to complete surfaces, such images of women preclude recognition of the female lack (of male genitals) beneath the surface of the image that signals male castration.[2] But here, men look at men as images, not with the effect of containing or limiting their identity but with a productive effect.

Identifying likenesses for the images, watchers produce more images and likenesses. This works for inclusion, as the likenesses suggest the familiar and inevitable quality of the strangers. The men know that Christmas's look will get him in trouble; they know the kind of horse and car that Brown is like. The likenesses imagined for the two men provide a sense of shared experience, of things known in common. The strangers become like the men who watch them, while Lena remains just as she is. Moreover, she becomes a person about whom all the men think alike. The likenesses produced for the male figures are inclusive but also expressive of differences; they indicate various views of the men watched. Male likenesses thereby allow for the expression of individual views in a metaphorical production of likeness that indicates the variety of white men.

The early observations of Lena, Joe, and Brown in *Light in August* indicate a gendering of reproduction according to which white women reproduce their histories and their bodies and white men reproduce images. A woman's looks tell others about herself. A man's looks tell others about the common experience of them all and also allow for the self-expression of individuals who interpret those looks. The exchanges of looks and images among white men constitute a collectivity that is akin to James's museum collection in *The Golden Bowl* or to, perhaps, the collective works produced by a repertory theater company. As when images in a museum are recognized as parts of art history rather than social or personal history, men's looks indicate various likenesses in the abstract terms of a public male collective. As a production of views, moreover, these looks and likenesses allow for the airing of various perspectives, opinions, and points of view, an airing that occurs as both an aesthetic and a political enterprise.

Indeed, Jürgen Habermas suggests that the twentieth-century democratic public sphere confuses imagery with thinking. An eighteenth-century public of autonomous persons engaging in the common terms of rational debate becomes in the twentieth century disparate persons and groups whose patterns of consumption mark their differences; they express no rational views, engage in no debate, and formulate no public policy. Eventually, according to Habermas, the publicity of the public sphere becomes controlled by advertising and other "public relations."[3] The media produce the figures that govern opinion, and representation occurs in the form of "public figures" rather than in the expression of differing views or opinions. Public debate is completely displaced by the public's consumption of representations in the media.

In *Light in August* white men represent themselves by reproducing images and acts; they also act as audience members who read and interpret these performances. Though Habermas argues that shared communication breaks down in a public sphere of consumers, Faulkner indicates that it does not. The audience of watchful men in Jefferson, at any rate, engages in communications of imagery. Though not rational debate leading to the formation of public policy, the exchange of images and likenesses does constitute a public sphere and determines who belongs within it: who participates in the free and open exchange of different views that occurs in it.

Like the expression of opinion in a democratic public sphere, the views expressed by white men are changeable. But public policy is not determined by any resolution of differing opinions. Nor is it determined, apparently, by the men who take part in it. As in Habermas's reading of the twentieth-century public sphere, in which advertising and publicity cause people to choose certain views over others, men do not seem responsible for the likenesses and differences they represent in public. They simply appear to be observing how things and persons look.

This public sphere is certainly as abstract an experience as the eighteenth-century sphere of public debate. Though not dealing in ideas, white male characters in *Light in August* are at one remove from their "actual" lives, and the scenery of their lives is all removable. Moreover, these men do not need to be together to be in relation to one another. As if watching productions of the media, they seem to recognize similar images in the persons and scenes they look at. Moreover, these images of likeness can be reproduced in their imaginations too, so that it is not necessary to be with others to experience the common repertoire of shows.

Acting Parts

These reproductions indicate that persons consume rather than produce their "views" or that they produce views already consumed. Moreover, if consumption is, as theorists have suggested, an experience of an unstable and various self,[4] participation in politics may mean changes of views caused not by changes in a man's thinking but by changes in the images provided by the media. The potential instability of individual identity is offset by other men's reproduction of the same likenesses. It is as if internal self-division is distributed among men, aired in the open rather than contained in the self. Exchanges of views and exchanges of parts, among men open to one another's views and to playing different parts, allows for a kind of de-alienation of the individual. On the one hand, the white male repertory of parts abstracts the individual from his particular experience. On the other, it provides images for and parts to be played by his internal other, as if to particularize his interior abstraction from himself. Relieved of his own history, such an individual may also be relieved of his own otherness.

McEachern is one of the men who behave as if playing a part. His behavior, even as he beats Joe, is impersonal and routine. "His voice was not unkind. It was not human, personal, at all. It was just cold, implacable, like written or printed words" (130). For such men, self-expression seems never to occur; expression is always a reading of something else. Yet to express the self impersonally and routinely is to be reliable. Joe prefers Mr. to Mrs. McEachern because "the man, the hard, just, ruthless man, merely depended on him to act in a certain way and to receive the as certain reward or punishment, just as he could depend on the man to react in a certain way to his own certain doings and misdoings" (146). Men can trust men, therefore, and become reliable themselves. Moreover, such behavior is both open and "clean," apparently because action has no interior motive or cause, no elements that are not clear and decisive. When Joe fights, as a child, with other boys, they "completely forget . . . why they had fought, if they had ever known" (138). "They just fought; it was as if a wind had blown among them, hard and clean" (137). When chasing Joe to his death, the moves of Percy Grimm are also impersonal and unthinking. He moves in "lean, swift, blind obedience to whatever Player moved him on the Board" (405).

Men can be relieved of indecision and insecurity by such impersonal action. They can also be relieved of internal doubleness by acting out multiple parts. Hightower, for example, takes the part of his dead grandfather as well as the part of grandson. His internal alienation, of the kind that tortures Quentin Compson, is openly expressed. Joe Christmas manages to project his internal alienation onto a scene in which other men take the part of his otherness. He begins the novel on the run, trying to escape "himself." He is "doomed with motion, driven by the courage of flagged and spurred despair; by the despair of courage whose opportunities had to be flagged and spurred" (197). At this point, experiencing internal splits—between courage and despair—Joe "might have seen himself as in numberless avatars" (197) because there is more within him than any single body or image can represent. But when Joe is finally chased by Grimm and the posse that comes after him, his initially interior division and escape are out in the open. His internal alienation takes a form that can be played and replayed in the sphere of white male representation.

Thus the symbolic realm of public representation offers figures—images for both self and other of white male individuals. The white male psyche is identified as a social script or a social production. As in a public sphere in which men debate their opinions, differences are aired in the open and expressed as belonging to various individuals.

This production of difference openly played by white men is achieved only with a sheer abstraction from "actual" pasts.

Escaping History

In the actual pasts of Christmas and Hightower, whose histories are given in the novel, there are other kinds of experience: closed, dirty, out of bounds to public representation. Such experience and its imagery are assigned both to white women and to black women and men. As in *The Sound and the Fury,* such persons are means of distinguishing white males. But in *Light in August* white women and black men and women pose a threat to white men if their necessity becomes apparent. Actually used as means of distinguishing white male figures, these characters cannot appear as necessary to white men without endangering white male distinction. Experiences of both white female and black characters in the novel are represented in common terms of darkness, formlessness, corruption, rot, swamp, slime, and other images of an undifferentiated mass that spreads and swallows white men. Such masses belong, according to the rules of the public sphere, in holes and secret spaces. Prohibited from public expression and recognition in any form whatever, they are acknowledged only as hidden and formless phenomena.

In the course of *Light in August,* the threat of racial and female blackness to white men is disposed of, which occurs when the struggles between white men and racial and female blackness are reproduced as struggles between white men only. The novel thereby replays the entry of male experience into the public sphere, clarifying the abstractions that must occur for an individual to enter life as a public figure. According to the terms of the novel, experience becomes reproducible and representable when it is cleaned up and set free from its ties to history. That is, it is freed from the actual scenes of the past in which events happened in a particular way. This means setting white men free from female and racial blackness, which is identified with historical cause in the novel and converted into lost causes when reproduced in the public sphere.

Whereas white men are joined together by the views that remove their common experience from actual historical scenes, Lena Grove, in the opening scene of the novel, is distinguished by views that place her in history. Lena's progress along the road, her late pregnancy, and her lack of a wedding ring are seen by men to indicate a past, a temporal development, a story in which she is coming after the man who fathered her child. Her body is identified as sequential, moving as inevitably as one moment comes after another. And her body appears as consequentiality, coming after Burch/Brown as the result of a time far removed but represented now in her body.

In *Light in August*, women and blackness are seen as something that comes after men, closes in on them, and chases them down. Lena threatens to hold Burch/Brown to his past by identifying him with consequence. Interfering with the removability of the scenery and the corresponding openness, mobility, and changeability of men's experience in public life, Lena moves in on Burch/Brown's life in Jefferson as if to stay. But the particular history which she represents and which would tie Burch/Brown to a consequential historical narrative rather than a removable and reproducible image is thwarted by the collective white male identity in Jefferson.

Bunch acts the part that Brown does not want to take. With no actual husband, Lena then has two men who have played, in part, the role of her husband. Her identity is further removed from her past when her baby is identified as Mrs. Hines's grandchild, by the doctor as well as the confused Mrs. Hines (348–49); then Lena " 'get[s] mixed up . . . and I think that his pa is that Mr—Mr Christmas too' " (359). The waitress Bobbie is also put in her place as a whore. Mocking her as Juliet, Max insists that he can see her relationship to Joe only as a bad act. Unlike white men who can take various roles convincingly, white women who assume multiple or changeable identities are associated with confusion and infidelity. Removed from consequentiality, the threat of history they embody becomes meaningless.

Lena is assigned a role when she is removed from the actual scenes of her past into a play in which the actors are interchangeable; she is identified, like Bobbie, as a "whore" (365). In the final scene of the novel, the last of the men who observe her actions takes her decisively out of history and consequence both. "I think she was just travelling. I dont think she had any idea of finding whoever it was she was following. I dont think she had ever aimed to, only she hadn't told him yet" (444). Byron Bunch reappears, unable to leave her but with no legal or moral responsibility for her or her child.

This particular replay of Faulknerian lost cause, in which man *as* cause disappears from view and women appear as whores whom men have trouble escaping, is a reproduction of crucial importance to the white male culture of Jefferson. The process by which a man achieves identity in this culture is a process of turning the self into a martyr to a lost cause, and martyrdom is achieved by all three of the central male characters of the novel.

Byron Bunch is the comic version of the martyr. Lena Grove is his "lost cause," a woman who seems unlikely ever to love him but whom he, for no clear reason, is stuck with. Christmas and Hightower achieve the distinction of tragic martyrs, also by means of women who are identified as sexually corrupt. These women, that is, are the causes produced for the men's martyrdom in the novel's tragic representations of their lives. Through the identification, in Joe Christmas's views of Joanna Burden, of female sexuality with darkness, the sexually corrupt white women take on the identity of black persons. And in this identification, blackness becomes another of white men's lost causes in the theatrical public sphere of the novel.

The lost cause is the only form in which racial blackness or females enter the public sphere of white male representations. Faulkner plays along with and reproduces these representations. But he allows for the recognition of something other than the tragedies white men produce to appear heroic. Also evident in the novel is the inability or refusal of white men to take responsibility for their history and actions. Black people and white women are the signs of lost cause, starting with Lena who has lost track of her baby's father. And they are used as such signs in productions of male martyrdom in which the lack of white male responsibility—perhaps the real lost cause—never appears.

Racial Blackness

Joe Christmas does not "look black" but believes that he is partly black. His fear of blackness as some part of himself he cannot escape is perhaps most explicit in the scene in which he walks through Jefferson one evening, first "between the homes of white people," looking "like a phantom, a spirit, strayed out of its own world, and lost."

> Then he found himself. Without his being aware the street had begun to slope and before he knew it he was in Freedman Town, sur-

rounded by the summer smell and the summer voices of invisible Negroes. They seemed to enclose him like bodiless voices murmuring, talking, laughing, in a language not his. As from the bottom of a thick black pit he saw himself enclosed by cabinshapes, vague, kerosene-lit, so that the street lamps themselves seemed to be farther spaced, as if the black life, the black breathing had compounded the substance of breath so that not only voices but moving bodies and light itself must become fluid and accrete slowly from particle to particle, of and with the now ponderable night inseparable and one. . . . On all sides, even within him, the bodiless fecundmellow voices of Negro women murmured. It was as though he and all other manshaped life about him had been returned to the lightless hot wet primogenitive Female. He began to run. (99–100)

Darkness seems to close in on Joe, with the street lamps farther apart than in the white neighborhood. But what is closing in on him is blackness, evident in no recognizable form, only in voices and smells. Although some language is spoken, Joe does not know it, and no signs exist of any culture. Without forms or signs to distinguish things, everything "becomes fluid," as "compounding" and "accretion" occur. It is then "as though" everything "manshaped" has merged into some female liquid.

As soon as he realizes that he has run out of the "black hollow," however, things take shape and spaces open up.

The Negro smell, the Negro voices, were behind and below him now. To his left lay the square, the clustered lights. . . . To the right the street lamps marched on, spaced, intermittent with bitten and unstirring branches. He went on, . . . passing again between the houses of white people. There were people on these porches too, and in chairs upon the lawns; but he could walk quiet here. Now and then he could see them: heads in silhouette, a white blurred garmented shape; on a lighted veranda four people sat about a card table, the white faces intent and sharp in the low light, the bare arms of the women glaring smooth and white above the trivial cards. (100)

In the white neighborhood things back off. The evidence of people is in visible forms and shapes so that their bounds are clear.

There are no smells, no voices, nothing that spreads through the air. The people playing cards, in particular, are both in focus—"intent," "sharp," "glaring"—and themselves clearly focused on a game, an organized activity with, presumably, definition, rules, and routine. Joe passes along, feeling that the street lamps also "march on." With clear forms and space in between them, the persons and objects in this scene are movable, whereas in the black neighborhood, the formlessness makes movement difficult. Only in the white neighborhood, then, are objects and scenery removable, a quality necessary to move experience into the public sphere.

When Joe enters the white neighborhood, he reproduces the figure of emergence that Faulkner uses to describe his body on the previous night. Then, Joe is standing naked by the road when a car passes him, and in the headlights, "he watched his body grow white out of the darkness like a kodak print emerging from the liquid" (94). Again when he emerges from the fluid black neighborhood into the distinct forms of the white neighborhood, Joe himself becomes a figure, and a man, subject to representation by media.[5] In these images of emergence, the white shape enters representation only in contrast to the black, shapeless mass. If this mass is the fluid needed to develop photographic negatives into positive prints or if it is, in the terms of the later passage, the fluid of the female body needed for the development of a human fetus, it is a means of development, a medium, necessary before entry into media of representation.

If white bodies must emerge from black fluid in order to be represented as white figures, blackness itself takes form only as the "doom and curse" of God and in Joanna Burden's eyes as a cross. Joanna tells Joe of her father teaching her that the black race was the curse of the white race.

> After that I seemed to see [Negroes] for the first time not as people, but as a thing, a shadow in which I lived, we lived, all white people, all other people. I thought of all the children coming forever and ever into the world, white, with the black shadow already falling upon them before they drew breath. And I seemed to see the black shadow in the shape of a cross. . . . At last I told father, tried to tell him. What I wanted to tell him was that I must escape, get away from under the shadow, or I would die. "You cannot," he said. "You must struggle, rise. But in order to rise, you must raise the shadow with you. But you can never lift it to your level. I see that now, which I did not see until I came down here. But escape it you cannot." (221–22)

Once represented as a doom and a curse by Joanna's father, black people are transformed from persons to things to nothing, a shadow. Then the shadow emerges "in the shape of a cross," to become the white man's burden.

In this form, blackness falls on white people, who can neither escape it nor "lift it to [their] level." Thus blackness enters the public sphere of white culture as a lost cause. But what falls altogether out of sight and is successfully escaped by white people according to this story is, first, the personal identity of black people and, second, the past in which black people were unable to escape the burdens put on them by white people. This history disappears, displaced by "timeless" imagery of mythic rather than historical dimensions, representing experience as repetitive and unalterable.

Joe Christmas finally emerges as a "Christ figure" in *Light in August* when he produces this process—that is, he removes himself from the scenes of his past and enters the scenery depicting blackness as a burden that he cannot escape. Beginning with no knowledge of his parents, Joe as well as others have only his looks to go by: he "looks white." Once those looks are rendered unreliable, his ignorance of his parents is joined to uncertainty about his race. In this uncertainty, as Eric Sundquist points out, Joe is like many people in the United States who are nevertheless identified as black or white.[6] The historical past is erased by the symbolic terms of racial distinction. To affirm the equation of his looks with white male likeness, Joe will take the role of a martyr to a lost cause. The specific lost cause he creates for himself is not racial but female blackness, the "Burden" of corrupt female sexuality that he identifies as Joanna.

Female Blackness

The exchange of one kind of blackness for another is made available to Joe at what is apparently his earliest experience of female sexuality. In the orphanage where he lives as a child, once "he discovered by accident the toothpaste which the dietitian used," Joe goes into the woman's room, quietly "like a shadow" (104), to eat it. When one day she comes in while he is there, Joe hides "beneath a cloth curtain which screened off one corner of the room" (105). She has a man with her, and Joe waits but begins to feel sick. "In the rife, pinkwomansmelling obscurity behind the curtain he squatted, pinkfoamed, listening to his insides, waiting with astonished fatalism for what was about to happen to him" (107). When he vomits, he is discovered.

The woman, "stupid enough to believe that a child of five not only could deduce the truth from what he had heard, but that he would want to tell it as an adult would" (107), asks the janitor to tell her what he knows of Joe. " 'You hate him too,' she said. 'You've been watching him too. I've seen you. . . . You know,' she said. 'You knew before the other children started calling him nigger. . . . And I've got to know. When he tells I will be fired' " (110–11). The janitor, who is eventually revealed to be Joe's grandfather and who believes both Joe and the dietitian are "evil," tells her to wait for God's will to be done. With no knowledge, the dietitian tells the matron Joe is black, and the two women arrange to have him adopted as soon as possible (123–25).

This is the earliest of the experiences in Joe's life that link women with secrecy. Attracted to the pink toothpaste, which is also like the "pink-and-white" dietitian (105), Joe is drawn into a world of obscurity and horror in which what is hidden inside or behind things is female and disgusting. Behind the curtain, Joe is terrified by his "insides," and once he throws up the pink ingredients of his stomach he is revealed to the woman as someone who knows her secrets of illicit sexuality. The dietitian, who wants to keep hidden what goes on inside her room, responds by inventing knowledge of Joe's "insides": that beneath an exterior that looks white enough he is "really" black. This is an even exchange: she attributes to him a hidden identity that will get him kicked out of the orphanage to prevent him from doing the same to her.

The grandfather wants no part in the revelation of hidden things, which he leaves to God. He also has a secret identity as Joe's grandfather; he claims to know that Joe's father was black, though that is his assumption rather than knowledge (328). Like other white men in the novel, he is interested only in what is revealed in looks and signs. "I just waited, on His own good time, when He would see fitten to reveal it to His living world. And it's come now. This is the sign, wrote again in womansinning and bitchery" (112). Blackness, heretofore secret and interior, is expressed in signs of "womanfilth" (115). The sinning female "reveals" Joe's blackness in a sign attributable, according to the white man, to both racial and female corruption.

Joe's presence as a white male observer marks the removability of the scene he witnesses to a different stage, on which it can be re-produced. But the woman moves first, to identify Joe as a male with no position in the world of white people and no capacity to participate in the reproduction of observations and views. She removes him from the scene altogether.

Joe reappears in nearby Jefferson many years later and begins an affair with Joanna Burden. He also watches Joanna, who in the first "phase" of their relationship reproduces conventional acts and ex-pressions of love.

> During that period (it could not be called a honeymoon) Christmas watched her pass through every avatar of a woman in love. . . . She surprised and took him unawares with fits of jealous rage. She could have had no such experience at all, and there was neither reason for the scene nor any possible protagonist: he knew that she knew that. It was as if she had invented the whole thing deliberately, for the pur-pose of playing it out like a play. Yet she did it with such fury . . . that on the first occasion he thought that she was under a delusion and the third time he thought that she was mad. She revealed an unex-pected and infallible instinct for intrigue. She insisted on a place for concealing notes, letters. (226)

Too personally involved to be playing a role, Joanna begins to dete-riorate or degenerate when she reveals an "instinct for intrigue." "Within six months she was completely corrupted" (227). Joe does not share Joanna's "blackness"; he leads "a life of healthy and normal sin" (227). But the small holes she has identified "for concealing notes, letters" seem to develop into great holes in which Joe is in danger of being swallowed up. It is in this second "phase," a term that suggests a natural and inevitable cycle, that Joe feels "as though he had fallen into a sewer" (224), and "he began to see himself as from a distance, like a man being sucked down into a bottomless morass" (227).

Although Joanna begins with conventional roles and reproduces recognizable poses, she goes "mad" and "wild."

> Now and then she appointed trysts beneath certain shrubs about the grounds, where he would find her naked, . . . in the wild throes of nymphomania, her body gleaming in the slow shifting from one to another of such formally erotic attitudes and gestures as a Beardsley of the time of Petronius might have drawn. She would be wild then,

in the close, breathing halfdark without walls, with her wild hair, each strand of which would seem to come alive like octopus tentacles, and her wild hands and her breathing: "Negro! Negro! Negro!" (227)

What are at first conventional white poses deteriorate into animal and "Negro" behavior. Then, as in the black neighborhood, things begin to close in on Joe, and there is a threat of being caught, in the closeness or by the "octopus tentacles."[7]

When Joe watches Joanna during this time, he sees her as "two creatures that struggle in the one body" (228). "One" of her "strove to drown in the black abyss of its own creating that physical purity which had been preserved too long now even to be lost. Now and then they would come to the black surface, locked like sisters" (228). This duality becomes, in the "third phase," a division between a ghostly daytime self and a "night sister." Watching Joanna working, Joe sees

beneath the clean, austere garments which she wore that rotten richness ready to flow into putrefaction at a touch, like something growing in a swamp. . . . And when he thought of that other personality that seemed to exist somewhere in physical darkness itself, it seemed to him that what he now saw by daylight was a phantom of someone whom the night sister had murdered and which now moved purposeless about the scenes of old peace, robbed even of the power of lamenting. (229)

Again Joanna is seen first in a recognizable and familiar form, and again that form disappears from sight and is replaced by something dark, rotten, and growing.

The descriptions of Joanna's corruption are physical but vague. They are dark, for one thing; they are shapeless, and they spread. To some extent Joanna seems diseased: "It was as though with the corruption which she seemed to gather from the air itself, she began to corrupt him" (227). Like a communicable physical decay, her corruption has no clear source or shape, and like a swamp it is neither reasonable nor resistible. It is doubly threatening and doubly "catching": Joe can be caught by dark things that reach out for him or by dark holes he falls into, by both threatening forms and formless threats. This uncontained corruption repeatedly exceeds the figures and poses of formal representation as it flows beyond the limits of distinct form. In keeping with this spreading corruption, Joanna at the end of the "second phase" has "begun to get fat" (228).

Male Martyrs

In her third "phase," Joanna decides to send Joe to one of the black colleges with which she is affiliated. "To school—A nigger school. Me" (241). It is at this point that he kills her. For some unexplained reason, Joe has never been able to leave Joanna. "Perhaps he realised that he could not escape. Anyway, he stayed" (228). Even when he murders her and then successfully evades the men chasing him, he walks openly into Mottstown and waits to be recognized and arrested (306). Then, when taken to Jefferson, Joe escapes jail only, "when free," to go "where he must have known he would be certainly run to earth" (388).

To escape, either from Joanna or, later, from the law, would be to become black and formless. This is what Joe feels when he changes boots with a black woman to escape the men who come after him; they, using dogs to track him, follow Joe's boots instead of him. "It seemed to him that he could see himself being hunted by white men at last into the black abyss which had been waiting, trying, for thirty years to drown him and into which now and at last he had actually entered, bearing now upon his ankles the definite and ineradicable gauge of its upward moving" (289). To turn this blackness into a form distinct from himself, Joe must take on Joanna Burden as an inescapable lost cause. Transforming her blackness into a cross, he can be a martyr, living up to his name, despite the fact that he is a murderer, a history that apparently does not interfere with his likeness to Christ.

Gail Hightower's experience of martyrdom is more deliberate than Joe's and more deliberately a reproduction of imagined male likenesses. Hightower as a young man "had come straight to Jefferson from the seminary, refusing to accept any other call," and "was still excited even after six months, still talking about the Civil War and his grandfather, a cavalryman, who was killed" in Jefferson after the end of the war (52–53).

On the train as he came with his wife to his church, Hightower, who grew up hearing stories of his grandfather, had clear pictures in his mind of Jefferson, though he had never been there.

> A handful of men . . . [r]iding for a hundred miles through a country where every grove and hamlet had its Yankee bivouac, and into a garrisoned town—I know the very street that they rode into town upon and then out again. . . . I know exactly how the house that we will some day own and live in upon the street will look. . . . [W]e can look out the window and see the street, maybe even the hoofmarks or their shapes in the air, because the same air will be there even if the dust, the mud, is gone—Hungry, gaunt, yelling, setting fire to the store depots of a whole carefully planned campaign and riding out again. . . . Try to see it. Here is that fine shape of eternal youth and virginal desire which makes heroes. (423)

The looks and looking that occur are means of reproducing a past of male predecessors. And the scene on the train is itself a reproduction of a past that occurred many years ago. In this more recent past, Hightower's wife was unable to see the "fine shapes" he pointed out to her. But although she did recognize the white male likenesses of Hightower's imagination, Mrs. Hightower became the lost cause of Hightower's martyrdom. His initial lost cause is his grandfather's civil war, but he makes do instead, like Joe, with bearing the burden of a corrupt woman.

This means a change of scenery—in fact, a whole new "campaign," one that is corrupt and run by a woman. Hightower always wanted to live in Jefferson—"he had been working for that since he was four years old" (422)—but he depended on his wife to get him assigned there. She planned her "campaign of abasement and plotting," "talking as though to herself of men, names, to see, to grovel to or threaten." And this campaign too is one Hightower watches: "He said, 'Yes. Yes. I see.' . . . It was as if he were saying *Yes. I see. I see now. That's how they do such, gain such. That's the rule. I see now*" (422). And in this way he learns about love and marriage as well: "So this is love. I see" (421); "*I see. That's the way it is. Marriage. Yes. I see now*" (422).

What Hightower sees watching his wife is what Joe sees watching Joanna: a corruption in which he takes no part. Mrs. Hightower's corruption is reinforced when it is transformed—or perhaps it spreads—into sexual corruption.

"She would slip off to Memphis now and then and have a good time. . . . Some folks claimed he knew about it. That he couldn't or wouldn't satisfy her himself and that he knew what she was doing. Then one Saturday night she got killed, in a house or something in Memphis. Papers full of it. He had to resign from the church, but he wouldn't leave Jefferson, for some reason. . . . That was pretty bad on the church, you see. Having strangers come here and hear about it, and him refusing to leave the town." (50–51)

As his wife acts out her illicit sexuality, the possibility that Hightower knows of it only sharpens his image as a martyr.

In his own memory, Hightower recognizes that he used his wife and her corruption "as a means toward [his] own selfishness" (428), in order to play the role he desired.

He seems to watch himself, alert, patient, skillful, playing his cards well, making it appear that he was being driven, uncomplaining, into that which he did not even then admit had been his desire since before he entered the seminary. . . . [A]llowing himself to be persecuted, to be dragged from his bed at night and carried into the woods and beaten with sticks, he all the while bearing in the town's sight and hearing, without shame, with that patient and voluptuous ego of the martyr, the air, the behavior, the *How long, O Lord* until, inside his house again and the door locked, he lifted the mask with voluptuous and triumphant glee. (428–29)

Seemingly unsophisticated, Hightower has "played the game" much more effectively than did his wife to get what he wanted. Here, looking back, he exposes to his own view the history and cause of his martyrdom. But the exposé that occurred in the media did not reach beneath the mask. The corruption with which Hightower was publicly linked in the newspapers, like the black fluid from which Joe's image emerges, is the contrasting darkness against which he emerged looking pure, white, martyred: the image, finally, of his grandfather.

But Hightower is overexposed. For one thing, he sees too much to be represented in the media of male likenesses, for what he sees is that, beneath his looks, he designed that likeness and sacrificed his wife to it. He sees the cause of the lost cause. People in the town saw him overexposed too, not only in the publicity that was distasteful to them but also in their suspicion that he knew about and did something to cause his wife's actions. Once overexposed, the forms of male public figures blur, lose distinction, like the sign he put up in front of his house: "Handpainted Xmas & Anniversary Cards / Photographs Developed" (50). Now, when Hightower sits in the dark, a mere shape looking out his window, the sign "is just a familiar low oblong shape without any significance at all" (51). Merging into the darkness, both he as public figure and his sign lose significant form. As with the figures and signs of the black characters of the novel, white characters pass by without noticing them.

Racial Symbolics

What might be called the racial symbolic in *Light in August* represents looks in peculiar ways, to be read in peculiar ways. So-called black and white people do not, or only seldom, look black and white. To say that Joe looks white is to employ the symbolic terms that convert mixed or indistinct experience into distinct forms. White women are represented, in symbolic terms, as limited to their bodily experience. Defined by physical limits, white women are not, however, limited to their appearance. Women's looks do not indicate their hidden holes and other secrets, thus white women's looks are not to be trusted, whereas white men's looks can be. In keeping with this distinction, women contain their own doubleness, as does Joanna Burden in Joe's eyes. She is haunted not by the spirit of someone else but by herself as phantom, and she embodies the struggle between purity and corruption that white men experience, in their imaginations if not their histories, between different men, different armies, different teams. White men exist free of physical limits. Their looks, as well as the likenesses recognized in their looks, move them into common identities. White men are bound together not by whiteness but by likenesses as imaginative as their whiteness.

Black persons in the novel are represented only vaguely. This is in keeping with the unrepresentable, formless "nature" of blackness in the experience of the white characters, except when it is transformed into the abstract form of a cross or other burden. Black men in this novel do not look at all, or if they do, no one can tell by their looks.[8] One confrontation, between Joe and a black man, occurs at night, and nothing is seen of the other man except his shape (102).

When Brown is looking for someone to carry a message to town for him, he meets a black man in daylight but can recognize little from the man's looks.

> Standing beside the porch now, materialised apparently from thin air, is a Negro who may be either a grown imbecile or a hulking youth. His face is black, still, also quite inscrutable. They stand looking at one another. Or rather, Brown looks at the Negro. He cannot tell if the Negro is looking at him or not. And that too seems somehow right and fine and in keeping: that his final hope and resort should be a beast that does not appear to have enough ratiocinative power to find the town, let alone any given individual in it. (381)

Unrecognizable and "inscrutable," this man is not characterized as a man but as "either a grown imbecile or a hulking youth" or a "beast." He does not appear to be looking at Brown. But it seems from this description that one can never depend on a black man's looks to know anything about him. Though detailed, this description provides no distinction for the man but rather a list of what cannot be distinguished, of characteristics that do not appear. Even in broad daylight, it might as well be night.

The black woman who sits on the porch during this encounter clearly looks at Brown: "With an aged an inscrutable midnight face she seems to contemplate him with a detachment almost godlike but not at all benign" (380–81). Not quite human either, this woman is, like the black man, "inscrutable." She takes part in the exchange between Brown and the black man, for whom she speaks and whom she tells what to do (382–83). Like Dilsey in *The Sound and the Fury,* this woman does not speak on her own behalf, which increases the sense of her "detachment."

Joe Christmas, however, enters into representation at the end of the novel as an image in white men's minds. In a sense, Joe's castration and death undergo double exposure, as both history and imagery. Insofar as his castration is inflicted on him because he had sexual intercourse with and killed a white woman, it is a historical act, part of the history of white men torturing black men that has been removed from scenes of representation. Because his castration reproduces the imaginary castration that is perhaps the favorite twentieth-century image of white male lost cause, as the sacrifice required for entry into the symbolic, Joe Christmas becomes the image of the white male martyr. And it seems that Faulkner thereby effects the removal of this scene from historical event. The image of Joe's castration, in which "the pent black blood seemed to rush like a released breath" and "to rush out of his pale body like the rush of sparks from a rising rocket," is an image whose orgasmic heights appear far removed from the experience of having genitals cut off.

Even as Faulkner depicts Joe's castration and death, he "cleans up" the scene. The female blackness and the racial blackness that come after men and close in on them earlier in the novel are displaced by this chase of a man by white men. This is an impersonal set of moves caused by "the Player" (406) rather than the participants. The white man who comes after Joe does not swallow or submerge Joe, as women and blackness threaten to do, but separates him from part of himself, castrating him and thereby causing "the pent black blood" to rush from Joe's body: "Upon that black blast the man seemed to rise soaring into their memories forever and ever. They are not to lose it, in whatever peaceful valleys, beside whatever placid and reassuring streams of old age, in the mirroring faces of whatever children they will contemplate old disasters and newer hopes. It will be there, . . . of itself alone serene, of itself alone triumphant" (407). This is a process in which imagery replaces history. As if he cannot be contained in his body, part of Joe's body rushes out of him, such that he, or "it," will be seen everywhere, in whatever scenery is available. And "it" will be serene and triumphant. The image seems to have lost its cause.

Like Hightower, Faulkner both wipes out history and calls attention to the removal of scenery that occurs in order to transform history into white male culture.[9] Joe's blood, seen as black, becomes like the black fluid out of which white male bodies emerge as photographs. Once the blood appears black, the actual blood is lost sight of, and blackness is transformed, again, into a formless fluid that needs to be eliminated for Joe to become a memorable image. As this image takes shape, Joe enters into white male culture in the novel: a culture in which persons' bodies are emptied of contents, and impersonal images provide racial likeness.

c h a p t e r f i v e

Black Spaces in *Sula*

In *Sula,* spacing—that is, closing down or opening up distances between things and persons—has extraordinary urgency. Houses and
bodies are the sites of hyperactive mechanisms of containment and
expulsion working to effect identity and distinction: of inside and
outside, of self and other. Spacing, moreover, becomes crucial to issues of representation and meaning in the Bottom, the place in Medallion, Ohio, in which most of the action of the novel occurs. Houston A.
Baker Jr. has called attention to the importance of place in *Sula:* "What
Morrison ultimately seeks in her coding of Afro-American PLACE is
a writing of intimate, systematizing, and ordering black village values," he suggests.[1] But although the manipulation of persons and
things in space can produce a symbolic order, Morrison seems more
concerned with the placement of experience that orderly representation misses.

Two places in the novel that indicate her concern to locate missing
experience are "the place where Chicken Little sank" in the river and
the place Eva Peace's missing leg once occupied, "the empty place on
her left side."[2] Neither of these is quite what one would expect a place
to be, for neither is the present location of anything. Like the empty
spaces in a symbolic order, these places mark an absence. But unlike
the lacks and open spaces that in works of Faulkner and James are
necessary to structures of meaning, the experience of missing in *Sula*
is a particular, historical experience. Absence is not represented by the
open spaces that characterize an expansive white consciousness; it is
experienced in the preoccupations of a historical consciousness with
what has been and might be.[3]

Placing Absence

Missing takes time and takes place in *Sula;* particular persons and things are missed from particular places. Although "the closed place in the middle of the river" (119) and the place where Eva's leg once was have nothing in them, they mark the absence of persons or parts of persons once present. Morrison thereby fills in spaces of a kind white culture identifies as empty. In *Sula,* this means converting such unoccupied spaces into places on the basis of previous occupants. Morrison locates missing persons and parts of persons in places they have formerly occupied.

Locating such occupants is one kind of preoccupation that occurs in the novel. A second kind of preoccupation, however, rather than locating missing occupants once present, places missing occupations, ones that never occurred at all. By this I mean that Morrison identifies both failed possessions of places and failed actions: various connections between occupants and their places that never took place. This second kind of preoccupation is a more absolute missing—that is, missing compounded by the prior as well as present absence of what is missed. It is nonetheless a historical experience, given characters whose past is one in which the overwhelming "meaning" of experience was negative.

Such a history is "missing" in that it is not composed of positive facts known and recorded. But it is a missing history in another sense too: as a history of missing, a history *made* by people's knowledge of what they would never become, places they would never hold, things they would never do.[4] In the first kind of preoccupation, people are aware of something that once was present; in the second kind, people miss things that might have been but never were. Thus Morrison places both missed presences and missed absences in *Sula.*

If the experience of missing is historical and specific, it is not abstracted into a component of cultural experience, as was the case when James confronted what white Americans were missing in the nineteenth century. Rather than being abstracted, missing is embodied in *Sula,* as missing persons and missing parts of persons become the focus of meaning. Preoccupations with absence in *The Sound and the Fury,* partly because absence seems not to be experienced bodily, can be universalized into abstract elements of white male psychology.

When Faulkner's Jason Compson misses the job he never had, that lack becomes a stable determinant of meaning in his life; it also becomes the means of identifying him with other white men. What the Compson men miss, repeated in form if not in content, becomes a means of relationship among them, providing consistency in their experience. Over time, the experience of missing, represented as lost causes, becomes a historical likeness too. Men make history by reproducing themselves in the imagery of lost causes.

But Morrison's characters in *Sula* are missing the means of production by which James's and Faulkner's white characters make history. Those characters can experience individual consciousness as a medium of cultural reproduction because they can assume the representative character of individual consciousness. Inner experience and cultural experience become exchangeable, through the projections and introjections by which cultural identity is produced and reproduced. Characters in *Sula* neither produce nor reproduce the kind of forms or the kind of spaces that give both consistency and diversity to white identity. What these characters recognize in themselves and in their community are inconsistencies: broken bodies, broken objects, broken relations between persons and between persons and things.[5] This means that they are able to produce meaning and community only by keeping experience within strict bounds.

The experience of missing what never was in *Sula* is not only an experience of missed objects but an experience of missed relations, missed connections. Such missing is clearest near the end of the novel, in 1941, when many people die at the construction site of the proposed tunnel. What the people of the Bottom see when they look at this place is not only what is there but what might have been there and is not there: all the things denied or negated by the fact that black people were never hired to work there.

> Their hooded eyes swept over the place where their hope had lain since 1927. There was the promise: leaf-dead. The teeth unrepaired, the coal credit cut off, the chest pains unattended, the school shoes unbought, the rush-stuffed mattresses, the broken toilets, the leaning porches, the slurred remarks and the staggering childish malevolence of their employers. . . .
>
> Like antelopes they leaped over the little gate . . . and smashed the bricks they would never fire in yawning kilns, split the sacks of lime-

stone they had not mixed or even been allowed to haul; tore the wire mesh, tipped over wheelbarrows and rolled forepoles down the bank. (161)

The first "thing" located in this place is hope; the second is promise. Both these relations to things were once alive and are now dead. The construction site seems preoccupied by them, and with their deaths numerous other losses are remembered. The losses recalled are things that these people did not do, things that they lost, things that broke or fell apart, but things that might have been done, kept, and changed for the better. What is missed here are hope and promise and the changes in things which they represent but which never happened.

When people turn to look at the objects actually present, these too are seen in terms of failed relations. The bricks, limestone, and wheelbarrows have been denied to the people of the Bottom as objects of their labor. What these people see, therefore, is not only the objects but also their own missing occupation with these objects: bricks not fired, limestone not mixed, wheelbarrows not used to haul. Characters' realization of what they are missing is a recognition both of lost objects and of missed relations to objects: the loss of hope, promise, repair, credit, attention, occupation. These relations are attachments of people and things that function as meaningful connections by occupying one with another. With neither their minds nor their bodies occupied in labor as a creative relation to the world, labor in which they might become means of production and change, these people are unable to use objects or themselves to form and reform the world around them.

The tunnel site, then, is preoccupied with absences. Missing absent attachments means a massive "displacement": people tear things apart, throw things around, and start a landslide that carries some of them to their deaths in the river and buries others in the tunnel. For most of their lives, therefore, these people do not allow themselves to recognize what they miss in this scene. The role of Sula in the Bottom is to take the place of the absences that preoccupy these people at the tunnel in 1941. What circulates through the community at the tunnel site are not images of self that reassure the self of consistency in and with others but losses that individuals recognize in their own and others' experience. This awareness of loss cannot enter into circulation except with destructive effects. To contain that circulation, missing is projected onto one person, whose identification with loss will keep it within bounds.

By identifying Sula as evil and rejecting her categorically, characters are able to keep their distance from absences they cannot afford to acknowledge. In this case, keeping order depends not on emptying space of occupants but on filling in spaces whose emptiness is unbearable. Sula, occupied with loss, takes the place of absences people cannot afford to miss. Morrison has said that she "wanted Sula to be missed by the reader. That's why she dies early."[6] To miss Sula is to recognize her occupation in and of the Bottom: what she did there and how she was a necessary part of the place, not only as a presence but because she took the place of absence.

Placing Experience

Various characters in Sula create order through spacing practices that allow them to control loss. The first personal perspective Morrison narrates, however, is not the perspective of any character but instead an outsider's view of the Bottom. Not really even personal, this perspective belongs to a seemingly generic "valley man."

> If a valley man happened to have business up in those hills—collecting rent or insurance payments—he might see a dark woman in a flowered dress doing a bit of cakewalk, a bit of black bottom, a bit of "messing around" to the lively notes of a mouth organ. . . . The black people watching her would laugh and rub their knees, and it would be easy for the valley man to hear the laughter and not notice the adult pain that rested somewhere under the eyelids, somewhere under their head rags and soft felt hats, somewhere in the palm of the hand, somewhere behind the frayed lapels, somewhere in the sinew's curve. He'd have to stand in the back of Greater Saint Matthew's and let the tenor's voice dress him in silk, or touch the hands of the spoon carvers (who had not worked in eight years) and let the fingers that danced on wood kiss his skin. Otherwise the pain would escape him even though the laughter was part of the pain.

A valley man is a European American, but he is identified in *Sula* not by race but by where he comes from: "white people lived on the rich valley floor in that little river town in Ohio, and the blacks populated the hills above it" (5). The identification of this man by his place begins a scene in which Morrison places experience where it cannot be seen and in which the watching man misses it. Because he does not see and does not go to certain places that are parts of the black people's experience, he perceives spaces as empty that for them are occupied by pain.

Seeing no sign of pain, the white man sees the people's laughter as excluding pain, whereas for them "the laughter was part of the pain." This difference in perception is located as Morrison identifies places that pain resides, such as "somewhere under their head rags." Preoccupied by pain, the bodies of these people are locations of both laughter and pain, which the white man cannot recognize because he is ignorant of certain other places too. There are places he could go—to the back of Greater Saint Matthew's or up close enough to touch the hands of the carvers—where the pain of the black people's experience would not escape him.

The white man stands at a distance from the black people in this scene, excluded and exclusive. But rather than being separated by an empty space of necessary detachment, a distance built into knowledge or representation, the white man could move into places in which he could feel what he is missing. It is not only in the experience observed, then, that something is missed in this scene, for the white man both fails to recognize certain preoccupations in the people he watches and has never been in the places occupied by their pain. His distances from the people he watches depend on excluding certain occupations—and certain missed occupations such as spoon carving—from knowledge and thereby converting places of occupation into empty spaces of separation.

Patterns of Containment

In the histories of the Bottom's inhabitants, Morrison goes on to redefine space as place. The occupants of the Bottom whose histories are first given in the novel include Shadrack, who was a soldier in the First World War, and Helene Wright, who came to the Bottom from New Orleans when she married. These are the first of the characters who practice strict containments and limitations of experience that keep things in their places.

Morrison first charts the need for such constraints in the story of Shadrack. Having seen a soldier's head blown off on a battlefield of the First World War, Shadrack reacted with a terror of things out of place.

> Before him on a tray was a large tin plate divided into three triangles. In one triangle was rice, in another meat, and in the third stewed tomatoes. . . . Shadrack stared at the soft colors that filled these triangles. . . . All their repugnance was contained in the neat balance of the triangles—a balance that soothed him, transferred some of its equilibrium to him. Thus reassured that the white, the red and the brown would stay where they were—would not explode or burst forth from their restricted zones—he suddenly felt hungry and looked around for his hands. . . . Slowly he directed one hand toward the cup and, just as he was about to spread his fingers, they began to grow in higgledy-piggledy fashion like Jack's beanstalk all over the tray and the bed. (8–9)

Shadrack is able to put a limit on the size of his hands as well as the dimensions of death by "making a place for fear as a way of controlling it" (14). He finds a place in the Bottom, founding National Suicide Day, in 1920, as a place for death: "If one day a year were devoted to it, everybody could get it out of the way and the rest of the year would be safe and free" (14). Having focused his fears on this containment, Shadrack himself can be focused and contained. "Once the people understood the boundaries and nature of his madness, they could fit him, so to speak, into the scheme of things" (15).

Like Shadrack, Helene experienced psychic chaos once when she left Medallion. With one slip, when she mistakenly gets into the "white" car on the train going south, she begins to lose control of her existence and slide back into an identity with her mother, "a Creole whore" (17), from whom Helene has spent her life trying to separate herself. Morrison traces this slide in a series of displacements:

> "What you think you doin', gal?"
> . . . So soon. She hadn't even begun the trip back. Back to her grandmother's house in the city where the red shutters glowed, and already she had been called "gal." All the old vulnerabilities, all the old fears of being somehow flawed gathered in her stomach and made her hands tremble. She had heard only that one word; it dan-

gled above her wide-brimmed hat, which had slipped, in her exer-
tion, from its carefully leveled placement and was now tilted in a bit
of a jaunt over her eye. (20)

Watching Helene, two black soldiers observe her exchange with the
conductor. Then, as Nel, Helene's daughter, watches them all, "for
no earthly reason" her mother "smiled dazzlingly and coquettishly
at the salmon-colored face of the conductor," and the two soldiers
suddenly "looked stricken" (21). "She saw the muscles of their faces
tighten, a movement under the skin from blood to marble" (21–22),
and "she resolved to be on guard—always. She wanted to make certain that no man ever looked at her that way. That no midnight eyes
or marbled flesh would ever accost her and turn her into jelly" (22).
Like Shadrack glaring at his rice and tomatoes, Nel watches the "custard" and "jelly" of her mother; she then resolves to resist their spread
and slippage. Never again to leave Medallion, Nel returns home to be
her own self: "I'm me. I'm not their daughter. I'm not Nel. I'm me.
Me" (28).

The stories of Shadrack and of Helene and Nel's trip to New Orleans offer different experiences of a need for containment. Both characters set limits to preoccupations. These are memories that occupy
their minds, but as memories of bodily disintegration they are, specifically, recollections of a loss of place. Shadrack, after seeing another
body come apart, fears that his own body cannot be kept within
bounds. Initiating National Suicide Day, he puts a limit to his fears, to
death, and to bodily disintegration by limiting suicide to one day of
the year and then "keeping" the holiday. Helene contains her fears by
keeping house and keeping up standards of propriety, both in her
house and in the Bottom.

But Helene's fears, and Nel's too, are apparently driven less by
what they see than by what others, particularly men, see in Helene.
Whereas Shadrack's body loses consistency in his own eyes, Helene is
watched by others who see her body as that of a "loose" woman,
"custard." Therefore Helene must contain not only her own slips but
the way she spreads into someone else when men look at her. On the
train south, she feels herself losing her place as Helene Wright and
slipping into an identity with her mother, the whore. Then she sees
herself losing her place in the men's eyes. They reflect not Helene
Wright or her mother but just another black woman in sexual com-

plicity with a white man. Once she begins to "slip," she spreads into this generalized identity because of history, memory, and fears of the men's own, preoccupations over which she has no control.

In the hospital, Shadrack is "relieved and grateful" when he is put into a straitjacket, "for his hands were at last hidden and confined to whatever size they had attained" (9). He is further relieved when he is able to see his reflection. "There in the toilet water he saw a grave black face. A black so definite, so unequivocal, it astonished him. He had been harboring a skittish apprehension that he was not real—that he didn't exist at all. But when the blackness greeted him with its indisputable presence, he wanted nothing more" (13). Helene, unable "to relieve herself" on the trip south because she is allowed no access to toilets, is perhaps without access either to the sense of presence that relieves Shadrack of his fears of nonexistence. As she sees herself reflected in men's eyes, she does not experience reflection as a means of bodily containment but as one other dimension in which she has difficulty keeping her place. Helene finds bodily relief in the grass but also in another "accomplishment": by the time she has reached Slidell, Louisiana, "she never felt a stir as she passed the muddy eyes of the men who stood like wrecked Dorics under the station roofs of those towns" (24). She is relieved here not by bodily containment but by getting rid of something in her body: the urine she expels, as well as the feelings usually stirred by men watching her.[7]

Patterns of Expulsion

Other women in the novel enforce more violent expulsions from their houses and their bodies, intent on getting rid of things and keeping their distance rather than keeping order. Whereas Helene Wright maintains strict standards and "the oppressive neatness of her home" (29), the Peace women inhabit a "household of throbbing disorder constantly awry with things, people, voices and the slamming of doors" (52). Their messy existence may not result from an indifference to limits, however; it seems instead one effect of a history of ejections and rejections by means of which the Peace women find relief in discharging fears rather than containing them. Walking out, throwing out, cutting off, sending things flying—these women affirm boundaries and their power over boundaries by getting rid of things.

Sula will walk out of Medallion on the day of Nel's wedding, as her grandmother Eva once walked out on her three children, to return "eighteen months later . . . with two crutches, a new black pocketbook, and one leg" (34). Eva's lost leg becomes the subject of various stories. "Somebody said Eva stuck it under a train and made them pay off" (31). But the stories Eva herself tells are of two kinds: "How the leg got up by itself one day and walked on off. How she hobbled after it but it ran too fast. Or how she had a corn on her toe and it just grew and grew and grew until her whole foot was a corn and then it travelled on up her leg and wouldn't stop growing until she put a red rag at the top but by that time it was already at her knee" (30–31). According to these two versions, Eva's body is subject to both excursions and incursions of parts.

On her trip south, Helene Wright defends against the inconsistency of "custard" with "the best protection: her manner and her bearing, to which she would add a beautiful dress" (19). Eva Peace deals with the inconsistency of her body not by means of consistent and beautiful forms but by making visible, even decorative, the difference between her absent and her present parts. "Nor did she wear overlong dresses to disguise the empty place on her left side. Her dresses were mid-calf so that her one glamorous leg was always in view as well as the long fall of space below her left thigh" (31). Rendering her inconsistency itself a consistent expression of her distinction, Eva in her refusals to standardize her identity nevertheless places it by securing the difference between self and other, opening to others' scrutiny the space of the missing leg.

Eva's interest in boundaries and spaces is as evident in her house as in her body. "Sula Peace lived in a house of many rooms that had been built over a period of five years to the specifications of its owner, who kept on adding things: more stairwars—there were three sets to the second floor—more rooms, doors and stoops. There were rooms that had three doors, . . . others that you could get to only by going through somebody's bedroom" (30). This house does not seem primarily a container so much as an excrescence. Eva keeps building, repeatedly pushing out and throwing up forms in additions whose messiness lies in the irregularity of access to them. Both over- and underaccessed, the parts of the house confirm Eva's control over ingress and egress. Spaces between are of more concern here than spaces per se, with an unusual amount of space given over to access.

Even rooms are reduced to ways in and out of other rooms, so that any space may become itself a spacing, a distance between: not so much a room, as room to get in and out.[8]

It is not that Eva and her house are open and free whereas Helene Wright and her house are constrained and closed. In terms of intent, the difference between the two is less than such oppositions suggest, because the primary concern of each woman seems her capacity to control and manipulate boundaries. Helene tries to preclude things slipping out of place; Eva lets things slip, even fly out of places in what may be an equally obsessive insistence on the permeability of boundaries. Hurling herself out a window of her bedroom to try to save her daughter Hannah, who has caught fire in the yard, Eva at another time burns up her son in his room because "there wasn't space for him in my womb" and "he wanted to crawl back in" (71).

Both women are primarily occupied, then, with controlling, or even patrolling, boundaries so as to control the definition of their own selves. Both mark off the self through representations that rule out certain parts of their experience. Helene with her good form—her beautiful manner, bearing, and clothes—represents herself with a consistency that she lacks in her body and in her history. Eva's equally careful representation of her body presents an absence that also sets limits to her bodily and historical inconsistency. One woman places her past out of bounds to maintain consistency. The other maintains and thereby controls inconsistency by putting her past into a space defined by what is missing from it yet emptied of history as well as the leg. Eva's past can "take shape" only as something missing: an inconsistent, unknown, and mysterious gap in her existence.

Sula's Perspectives

There are at least three distances at which characters in the novel experience the representations that provide their identity, two of which I have already discussed. In the water in a toilet, Shadrack sees his definite identity as a black man reflected back at him. As in Lacan's "mirror stage," this experience of reflection defines the self as other. If Shadrack sees his ideal self reflected in a toilet, that reflection is both ideal and abject. Yet he is nevertheless reassured that he is "real" by the reflected image (13).[9] Helene Wright and Eva Peace, I have argued, produce for themselves, by manipulations of things and bodies in space, definitive representations such as Shadrack finds in reflected images. For these women, definition is not provided by reflections. But they nonetheless, as they fill in and empty spaces, provide definite forms of and limits to meaning.

Eva's daughter and granddaughter both, like her, get rid or get out of things by increasing distances between one thing and another. As a child, Sula understands the defensive value of cutting off parts of her body; she scares away the white boys who chase her by chopping off the end of her finger (54–55). Later she lets fly a whole body when Chicken Little "slipped from her hands and sailed away out over the water" to his death (60–61). This is just after she herself has been "sent . . . flying up the stairs" by her mother's announcement that she does not like her (57). Sula, however, seems not to experience her manipulations of space as representative. Whereas Eva is characterized in stories as having cut off her leg, Sula actually cuts off part of her finger. And whereas her mother sends her flying figuratively, she sends Chicken Little's body through the air and kills him. Yet Sula does not control such acts; she does not mean them, and they effect no meaningful forms of experience for her. It is as if Sula does not have the distance from such events necessary to experience control of them.

On the one hand, Sula, like her mother and grandmother, is identified with breaks and separations. On the other, she does not use breaks and separations to give form or consistency to her experience. Unlike Eva, Sula does not place or contain inconsistency so as to limit it; she simply allows a place for losses, breaks, and separations that occur. She does not attempt to repair or reform or connect things that break or exercise any other control over them; she lets things go. Morrison says that Sula is "like any artist with no art form" (121), and Sula does not use form to control experience. Nevertheless, she experiences definition, which occurs through the location of absence rather than in the re-presentation of forms. Because she does not use form to provide definition, Sula realizes the form and definition given to experience by absence. It is her recognition of the definitive power of missing that makes Sula's perspective extraordinary.

The ways in which Sula breaks meaning apart are to some extent familial. The Peace women enforce emotional distances, for example, with their tendency to throw things around. Because of such distances Sula can be identified, as Hortense J. Spillers argues, as "a figure of the rejected and vain part of the self—ourselves—who in its thorough corruption and selfishness cannot utter, believe in, nor prepare for, love."[10] Sula's emotional detachment is evident in certain physical distances she maintains, such as "standing on the back porch just looking" as her mother burns to death (78). With this perspective, Sula goes beyond the bounds even of her family's sense of proper distance. She repeatedly opens up what Spillers calls "subperspectives, or *angles onto* a larger seeing" because she disconnects elements of meaning that other people connect.[11]

Sula's capacity to "just look" depends on experiencing no emotions or intentions that connect her to objects and no meaningful links, either, between one experience and another. She can look at things without presuming anything about them, holding to no assumptions that would affect the "clarity" of her perception. She thereby calls into question assumptions other characters hold. When Jude comes home from work expecting commiseration from Nel, for example, Sula looks at his experience another way.

> [He] told them a brief tale of some personal insult done him by a customer and his boss—a whiney tale that peaked somewhere between anger and a lapping desire for comfort. He ended it with the observation that a Negro man had a hard row to hoe in this world. . . . Sula said she didn't know about that—it looked like a pretty good life to her. . . .
>
> " . . . White men love you. They spend so much time worrying about your penis they forget their own. . . . And white women? They chase you all to every corner of the earth, feel for you under every bed. . . . Now ain't that love?" (103)

Sula's insistence on looking at things another way provides Jude the relief of laughter rather than the comfort of monotonous sympathy. But this relief depends on disconnection and detachment.

What occurs in such scenes is similar to what occurs when Henry James's Adam and Maggie Verver produce new views of persons and situations in *The Golden Bowl*. Yet although James identifies those views as occurring in clear or open space, Sula's way of looking at things suggests that the Ververs do not merely look. Compared with Sula, the Ververs look at things with many assumptions, with what might be called a "backing": made up, for example, of the belief that they can change situations, if not persons, by viewing them differently.[12] Adam Verver's consciousness is one other open space that Morrison might view as preoccupied. Backed by such beliefs, the Ververs view objects in relations. Backed by no belief in relations, "just looking," Sula makes clear that Jude's experience is invisible. To look at it, it could be anything.

Dead Losses

Not only does Sula break with conventionally gendered identities because she actively looks at others,[13] but her perception also causes breaks within certain constructions of meaning at work as symbolic orders. As Mae G. Henderson argues, the effect of Sula's breaks with meaning is "to disrupt or subvert the 'symbolic function of the language.'"[14] Yet this effect is not exactly deconstructive. Although Sula certainly breaks apart meanings others assign to experience, she fails to produce the sense of contested meaning that deconstruction produces when a struggle for meaning is revealed within apparently masterful structures. In others' eyes—within the community, and from the reader's perspective—Sula has a deconstructive effect, because she becomes a scapegoat, a necessary presence who is also an outcast. But in Sula's personal experience there is none of the tension of deconstruction. She is capable of imagining anything as anything, and her "gift for metaphor" (121) suggests that she can imagine anything in the place of anything else. But her displacements lack the consistency necessary to both constructed and deconstructed meaning.

Whereas deconstruction contests the limits that hold meaning secure, Sula destroys meaning. One could say that she demeans experience, for she converts meaningful experience into sheer loss. Her losses are never recouped and her breaks never repaired, because they never assume a form that gives them consistency. Though an "artist," Sula lacks occupation as well as form, and her disengagement precludes meaning.

When Sula experiences consistency, it occurs only as an event in time, something that cannot be consistently maintained. There are several points in the novel when Sula attempts to hold herself together or imagines doing so. But in each case her hold breaks, and she comes apart. Her experience of sexual intercourse is described in these terms; her body feels both pulled together and dispersed. "Particles of strength gathered in her like steel shavings drawn to a spacious magnetic center, forming a tight cluster that nothing, it seemed, could break. . . . But the cluster did break, fall apart, and in her panic to hold it together she leaped from the edge into soundlessness" (123). When she is making love to Ajax, she thinks about "his face in order to confine, for just a while longer, the drift of her flesh toward the high silence of orgasm" (130). But she only contains the slippage of her own body by imagining that she can split his apart.

> If I take a chamois and rub real hard on the bone, right on the ledge of your cheek bone, some of the black will disappear. It will flake away into the chamois and underneath there will be gold leaf. . . .
>
> And if I take a nail file or even Eva's old paring knife—that will do—and scrape away at the gold, it will fall away and there will be alabaster. . . .
>
> Then I can take a chisel and small tap hammer and tap away at the alabaster. It will crack then like ice under the pick, and through the breaks I will see the loam. (130)

Breaking away his face, in bits, Sula exercises no imaginative containment of her own body or his.

What might be parts of a struggle for representative order, then, occur as displacements with no meaning. Sula breaks apart bodies, in fact and in imagination, whose parts remain split apart. And as she claims to mean nothing by such actions, she also breaks apart the meaningful constructions that attach motive, intention, and logical causes to events. As she says of Ajax: "It's just as well he left. Soon I would have torn the flesh from his face just to see if I was right about the gold and nobody would have understood that kind of curiosity. They would have believed that I wanted to hurt him just like the little boy who fell down the steps and broke his leg and the people think I pushed him just because I looked at it" (136–37). Attaching events to motives and feelings, others in the Bottom combine parts of experience that Sula separates. The neutrality of Sula's curiosity is seen by others as moral intention, and events are made meaningful by being made to add up. But those who accumulate meaning by weaving persons, things, and events together in this way become "spiders" in Sula's eyes, and she has contempt for them and their webs (120).

Neither weaving meaning together nor moving along the diverting paths of Derridean *differance*, Sula does not make the kinds of connections necessary to either a construction or deconstruction of meaning.[15] Perhaps, Morrison suggests, this is because Sula herself does not add up; her identity is not the result of accumulation but instead an experience of inconsistency.

> As willing to feel pain as to give pain, to feel pleasure as to give pleasure, hers was an experimental life—ever since her mother's remarks sent her flying up those stairs, ever since her one major feeling of responsibility had been exorcised on the bank of a river with a closed place in the middle. The first experience taught her there was no other that you could count on; the second that there was no self to count on either. She had no center, no speck around which to grow. In the midst of a pleasant conversation with someone she might say, "Why do you chew with your mouth open?" not because the answer interested her but because she wanted to see the person's face change rapidly. She was completely free of ambition, with no affection for money, property or things, no greed, no desire to command attention or compliments—no ego. For that reason she felt no compulsion to verify herself—be consistent with herself. (118–19)

Morrison here suggests that an ego is some kind of accumulation that Sula cannot amass because of distances she keeps. On the one hand, Sula does not "accumulate" because she cannot feel love. But to use the more physical terms of Morrison's descriptions, Sula fails to attach one thing to another. With no interest in acquisition, accumulation, or drawing anything like others' attention toward herself, Sula simply does not function in terms of combination, collection, or accretion.

Sula functions in terms of slippage. Her mother "slips" when she says she does not love her daughter within Sula's hearing. Sula's hand slips when she cuts off part of her finger, and Chicken Little slips out of her hold when he flies to his death. Giving her nothing "to count on," such slips give her no possibility of accumulation. Neither self nor other takes shape or acquires form in Sula's experience. Other characters in the novel can control slippage, with forms that set limits to things in time and space. But Sula has no form of keeping anything, and so every slip turns into a dead loss.

Missing Images

How such experience might enable definition to occur is suggested most clearly when Ajax leaves Sula. Throughout the novel, Sula remains unable to hold onto anything—and this despite the fact that, with Ajax, she "began to discover what possession was. Not love, perhaps, but possession or at least the desire for it" (131). The first effect of this desire is to drive Ajax away. Once he is gone, moreover, Sula can find no "evidence of his having ever been there" (134).

The one thing of his that she finds is his driver's license, but that, bearing a different name, does not allow Sula to recover Ajax so much as it makes her feel she never knew him at all.

> Albert Jacks? His name was Albert Jacks? A. Jacks. She had thought it was Ajax. All those years. Even from the time she walked by the pool hall and looked away from him sitting astride a wooden chair, looked away to keep from seeing the wide space of intolerable orderliness between his legs; the openness that held no sign, no sign at all, of the animal that lurked in his trousers; looked away from the insolent nostrils and the smile that kept slipping and falling, falling, falling so she wanted to reach out with her hand to catch it before it fell to the pavement. (135)

As a representation of Ajax, the driver's license signals only absence. It gives Sula nothing to hold on to, generating memories of repeated slippages: open spaces that hold no sign, eyes that look away, open smiles that also slip away.

"In psychoanalytic terms," says Elisabeth Bronfen, "the healthy trajectory from mourning to remembering or commemoration is marked by a freeing of libidinal energies from the first lost object that must be reinvested in a second surrogate object, who may be perceived in the image of the deceased."[16] Sula cannot attach herself to a substitute object, nor can she remember Ajax *as* an object. The images she recalls are not those of the deceased but those of decease, as she finds, in her house and in her memory, things already missed, or signs and images of him *as* missing, in part and whole. Imagery does not occur except in narrative, in which form images dissolve.

Because images do not take shape in her mind, Sula cannot get hold of either Ajax or herself. The forms in which she represents herself to herself are as inconsistent as the forms in which she remembers Ajax.

When I was a little girl the heads of my paper dolls came off, and it was a long time before I discovered that my own head would not fall off if I bent my neck. I used to walk around holding it very stiff because I thought a strong wind or a heavy push would snap my neck. Nel was the one who told me the truth. But she was wrong. I did not hold my head stiff enough when I met him and so I lost it just like the dolls. (136)

Here Sula realizes two different forms, in the paper dolls and in the expression "I lost my head," which depict figuratively the human body or part of it. If her "gift for metaphor" is at work here, the attempt at representation nevertheless fails to produce any difference between the figures and the body. Sula might use the figure to distance herself from loss, by displacing loss from herself to the doll. Instead, she sees the figure's likeness as a mere repetition of her self, and as such, it is subject to the same slippage she is. Such representations provide no relief from her experience of loss because the initial displacement of loss, from her body to figures of the body, travels back to inhabit the same place as the body. One thing does not stand for another; both together fall apart.

Identifying, as usual, breakages rather than the attachments and combinations that would enable her to give her experience meaning, Sula experiences missing, not mourning. Instead of recovering parts of the lost Ajax, she experiences his absolute absence.

He had left nothing but his stunning absence. An absence so decorative, so ornate, it was difficult for her to understand how she had ever endured, without falling dead or being consumed, his magnificent presence.

. . . His absence was everywhere, stinging everything, giving the furnishings primary colors, sharp outlines to the corners of rooms and gold light to the dust collecting on table tops. When he was there he pulled everything toward himself. Not only her eyes and all her senses but also inanimate things seemed to exist because of him, backdrops to his presence. Now that he had gone, these things, so long subdued by his presence, were glamorized in his wake. (134–35)

What happens here is not traditional figuration, according to which forms contain meaning by the consistency and definiteness of their boundaries. Here, figuration depends not on an internal consistency and presence but on an external suffusion of absence. Absence, that is, spreads around things, and as it does they become decorative and ornate; they begin to function as figures.

In this passage, absence assumes the decorative and ornamental role taken by figure in traditional metaphysics. According to tradition, metaphysics, like architecture, composes meaning in layers of construction, from the ground up. Mark Wigley discusses the identification of philosophy with architecture in these terms: "Philosophy's traditional description of itself and its object as building invokes and sustains a particular image of architecture as a mechanism that precedes and controls the decorative images attached to it through its structural bond to the ground." In Derrida's "displacements of the traditional architectural figure," Wigley clarifies, "structure is no longer simply grounding through a continuous vertical hierarchy from ground to ornament, but a discontinuous and convoluted line. . . . The sense of structure is actually produced by the supplementary layers of representation that appear least structural."[17] Morrison depicts an absence functioning as "ground" in terms that resemble Derrida's deconstructive analysis, insofar as the ground against which figures take form is not solid. But the crucial fact about the "background" that glamorizes Sula's things is that it is occupied by an absence. Not solid but not empty either, the ground for figuration is a missing person.

Given the absence of Ajax, each thing in the room acquires sharp edges as a separate form. What is missing is any relation between these objects, which were seen in Ajax's presence relative to him. Sula does not see things relative to one another; there is no center or standard to which to relate the things she sees. This is a crucial characteristic of Sula's vision. She does not merely break forms apart but perceives things without the connections between them afforded by relations. And this means that Sula has a strange experience of things and people which does not, perhaps, produce meaning but which does produce definition.

Sula's definition of things is described when she returns to the Bottom after years of absence and Nel realizes Sula's effect.

> Was there anyone else before whom she could never be foolish? In whose view inadequacy was mere idiosyncrasy, a character trait rather than a deficiency? . . . Sula never competed; she simply helped

others define themselves. Other people seemed to turn their volume on and up when Sula was in the room. More than any other thing, humor returned. She could listen to the crunch of sugar underfoot that the children had spilled without reaching for the switch; and she forgot the tear in the living-room window shade. . . .

Sula would come by of an afternoon, walking along with her fluid stride, wearing a plain yellow dress the same way her mother, Hannah, had worn those too-big house dresses—with a distance, an absence of a relationship to clothes which emphasized everything the fabric covered. When she . . . stepped inside, the dishes piled in the sink looked as though they belonged there; the dust on the lamps sparkled; the hair brush lying on the "good" sofa in the living room did not have to be apologetically retrieved, and Nel's grimy intractable children looked like three wild things happily insouciant in the May shine. (95–96)

For Nel at least, Sula's presence has a glamorizing effect similar to the effect of Ajax's absence for Sula. Here, too, this effect seems due to an absence of relations.

Sula sees things without relating them to anything else. Most strikingly, she does not recognize inadequacies, deficiencies, or anything wrong with things that are broken, dirty, or out of place. To do so, she would have to see things relative to what they should be, holding in her mind an image of how they would look if they were "right." But Sula's mind, not preoccupied by those forms or relations, does not reproduce them. She looks at things in an absence of relation. Thus it is that she dresses "with a distance, an absence of a relationship to clothes." Clothing might represent or reform the body, making it look different, which is the case with Helene Wright's clothing, for example. But for Sula there is no relation between her body and her clothes, which therefore do not seem to contain or alter her body at all.

Sula does not see things and think of what they might be or might have been. She sees with an absence of the relations that would connect what is to what is not or to other things present. Such items as dirty dishes and the dust on the lamps seem to belong, therefore, where and as they are. This sense of belonging is different from a sense of place, because there is no relation between things and because there is no occupation with things. Sula emphasizes instead the absence between things and between things and persons, and in this she may be a sign of things to come. In 1965, when Nel misses the Bottom, she also misses places: "Maybe it hadn't been a community, but it had been a place. Now there weren't any places left, just separate houses with separate televisions and separate telephones and less and less dropping by" (166).

Sula's Place

Helene Wright and Eva Peace maintain consistency in their lives either by ruling out of bounds or carefully containing within bounds their histories of bodily loss of control: those events, for example, when Helene turned to "custard" and Eva lost her leg. One character holds herself together, whereas the other displays her broken body, but both work to set bounds to the inconsistency of their identities. When the people of the Bottom band together against Sula, yet another pattern of containment is practiced. Eventually, Sula becomes a "pariah" (122), but people do not throw her out. "The presence of evil was something to be first recognized, then dealt with, survived, outwitted, triumphed over" (118). Confusing and dangerous as she is, Sula comes to be a means of limiting evil, a way to keep others safe and secure, a means, even, of keeping others good.

These uses depend on seeing Sula herself as a consistent phenomenon. In others' eyes, she amasses weight and accumulates consistency, as evidence of her evil is collected. The past is one source of evidence. "Everybody remembered the plague of robins that announced her return, and the tale about her watching Hannah burn was stirred up again" (112). The present is another source: "she came to their church suppers without underwear" (114); Shadrack is seen to "tip his hat" to her (17); and "Sula did not look her age" (115). Things that have not appeared evil before are suddenly recognized as such; thus the meaning of Sula's birthmark is suddenly "cleared up" (114). On the other hand, evil acts that have not before been attributed to her are suddenly reported as fact. In this collecting process, with "the weighty evidence piling up" (115), Sula is given "the final label." The men "said she was guilty of the unforgivable thing—the thing for which there was no understanding, no excuse, no compassion. . . . They said that Sula slept with white men. . . . [A]ll minds were closed to her when that word was passed around. . . . Every one of them imagined the scene, each according to his own predilections—Sula underneath some white man—and it filled them with choking disgust" (112–13). As others' minds close to her, they also keep thinking about her. And they reproduce, with variations, a scene in which Sula sleeps with a white man. The "choking disgust" these characters can reiterate each time they imagine such scenes provides a constant replay of their disconnection from Sula. In repeated replays, they both contain evil within her and distance themselves from the forms she takes in their imaginations. Here as elsewhere in *Sula,* seeing—imaginative vision as well as "just looking"—is identified with separation.

For all the disgust and disconnection produced in this process, Sula is not placed outside the group, which in fact comes to depend on her for its own sense of place. Once she is identified as a total evil, she becomes necessary to the Bottom as something like a moral standard, a limit marking off right from wrong. Perceived as a generalized evil, Sula serves to make other people appear relatively good. Teapot's Mamma, called this "because being his mamma was precisely her major failure" (113–14), suddenly becomes a devoted mother when she can blame Sula for hurting her son. When Teapot falls down, Teapot's Mamma "told everybody that Sula had pushed him" and then "immersed herself in a role she had shown no inclination for: motherhood. The very idea of a grown woman hurting her boy kept her teeth on edge. She became the most devoted mother: sober, clean and industrious" (114). Once "an indifferent mother" (113), Teapot's Mamma assumes the role of a good mother to be different from Sula. Sula is seen to be what Teapot's Mamma was formerly—"a grown woman hurting her boy"—and Teapot's Mamma, sticking Sula with her own evil, becomes perfectly good. Other women, because Sula "lay their husbands once and then no more," become better wives: "to justify their own judgment, [they] cherished their men more" (115).

Moral ambivalence is erased as these characters become more loving of one another and as Sula comes to be more hateful. They can become good because she has become evil. "Once the source of their personal misfortune was identified, they had leave to protect and love one another. They began to cherish their husbands and wives, protect their children, repair their homes and in general band together against the devil in their midst" (117–18). The images and roles by which characters identify themselves and Sula suggest that through their rejection of her they enter a symbolic order of relations.

Sula in effect is the relation between them. She becomes what others are not, and others are seen in relief against her and distinguished by their difference from her. Sula not only inhabits the space that provides moral distinction but also is both a means of distinguishing others and a means of bonding others together; she is used by others to externalize difference, which she keeps beyond the bounds of those whose security lies in their consistency. They hold together insofar as they can use Sula to contain the differences that would otherwise divide them.

Sula relates people in the Bottom because she is an excuse for them to band together and because she is a standard against which they acquire relative value. She functions as she remembers Ajax functioning for her: as a presence who "pulled everything toward himself" (134) and gave things a center. But she remains an "absence of a relationship" in that what collects around her are negations: what others are not and do not want to be. Sula is the figure constructed by others in patterns of collection and containment, a figure on which their gossip and their imaginations can focus their own negation. She is a center, a mass, of negation. For this reason, when she dies people are glad to be rid of her. But they have achieved a more stable order through her. The symbolic order in which persons are fit into distinct roles depends here on the rejection or abjection of somebody beyond the bounds of distinction. Once Sula is gone, therefore, chaos occurs.

Sula's place in the Bottom, then, is a place of absence: she is identified as evil and as what others are not; she is seen as having no place there. Sula places absence in another sense too: as the location of evil and the reference point for others' negation, she takes the place of evils that are absent from the Bottom, specifically those of racism practiced by white people. Identifying Sula as evil allows characters to contain both good and evil within their midst and thereby to avoid making any reference to the white people outside the Bottom. Insofar as they can confine evil to Sula, characters use her to contain their anger at those evils they are powerless to remedy.

Missing Sula

When Sula dies, nobody misses her. People "felt that either *because* Sula was dead or just *after* she was dead a brighter day was dawning" (150–51). But without Sula, the Bottom begins to come apart. "Mothers who had defended their children from Sula's malevolence (or who had defended their positions as mothers from Sula's scorn for the role) now had nothing to rub up against. The tension was gone and so was the reason for the effort they had made. Without her mockery, affection for others sank into flaccid disrepair" (153). As people let go of the bonds that gave them coherence, "a falling away, a dislocation was taking place" (153); this loss of place is realized on National Suicide Day, at the construction site of the proposed tunnel.

As people recognize their absence of relation in that place, they experience firsthand the losses that Sula kept from them. These are primarily, as I mentioned earlier, losses of relation, of any connection between people and the objects they see, any attachment forged by labor, hope, or promise. Without such connections, they see things for which they had hoped but which never existed—school shoes and repaired teeth—as well as things which existed but which were cut or broken—coal credit and toilets. Like the leaning porches and slurred remarks of the employers whose malevolence is "staggering," these objects are characterized by an indistinction or a slippage of form, so that they are not what they should be.

Without Sula among them, it is as if people must themselves experience the absence of relationship she contained. They lose their place: slipping out of control, breaking all the tools and equipment they can, and moving into a sheer absence of relationship.

> They didn't mean to go in, to actually go down into the lip of the tunnel, but in their need to kill it all, all of it, . . . they went too deep, too far . . .
>
> A lot of them died there. The earth, now warm, shifted; the first forepole slipped; loose rock fell from the face of the tunnel and caused a shield to give way. . . . With the first crack and whoosh of water, the clamber to get out was so fierce that others who were trying to help were pulled to their deaths. (161–62)

Slipping to their deaths, these characters realize Sula's absence. As they move into identity with her, even the ground comes apart, and they feel what they are missing.

In *Sula,* people in the Bottom amass an identity of evil called "Sula" that functions somewhat like the "background" of racism Morrison identifies in white American literature. But the need for such a ground, as well as its effects, are different. One might say there is a projection of evil within the black community useful to withstanding the projections practiced upon the community by whites. Under pressure from external forces of racism, people in the Bottom distribute their moral variations among themselves to contain what they can project into the white population only at the risk of their own lives. What they contain is not only the evil that would more accurately be located outside their community but also their own rage, which, because limitless, cannot be stopped once let loose.

A different kind of displacement occurs to prevent Nel from knowing what she is missing when Sula dies. After Sula's affair with Nel's husband and after Jude leaves, Nel is repeatedly bothered by the awareness of something that will not go away.

> There was something just to the right of her, in the air, just out of view. She could not see it, but she knew exactly what it looked like. A gray ball hovering just there. . . . To the right. Quiet, gray, dirty. A ball of muddy strings, but without weight, fluffy but terrible in its malevolence. She knew she could not look. . . .
>
> She spent a whole summer with the gray ball, the little ball of fur and string and hair always floating in the light near her but which she did not see because she never looked. (108–9)

Sula looks straight at things, which, clear-cut and disconnected, she does not hang onto. For Nel, though, experience leaves aftereffects, and in this messy and irritating form, Sula seems something she cannot either face or get rid of. Only many years later, after visiting Eva in "the home for the aged" (167), does Nel remember why.

Eva does not seem to recognize Nel, whom she confuses with Sula. Nel is dislocated from her own identity when Eva accuses her of killing Chicken Little, who flew out of Sula's hands and drowned while the three of them were playing by the river.

> What did old Eva mean by *you watched?* How could she help seeing it? . . . But it was there anyway, as it had always been, the old feeling and the old question. The good feeling she had had when Chicken's hands slipped. She hadn't wondered about that in years. "Why didn't I feel bad when it happened? How come it felt so good to see him fall?"
>
> All these years she had been secretly proud of her calm, controlled

behavior when Sula was uncontrollable, her compassion for Sula's frightened and shamed eyes. Now it seemed that what she had thought was maturity, serenity and compassion was only the tranquillity that follows a joyful stimulation. (170)

Here Morrison suggests how Nel displayed and elaborated her own character on occasions provided by Sula: how she staged her own kindness and strength against the backdrop of Sula's fear and shame. Eva, by identifying Nel with Sula, calls forth questions and doubts that disturb the clear distinctions Nel has created between Sula and herself.

Eva transforms the routine visit to the nursing home, when Nel goes through the forms of politeness and responsibility, into an improvised exchange of call-and-response that disturbs Nel's status quo. Accustomed to calling attention to absences, such as her missing leg, Eva refuses to accept Nel in the self-satisfied and patronizing terms in which she presents herself. " 'You've got a pretty room, a real pretty room, Miss Peace,' " Nel says of one of the "sterile green cages" in which Eva lives (168, 167). Eva responds with open hostility and her accusation of murder: " 'You. Sula. What's the difference?' " (168). In this exchange, Eva, like Sula, calls for a critical review of things that others take for granted.

Calling for response, Eva transforms identity and difference into processes of meaning in the making rather than fixed structures of meaning. Once Eva has refused to admit the difference between Nel and Sula, Nel, walking home, responds in agreement. " 'We was girls together'. . . . 'O Lord, Sula,' " she cried, " 'girl, girl, girlgirlgirl' " (174). This construction suggests that there was no difference between them. It is with this recognition that "a soft ball of fur broke and scattered like dandelion spores in the breeze" (174). Perhaps because she now admits her own confusion with Sula, the messy pile of stuff Nel has imagined herself keeping out of sight disperses. But the most important change in the final scene is the recognition Eva makes possible, not of any particular identity but of the dependence of distinctions on both what is seen and what is pushed out of sight.

Sula's presence in the Bottom calls for response. She never fades into the background but demands attention as she breaks the rules and ignores others' interests. People hate Sula, and there is evident justification for their hatred. But many unseen reasons also exist for their hatred and for Sula's behavior as well as their own behavior. Sula demands responses not only by what she does but by calling attention to things people in the Bottom are missing. To see these characters' identities as responses to what is missing is to insist not only on the invisible elements of racial and cultural identity but also that the production of African American identity has proceeded, by means perhaps unseen and unrecognized, as a powerful cultural production because of persons' refusal to limit that identity to the dimensions of white visual culture.

Off the Record

Jazz and the Production of Black Culture

In *Sula,* the most highly individualized character distinguishes herself by cutting relations to others altogether. To the extent that the community bonds together, it does so by means of Sula: she realizes what they are not, and they become consistent in their opposition to her. In *Jazz,* however, it is not scapegoating or exclusion by which characters produce consistency and community. Morrison identifies music as a medium of black culture that is a means of experiencing both differences and likenesses, both past and present, among African Americans. Jazz produces, moreover, not only consistency among various persons but also a bodily consistency of individual identity that is missed by characters in *Sula.*

Initially, however, "the City" of *Jazz* seems to produce more disconnection than connection. "The wave of black people running from want and violence" and into the City "crested in the 1870s; the '80s; the '90s but was a steady stream in 1906 when Joe and Violet joined it."[1] Morrison's "City" draws people because it has no part in their past; it is not haunted. "Part of why they loved it was the specter they left behind" (33). Moreover, the City has the effect of cutting connections between people because it brings out stronger, more distinct individual identities.

> There, in a city, they are not so much new as themselves: their stronger, riskier selves. And in the beginning when they first arrive, and twenty years later when they and the City have grown up, they love that part of themselves so much they forget what loving other people was like—if they ever knew, that is. I don't mean they hate

them, no, just that what they start to love is the way a person is in the City; the way a schoolgirl never pauses at a stoplight but looks up and down the street before stepping off the curb; how men accommodate themselves to tall buildings and wee porches, what a woman looks like moving in a crowd. (33–34)

This attention to "the way a person is" means that sensations replace deeper feelings, feelings that attach persons to one another. "Little of that makes for love, but it does pump desire" (34).

It is the striking effects—of contrasts and of motion—that are noticed.

The woman who churned a man's blood as she leaned all alone on a fence by a country road might not expect even to catch his eye in the City. But if she is clipping quickly down the big-city street in heels, swinging her purse, or sitting on a stoop with a cool beer in her hand, dangling her shoe from the toes of her foot, the man, reacting to her posture, to soft skin on stone, the weight of the building stressing the delicate, dangling shoe, is captured. And he'd think it was the woman he wanted, and not some combination of curved stone, and a swinging, high-heeled shoe moving in and out of sunlight. He would know right away the deception, the trick of shapes and light and movement, but it wouldn't matter at all because the deception was part of it too. Anyway, he could feel his lungs going in and out. There is no air in the City but there is breath, and every morning it races through him like laughing gas brightening his eyes, his talk, and his expectations. (34)

What catches the man's eye are visual contrasts and combinations. These are produced by movements such as clipping, swinging, and dangling as well as by contrasts between textures, as of stone and skin, and between weights, as of the building and the shoe. It does not matter that the man is deceived into thinking he wants the woman, because "the deception was part of it too." Deception about the object of desire is one more effect, like motion and light, which, like deception, are temporary, external, and distinct from the woman herself.

Such experience has surfaced in several senses. The man does not feel his blood churn, as in the country, but feels "his lungs going in and out," like the shoe "moving in and out of sunlight." Objects of such feelings have also surfaced, from persons to the effects of stone and light. Breath like laughing gas speeds things up and brightens them, providing effects similar to those of the woman's moving body.

Deceptive effects provide sensations as valuable as those caused by actual objects or events.

The contrasts that are sensational do not occur as contrasts of surfaces and depths. Unlike a contrast between figure and ground, in which a blank background provides depth to distinguish a figure, these oppositions that sharpen perception occur between one shape or sensation and another, as with breath going in and out or skin seen against stone. This groundlessness indicates a lack not only of spatial depth but also of temporal depth. Things and persons are not seen in relation to what they or other things were in the past. What is absent is not necessary to desire, which is "pumped" by the effects of vivid, visible changes and contrasts in objects seen.

There is little evidence, then, even in the visual dimensions of Morrison's City, of the kind of background that she has identified as necessary to the distinction of American whites. Such a background is composed of a dark mass of figures, used for the purpose of distinguishing other figures. Relieved of their own moral ambiguity, the whites who project their own "darkness" onto undistinguished background figures then stand out, in relief, from that background. But here in Morrison's City, figures are perceived distinctly because of contrasts provided by movement, occurring from one moment to the next. Such movement, like the rhythm of music, provides its own relief. Or, if a contrasting background causes figures to stand out, that effect happens sensationally too, in a brief combination, as temporary as an improvisational figure in a performance of jazz.

The narrator sees such a vision when a bright sky produces a silhouette of figures.

> A colored man floats down out of the sky blowing a saxophone, and below him, in the space between two buildings, a girl talks earnestly to a man in a straw hat. He touches her lip to remove a bit of something there. Suddenly she is quiet. He tilts her chin up. They stand there. Her grip on her purse slackens and her neck makes a nice curve. The man puts his hand on the stone wall above her head. By the way his jaw moves and the turn of his head I know he has a golden tongue. The sun sneaks into the alley behind them. It makes a pretty picture on its way down. (8)

Outlined against the sky and framed by the two buildings, this image is purely visual, with even speech seen. It is a vision of surfaces, profiles, edges. As in the descriptions of the way people are in the city, these forms are seen with little particular content.

Musical Media of Cultural Production

The views of persons the narrator of *Jazz* sees throughout the City provide public images of individuals that, like figures of white persons in the public spheres of James's and Faulkner's fiction, seem abstracted from particular human identities. The memorable views that are produced and collected in the early pages of *Jazz* are not, however, abstracted from time. It is the essence of these visions that they be seen in time, so that the rapid changes which "catch the eye" are noticeable. As the setting sun in the above passage suggests, the sensational images of the City do not last. This may be part of the "relief" that such views offer to persons in the City.

In the model of relief that Morrison identifies with the construction of American whiteness in *Playing in the Dark,* whites relieve themselves of their own internal contradictions. In these images of city life in *Jazz*, black persons experience relief in rhythms of movement that relocate change in the present, replacing history with tempo. The City provides both backing and variation according to a musical model, in which the steady rhythmic burden of the bass or of the chorus in song backs up variations and solos.

These views of persons in the City provide relief not only from history but also from what is inside persons, by focusing attention on the surfaces and edges of people's bodies. This provision of relief bears little resemblance to the abstracted views of persons in white public spheres, which empty individuals of particular contents. Morrison's characters have already been emptied; that is part of their history. And part of what they are relieved of in the City is what characters feel as an "inside nothing." The temporality of these images provides several kinds of relief. There is the relief of rhythm—of tempo—in the movements of figures. And there is the relief of the sun going down and of death. Both free characters of their "inside nothing."

In *Jazz*, Morrison explores the power of black music to do much more than provide such relief. Identifying various ways in which persons reproduce the relations of call-and-response that have characterized black musical performances for centuries, Morrison produces a responsiveness in her City that relieves individuals of separateness. She thereby suggests that separateness is among the impositions of white culture on black experience. Beyond the images with which white Americans cultivate distinction, Morrison identifies responsive relations among black persons, relations with the power to "back" both people's resistance and their productivity.

In *Light in August* Faulkner imagines Joe Christmas's body, seen one night in the headlights of a passing car, developing into a white image, like a photograph from a negative. Near the end of *Jazz*, Morrison suggests why a photograph cannot reproduce black identity.[2] Speaking of Joe and Violet, the narrator remembers them in a sort of racial construction that is sharply focused but not distinctly visible.

> When I see them now they are not sepia, still, losing their edges to the light of a future afternoon. Caught midway between was and must be. For me they are real. Sharply in focus and clicking. I wonder, do they know they are the sound of snapping fingers under the sycamores lining the streets? When the loud trains pull into their stops and the engines pause, attentive listeners can hear it. Even when they are not there, when whole city blocks downtown and acres of lawned neighborhoods in Sag Harbor cannot see them, the clicking is there. In the T-strap shoes of Long Island debutantes, the sparkling fringes of daring short skirts that swish and glide to music that intoxicates them more than the champagne. . . . The click of dark and snapping fingers drives them to Roseland, to Bunny's; boardwalks by the sea. Into places their fathers have warned them about and their mothers shudder to think of. Both the warning and the shudder come from the snapping fingers, the clicking. And the shade. Pushed away into certain streets, restricted from others, making it possible for the inhabitants to sigh and sleep in relief, the shade stretches—just there— at the edge of the dream, or slips into the crevices of a chuckle. . . . It bunches on the curbstone, wrists crossed, and hides its smile under a wide-brim hat. Shade. Protective, available. Or sometimes not; sometimes it seems to lurk rather than hover kindly, and its stretch is not a yawn but an increase to be beaten back with a stick. Before it clicks, or taps or snaps its fingers. (226–27)

What comes into focus here, not through the click of a camera but with the clicking of fingers, is an embodied form of cultural reproduction that is continuous rather than momentary, communal rather than individual. What moves and is tracked through the passage and through the scenes and figures depicted is, first, a sound—the clicking—and, later, a "shade."[3] Here, as Farah Jasmine Griffin emphasizes, Morrison is clearly "reveal[ing] the black presence lurking in the shadows of the American literary imagination."[4]

Neither the heard nor the seen presence on which the passage focuses is individualized. Indeed, to say that production here is embodied is somewhat inaccurate, because it is only parts of bodies that produce the collective sound. Focusing attention on what cameras do not reproduce, this passage represents both what is unseen or unnoticed by observers and what is always only part of "the picture." The clicking fingers are merely parts of bodies, and whether heard as responses to music or as a beat that calls music forth, their sounds are simply part of musical production. The auditory dimensions of this representation do not, therefore, complete any picture. They provide a more inclusive representation of experience than imagery provides, at the same time as they insist on the partial character of any particular views or sounds. The increased accuracy of this representation is due in part to its inclusion of more than visible dimensions of experience and in part to its implicit acknowledgment of its own incompleteness.

Rather than merely indicating that African American culture does not fit the picture produced by the media of white modernity, I mean to stress the critical take Morrison produces on those media. In *Jazz*, the exchanges which occur among characters and which provide a "backing" for individuals are marked by a double consciousness that is critically aware of different perspectives within African American culture and also of deep divisions between black and white cultures. In the black public sphere of Morrison's City, it is not individual points of view so much as "double takes" that are necessary to political representation, because of the double experience of black culture and white culture. According to the double take Morrison offers on white modernity, its visual media are not only inadequate means of representing African American experience but also media that, even as they allow for the consolidation of individual and racial identities, necessarily impose particular losses on human experience.

The losses that predominate in *Sula*, I have argued, are lost relations. These losses are realized but not redressed, as Sula herself takes the place of loss in the community. In *Jazz*, characters take the place of loss in a different sense. The greatest loss suffered by each of the three central characters of the novel—Joe, Dorcas, and Violet—is the loss of a parent. Whereas the person who is lost cannot return, Morrison suggests that the lost relation may be reconstituted. The parent-as-relation is an emotional relation as well as a "blood relation." The sense of a blood relation identifies persons within families as separate bodily containers of common identity. Morrison, however, identifies persons in their social and emotional relationships with each other. In shifting emphasis from lost objects to lost relations, she insists on the communal constituents of individual identity and on the capacity of response to provide identity.

One might argue that the Lacanian mirror stage also does this, because the individual achieves identity at this stage only when his or her body takes shape in the eyes, or as if in the eyes, of another person. But according to this theory too, the individual assumes identity as a whole, coherent, and separate body. Morrison instead identifies bodies in relation and a belief in bodily consistency as dependent on others' continued responses to the self. Others' responses to the self thereby become part of the self, which is experienced as consistently in relation rather than as initially constituted in relations that provide a sense of both internal and external separation.

According to this distinction between a Lacanian model of self-as-other and the relational identity of characters in *Jazz*, the mobility of human images in the novel is more like musical variations than "moving pictures." Whereas film represents mobilized images, Morrison's cultural media of relations extend identity beyond images. When she focuses attention on the shade, she does not merely see what white views have missed. She represents what cannot be viewed: dimensions of experience that require different dimensions of representation if they are not to be lost.[5]

Playing Records

There is evidence of a critical perspective on modern media in *Jazz* in the disconcerting changes in the narrator's perspective on her characters.[6] Early in the novel, the narrator provides musical parallels to life in the City that by the end of the novel are recognized as wholly inadequate. For example, the narrator insists at first that the backing provided by the City is a matter of plan and design: "Do what you please in the City, it is there to back and frame you no matter what you do. And what goes on on its blocks and lots and side streets is anything the strong can think of and the weak will admire. All you have to do is heed the design—the way it's laid out for you, considerate, mindful of where you want to go and what you might need tomorrow" (8–9). Later, the narrator sees even less choice in the City, which offers only illusions of freedom while keeping people not only on track but in a circular groove.

The narrator says of Joe and his love for Dorcas:

> Take my word for it, he is bound to the track. It pulls him like a needle through the groove of a Bluebird record. Round and round about the town. That's the way the City spins you. Makes you do what it wants, go where the laid-out roads say to. All the while letting you think you're free. . . . You can't get off the track a City lays for you. Whatever happens, whether you get rich or stay poor, ruin your health or live to old age, you always end up back where you started: hungry for the one thing everybody loses—young loving. (120)

The City keeps people going back over the same ground repeatedly, as if replaying the music on a phonograph record. The consistency of experience is provided, despite variations, by a form of backing up, to the loss that is the starting point.

Among the characters who replay their losses, most want to regain parts of themselves rather than objects lost in the past. Violet, Joe, and Dorcas are orphans. As a child Joe names himself Joe Trace because he is told his parents "disappeared without a trace" (124). Violet was also left behind when her mother threw herself down the well at home in Virginia. Dorcas's parents were killed in the East St. Louis riots. Her father was "pulled off a streetcar and stomped to death," and her mother was burned to death the same day, "when her house was torched" (57). Perhaps because Violet, Joe, and Dorcas identify themselves as something left behind or perhaps because they have lost parts of themselves along with their parents, it is part of the self that each tries to recapture.

Joe begins his affair with Dorcas not because of desire for her but because he has lost all trace of the feelings he experienced when he fell in love with Violet, his wife. "Convinced that he alone remembers those days, and wants them back, aware of what it looked like but not at all of what it felt like, he coupled himself elsewhere" (36).

> He recalls dates, of course, events, purchases, activity, even scenes. But he has a tough time trying to catch what it felt like.
>
> He had struggled a long time with that loss, believed he had resigned himself to it, that old age would be not remembering what things felt like. That you could say, "I was scared to death," but you could not retrieve the fear. That you could replay in the brain the scene of ecstasy, of murder, of tenderness, but it was drained of everything but the language to say it in. (29)

Feeling like an observer of the scenes of his own life, Joe can recall the past only from the outside. Not only is the past drained of its inner life, but memory itself seems unable to capture, by means of images and words, anything but the forms of life.

When he begins his affair with Dorcas, however, Joe seems to lose track of just which feelings he wants to get back. When he speaks to Dorcas of his "inside nothing," it is not his loss of feeling for Violet but the emptiness caused by his missing mother that Joe talks about (37–38). He tracks his losses further back, going over older and older ground, and he eventually will track Dorcas through the City as he once hunted for his mother through the woods in Virginia (180).

When he tracked his mother, though, Joe was never able to find her, even when he found the place she lived, a cave in the woods. "The color of the stone walls had changed from gold to fish-gill blue by the time he left. He had seen what there was. A green dress. A rocking chair without an arm. A circle of stones for cooking. Jars, baskets, pots; a doll, a spindle, earrings. . . . Also, a pair of man's trousers with buttons of bone. . . . But where is *she?*" (184). Even with all her "effects," Joe still cannot locate the person he wants. His mother's effects include the feel of the place as well as her belongings, but as in the City these sensational evidences of a person leave out the person herself.

It is this emptiness that Joe replays, as if there is no actual feeling to get back, only a lack of feeling. When Joe misses what language leaves behind and when he attempts to recapture this, he is missing both feelings and persons. His own self can be identified as something left behind, as are the traces of his mother he finds in the cave. Hoping to recapture what was left behind, Joe only replays the feeling of an "inside nothing," as if he and his mother are what was lost.

Dorcas, who also has an "inside nothing" (38), ends her life replaying a blues scenario in which she is killed by her lover when he finds her dancing with her new man. Dorcas finds in such images and stories, of helpless women who lose their lives, roles that she wants to replay. " 'Everything was like a picture show to her, and she was the one on the railroad track, or the one trapped in the sheik's tent when it caught on fire' " (202). The feeling Dorcas has kept from East St. Louis is a feeling of burning. "Back in East St. Louis, as the little porch fell, wood chips—ignited and smoking—exploded in the air. One of them must have entered her stretched dumb mouth and traveled down her throat because it smoked and glowed there still" (60–61). When Dorcas stands with her aunt, Alice, viewing the parade of "men marching down Fifth Avenue to advertise their anger over two hundred dead in East St. Louis" (57), she "watched the black unblinking men, and the drums assured her that the glow would never leave her, that it would be waiting for and with her whenever she wanted to be touched by it" (61). Here, as is true with Joe, it is not people but a feeling that she wants to keep; the feeling will not leave her, will wait for her, will touch her.

If Dorcas is able repeatedly to feel this burning glow, however, the burning changes to a sexual fire as she grows up. She is reminded of her burning, for example, when she listens to the stories told by Neola Miller, one of the sisters who look after Dorcas and other children after school. Neola has one paralyzed arm. This happened, the narrator says, when the man Neola was to marry "left the state. The pain of his refusal was visual, for over her heart, curled like a shell, was the hand on which he had positioned the ring" (62). Neola stops reading scripture and begins telling stories each afternoon when her sister falls asleep.

One of her stories is about a woman who cannot leave a man "who was no good to (or for) her"; another is about a fourteen-year-old girl who runs away from home to follow a boy who has joined the army.

> So they could see, couldn't they, the power of sin in the company of a weak mind? The children scratched their knees and nodded, but Dorcas, at least, was enchanted by the frail, melty tendency of the flesh and the Paradise that could make a woman go right back after

two days, two! or make a girl travel four hundred miles to a camp-town, or fold Neola's arm, the better to hold the pieces of her heart in her hand. Paradise. All for Paradise. (62–63)

Here burning and melting flesh have shifted their referents, from the fire in which Dorcas's mother burned to the sin that can consume the frail flesh of any weak mind. This tendency to melt calls a woman right back to a "no-good" man. Desire drives Dorcas back, too, even as it drives her forward; she seeks out men and sexual experience but also gets back to the burning of her mother.

Language obscures the difference between sexuality and loss by equating two kinds of "burning" experience and enabling Dorcas to feel one as the other. Both Dorcas and Joe turn the future into the past by activating the ambiguity of language and the distance between language and feeling. Language provides a means of missing in both cases: Joe misses feeling, and Dorcas misses the difference between sexuality and destruction. In part this results from the stories she is told, the myths of the blues, and so forth. But both in substance and in form, language takes her "right back."

Lost Parts

Neola's paralyzed arm is, like the "inside nothing" of Joe and Dorcas, a part of her that she no longer feels and that no longer can be moved. Morrison again sees the loss of another person as a missing part of the body in the story of Golden Gray. He is the child of the white woman whom True Belle, Violet's grandmother, worked for in Baltimore. Golden Gray is only told that his father is alive—and black—when he is grown.

> Only now, he thought, now that I know I have a father, do I feel his absence: the place where he should have been and was not. Before, I thought everybody was one-armed, like me. Now I feel the sur-gery. . . . I am not going to be healed, or to find the arm that was removed from me. I am going to freshen the pain, point it, so we both know what it is for.
>
> And no, I am not angry. I don't need the arm. But I do need to know what it could have been like to have had it. It's a phantom I have to behold and be held by. . . . This part of me that does not know

me, has never touched me or lingered at my side. . . . This arm that never held itself out, extended from my body, to give me balance as I walked thin rails or logs, round and slippery with danger. When I find it, will it wave to me? . . .

Who will take my part? Soap away the shame? (158–59)

Gray feels the loss of his father only once he is told that his father is alive; it is as if he is missing an arm. He can imagine much about his father's absence: all the things a father might have done that he did not do. But this is a missing history, an imagination of what might have been. There is nothing to be recovered but the pain of the separation, the only physical evidence of the missing part.

Again experience is reduced to sensation, and experience of others is limited to one's own sensations, because others are missing. To "point" the pain, Gray thinks will give it meaning and purpose, providing cause and effect. Yet there is no real cause for these effects. Gray wants to feel the pain and thereby see what he is missing, but he cannot feel anything but missing. The relationship is what he missed, the relationship which is represented in his mind as an arm that belongs to both himself and his father. That part of his father is part of him, and his father can take Gray's part so that Gray will not be alone and ashamed. This relationship itself cannot be realized except as a phantom: something which can be seen, felt, and imagined but which has never existed.

The construction of masculine and racial identity that Faulkner depicts in terms of lost cause depends on a symbolics of loss. The symbolics of loss required for this identity means the active cultivation of loss: loss is cultivated, or imagined, as the mark of identity. As an imaginative construction, the lost cause entails no recovery of losses. Moreover, as an imaginative construction, the lost cause provides roles to be played that give likeness to various white men. Quentin Compson, then, can take his grandfather's part, and Quentin's father has already taken Quentin's part.

As historical constructions, however, lost causes are experienced by Morrison's characters as lost parents who are unknown, not as marks of identity. They have no symbolic value in any construction of racial or individual identity. They are experienced as "inside nothings," both in the sense that the child has no knowledge of the inner self of the lost parent and in the sense that the child misses the inner feeling of loving and being loved by the lost parent. The subject who experiences these losses may feel that part of the self is missing—the part that would be taken by and shared with a parent. This missing part may also be physical: the hand or arm that might have been taken.

It is because of these missing parts, it would seem, that people in the City live on the sensational surfaces of experience that is emptied of inner reality, of both depths of feeling and depths of attachment. The parts that the people in the City can take reproduce, moreover, the inner loss. Even as they aim to take the form and heed the design of the City, the very reproduction of form marks the internal emptiness of the reproduced figures. And if people, unable to recapture people lost to them, seek to regain lost feelings, they reproduce their own experience as merely a way of being, a way of feeling. Broken into parts, persons and community also experience a breakdown of response among their parts.

Violet

In Violet's experience, the missing of people takes on yet other dimensions. Like other characters in the City, she perceives effects and sensual impressions rather than persons. Yet Violet also sees persons as playing various parts, from different perspectives, and as interchangeable in their parts. After Dorcas's death, Violet seeks out Alice and talks to her about Dorcas. " 'Another time I would have loved her too. Just like you did. Just like Joe' " (109). Violet sees this possibility because she recognizes that Dorcas is young enough to be the daughter that Violet, who has had three miscarriages, has lost. "Who lay there asleep in that coffin? Who posed there awake in the photograph? The scheming bitch who had not considered Violet's feelings one tiniest bit, who came into a life, took what she wanted and damn the consequences? Or mama's dumpling girl? Was she the woman who took the man, or the daughter who fled her womb?" (109). Violet not only misses her mother, who killed herself when Violet was a child, but her own daughter, "that last miscarried child" whom she never knew (108).

Like other characters who miss persons they never knew, Violet thinks of her daughter in terms of externals, especially in terms of what mother and daughter would do together. "Who would she favor? What would her speaking voice sound like? After weaning time, Violet would blow her breath on the babygirl's food, cooling it down for the tender mouth. Later on they would sing together, Violet taking the alto line, the girl a honeyed soprano. . . . Later on Violet would dress her hair for her the way the girls wore it now" (108). This is a sensational depiction—of looks, sounds, tastes—according to which any female child could take the part of the missing daughter. Yet these images also depict a part of Violet's life that could exist only in relation to the lost daughter. Like the lost relationship that Golden Gray imagines when he thinks of the father he never knew, these images are missing parts of Violet's life that are imagined as responses of persons to one another.

Because they are abstracted from Violet's actual experience, the parts—the face, the hair, the voice—of her daughter, like the alto and soprano parts of the songs, are roles many people might play. In the course of the novel, as Violet attempts to regain not only her husband but the self she has lost track of, she recognizes that she has understood both Joe and herself in impersonal terms. Because she saw him initially as anybody would have seen him, Violet also sees that she is exchangeable with other women who look at him. And this leads her to recognize various exchanges of identity among herself, Joe, and Dorcas.

> I picked him out from all the others wasn't nobody like Joe he make anybody stand in cane in the middle of the night; make any woman dream about him in the daytime. . . . Any woman, not just me. Maybe that is what she saw. Not the fifty-year-old man toting a sample case, but my Joe Trace, my Virginia Joe Trace who carried a light inside him. . . . What did she see, young girl like that? . . . And also what did he? A young me with high-yellow skin instead of black? A young me with long wavy hair instead of short? Or a not me at all. . . . Somebody golden, like my own golden boy, who I never ever saw but who tore up my girlhood as surely as if we'd been the best of lovers? . . . Is that what happened? Standing in the cane, he was trying to catch a girl he was yet to see, but his heart knew all about, and me, holding on to him but wishing he was the golden boy I never saw either. Which means from the very beginning I was a substitute and so was he. (96–97)

These substitutions occur when memories of "my Joe Trace" with "a light inside him" are displaced by a prior image of desirability.

Though never seen, the desirability of the "golden boy" of Violet's imagination has been cultivated by the stories True Belle told her grandchildren about Golden Gray. It is such "golden" images, not the looks of actual dark-skinned persons or the particular choice of the lover, that direct desire. The desirable images are drained of the color and particularity of actual persons and direct desire instead to missing persons.

This orientation toward people, according to which they are exchangeable and can take the same parts, involves an impersonality that Morrison identifies with the visual forms and language that rule white culture. The impersonality and exchangeability of persons occurs through images that empty persons of particularity, moreover, in a specific way. These images "whiten" black persons, thereby constituting desirability as what black persons are missing. Like one of the scenes replayed in Joe's memory, "drained of everything but the language to say it in" (29), these images are forms, outlines, and surfaces of experience that empty feeling as well as objects of desire.

Oriented toward loss, these characters experience emptiness not only because of their own histories of loss but also because of the white cultural production of desire as a reproduction of images. What is missing in this reproduction of desire is not merely an originary absence necessary to move the subject into the substitutions of representation. As the trajectory of desire moves toward increasingly "white" characteristics, blackness is missing to desire and missing, therefore, from the substitutions that constitute desire. Black persons become substitutes for white images of desire, but they seem to do so only in parts: skin that is light, hair that is wavy. This is a form of dismembering in which the self recognizes in different parts of the body different degrees of both potential alienation and potential desirability.

Critical Culture

In the story of Golden Gray, who is a product and reproducer of white culture, as he goes in search of his father, Morrison presents the character in *Jazz* most dependent on visual representations. Traveling through Virginia in his carriage, Gray startles a woman, "a naked berry-black woman" (144) who runs from him, slips and falls, and is knocked unconscious. He wraps her in his coat and puts her on the seat beside him. "He does not see himself touching her, but the picture he does imagine is himself walking away from her. . . . He is uneasy with this picture of himself, and does not want to spend any part of the time to come remembering having done that" (145). It is his imagination of how he will appear, to himself and others, that motivates Gray's behavior throughout this story. "No one is looking at him, but he behaves as though there is" (153), as he refers to images of himself as the criteria of appropriate behavior rather than acting with direct reference to the woman, his feelings, or his immediate surroundings.

Caught up in images, Gray worries more about the state of his clothes than the condition of the unconscious woman (151). And "he is shaping a story for himself to tell somebody, to tell his father, naturally": seeing it a certain way.

> He thinks his story is wonderful, and that if spoken right will impress his father with his willingness, his honor. But I know better. He wants to brag about this encounter, like a knight errant bragging about his coolness as he unscrews the spike from the monster's heart and breathes life back into the fiery nostrils. . . .
>
> Why doesn't he wipe her face, I wonder. She is more savage perhaps this way. More graphically rescued. If she should rise up and claw him it would satisfy him even more. . . . Aw, but he is young, young and he is hurting, so I forgive him his self-deception and his grand, fake gestures. (154–55)

In the story that Golden Gray is both reproducing in his imagination and using as a standard for his behavior, he looks the more brave and honorable as the woman looks more savage and monstrous.

In a sense, Gray is both audience and actor in the scenes of honor he imagines. He in effect reproduces an audience that will see what he sees in the images he reproduces. The replaying of white parts established by myth, legend, and tradition, as is the case in works of James and Faulkner, meets with little variation of interpretation. Playing roles of dove, gunfighter, or civil war general, white characters of James and Faulkner do not expect or receive criticism. Simply to invoke these images is enough to produce uncritical reception by persons whose reception of images is difficult to differentiate from their reproduction of images.

The pressure exerted by the public on such characters as Milly Theale and Joe Christmas is a pressure to conform to already received images. Thus the sensational publicity and gossip that circulate in London society about Milly Theale produce a sexual past that places her in a context which everyone knows. Joe Christmas, too, cultivates—or Faulkner cultivates for him—a sensational identity in cliché terms. According to these, black men are equated with sexual and racial violence, and so Joe's is also the same old story. As when Milly Theale plays a dove and becomes difficult to read as anything but innocent, Golden Gray hopes to reproduce an image of himself, in his own mind and in the minds of others, that will be clearly heroic.

When black characters in *Jazz* reproduce images of themselves from cultural media, however, there is little automatic agreement about their identity. As in the above passage when the narrator sees through Gray's "fake gestures" and monstrous imagination, the critical perspectives of characters repeatedly insist on looking behind the scenes of cultural production. There seem to be a number of reasons for the variety of perspectives that constitutes Morrison's urban community. For one thing, black characters live with a degree of self-consciousness that whites do not appear to have. Because of racism, blacks are or become more conscious of the unrepresentative character of images produced by white media and of various interpretations of those images.

Morrison's characters, moreover, produce various interpretations themselves. From the beginning of the novel, the gossipy tone of the narrator, who also reports others' opinions and who makes mistakes in voicing her own, adds to the dubious and debatable quality of the characters' experience. The critical perspectives of various persons result both in disagreement and debate and in choice. For Morrison both groups of persons and individuals become more active producers of meaning in the face of the unreliability of meanings produced in white culture.

Equally important to characters' increased critical perspectives is the fact that, in the media of black cultural expression in the novel, variation takes precedence over reproduction. Debate and argument occur throughout the novel as media through which people represent and exchange their experience. I have argued that the "views" expressed by characters in James's and Faulkner's novels indicate a shift in the dominant white culture from a political to an aesthetic model of cultural expression. But the views of Morrison's black characters are not abstracted from history or from political experience. Faulkner's white men reproduce images for each other that mark their ability to take part in a production of identity shared by other white men. According to this model, the more views the better, because the quantity marks the variety and inclusiveness of the collectivity. But the views of Morrison's characters are not simply represented and collected.

In *Jazz*, views cannot be collected as a series of finished perspectives because they keep changing in relation to new views produced. One example of this occurs in the meetings between Violet and Alice that take place regularly after Dorcas's death. In one conversation, Alice begins by rejecting Violet's violence: " 'I don't understand women like you. Women with knives' " (85). But Violet's repeated questions force Alice to remember the loss of her own husband to another woman and how "every day and every night for seven months she, Alice Manfred, was starving for blood" (86). This identification with Violet is produced by Alice's memory, but it is Violet's questions that call up Alice's memory. Moreover, the identification is an emotional likeness. The production of identity requires the participation of multiple persons. It involves memory and history, creating emotional rather than visual likenesses.[7]

In their sense of self as well as in their relations to one another, these characters make evident social processes of expression and community that have been historically characteristic of numerous black religious and aesthetic practices. The call-and-response structure of "many African American oral traditional forms, from sermon to interjective folktale to blues, jazz and spirituals," for example, provides a medium of both involvement and improvisation among persons.[8] Within this tradition it is not the contents of the expressions that provide continuity so much as the continued practice of an exchange of expressions. Expressions are not only important as representations that accumulate to voice and increase the dimensions of black culture but also as media in which African Americans experience and transmit their relatedness.

Such traditions of community mean that Morrison locates much of the racial identity of African Americans outside representation and reproduction; hence her characters' awareness of multiple meanings. As a nonrepresentative medium, music works to bond persons with sounds, rhythms, and patterns of repetition that evoke a sense of continuity and consistency which is not imaged. The lyrics of jazz and blues songs, moreover, may represent multiple registers of meaning which are important to the cultural value of the lyrics but which are recognizable only if reference is made beyond the terms of their representations. In this realm of unrepresented or underrepresented experience, which is a realm of responses to representations, Morrison locates much of the strength of black culture.

Paul Gilroy argues in *The Black Atlantic* that for historical reasons,

> The stories which dominate black popular culture are usually love stories or more appropriately love and loss stories. That they assume this form is all the more striking because the new genre seems to express a cultural decision not to transmit details of the ordeal of slavery openly in story and song. Yet these narratives of love and loss systematically transcode other forms of yearning and mourning associated with histories of dispersal and exile and the remembrance of unspeakable terror.[9]

These love stories, Gilroy argues, "are a place in which the black vernacular has been able to preserve and cultivate both the distinctive rapport with the presence of death which derives from slavery and a related ontological state that I want to call the condition of being in pain."[10]

The very multiplicity of these registers of private, public, historical, political, and emotional experience in the love stories characteristic of popular African American songs is not the result of aesthetic ambiguity but of historical, political experience. As Gilroy points out, "art, particularly in the form of music and dance, was offered to slaves as a substitute for the formal political freedoms they were denied under the plantation regime. . . . In contradistinction to the Enlightenment assumption of a fundamental separation between art and life, these expressive forms reiterate the continuity of art and life."[11]

Such continuity is evident when stories of "love and loss" in the blues, for example, are taken to refer to the separations forced on enslaved people. Moreover, such political meanings were often improvisational. As Gayl Jones points out, "During the time of slavery, spirituals often carried coded messages about a planned escape or rebellion."[12] With these multiple registers of meaning at work, the music that is for Morrison in *Jazz* the central expressive medium of black culture indicates the interpretive complexity necessary to the realization of African American identity.[13]

The production of black culture in *Jazz* occurs in exchanges among characters that reflect such multiple perspectives. Rather than exchanging either images of likeness or words whose meaning is assumed to be clear, characters enter into exchanges in which referents are suspect. Any image or word, then, calls for a critical response. Or characters may imagine ideas and images of themselves that do not quite take shape: ideas of identity that are not visible or visualizable. In doing so, characters produce identities whose connection depends on thinking and feeling rather than bodily resemblance. What becomes critical to black identity is not how people look but how people respond to one another.

Morrison's characters may themselves reproduce desirable images of whiteness. Violet becomes aware of doing so at the cost of a coherent identity. Violet has lived all her life identifying her ideal object of desire in the image of Golden Gray because her " 'grandmother fed me stories about a little blond child.' " Moreover, she used these images to imagine the self she wanted to be: " 'I thought of him as a girl sometimes, as a brother, sometimes as a boyfriend. He lived inside my mind' " (208). At the end of the novel, Violet sees that she has lost track of parts of herself in her attempt to conform to this alien image and decides to see herself in a different image. " 'Now I want to be the woman my mother didn't stay around long enough to see. That one. The one she would have liked and the one I used to like before' " (208). This shift of reference, from the image of Golden Gray in her own mind to the image of herself in her mother's eyes, occurs as a shift from a visual likeness to emotional liking as the measure of the self. This image is, in a sense, an image of relation, a reproduction of a responsive reflection among persons.[14]

Alice Manfred develops a critical perspective not on images produced in her family but on those produced in the market. Alice, though she likes women's fashions, cannot easily adopt new styles: "Especially the coats slung low in the back and not buttoned, but clutched, like a bathrobe or a towel around the body, forcing the women who wore them to look like they had just stepped out of the bathtub and were already ready for bed" (55). Alice's is not a moral but a pragmatic perspective, owing to her experience "south of 110th Street," where she is identified as a sexual object no matter what she is wearing. "That was where whitemen leaned out of motor cars with folded dollar bills peeping from their palms. It was where salesmen touched her and only her as though she were part of the goods they had condescended to sell her" (54). Alice carries in her mind, then, both desirable images of fashionable clothes and images of white people whose reception of her is not determined by her clothes but seems to remain static whatever her appearance.

Aware that white people's views of her are determined at some level deeper than her looks, Alice may not be confronted simply with a different code applied to black people. White people's "readings" of Alice appear not to be coded, or only largely so, insofar as white people perceive black people as undifferentiated from one another. Here a black character's awareness of hidden registers of meaning clearly is useful in reading black and white cultural expressions. For Alice and Violet, then, the self is understood less as an image than in terms of how others—white people, Violet's mother—might see her, and this response is not represented as a merely visual phenomenon.

Dorcas is a character who does not develop much critical consciousness of the images of cultural media; she remains until her death devoted to looks: " 'She was always talking about who was good looking and who wasn't' " (200). Dorcas reproduces her identity in the images not of white but of black culture, specifically musical culture. When she first came to the City, after the deaths of her parents in East St. Louis, "Dorcas lay on a chenille bedspread, tickled and happy knowing that there was no place to be where somewhere, close by, somebody was not licking his licorice stick, tickling the ivories, beating his skins, blowing off his horn while a knowing woman sang ain't nobody going to keep me down you got the right key baby but the wrong keyhole you got to get it bring it and put it right here, or else" (60). Dorcas likes danger (202). She likes to be bad, to answer the call of the City to "come and do wrong" (67).

Dorcas does wrong with Joe but then shifts her love to Acton, who makes her feel more wrong: not in the sense of breaking rules but in the sense of inadequacy: " 'Acton, now, he tells me when he doesn't like the way I fix my hair. Then I do it how he likes it. I never wear glasses when he is with me and I changed my laugh for him to one he likes better. I think he does. I know he didn't like it before. And I play with my food now. . . . Acton gives me a quiet look when I ask for seconds' " (190). Acton "looks angry" too when Dorcas is shot and her blood gets on his jacket; " 'it is not clean the way it was before and the way he likes it' " (192).

Highly conscious of how things look, Dorcas is also strongly aware of other people looking at her. She drops Joe and takes up with Acton, she says, because she wants other girls to admire the man she is with. She has been secretive about Joe not only because he is married but also because she is not sure of others' response to him: "I sort of hinted about Joe and me to Felice and she laughed before she stared at me and then frowned" (189). Dancing with Acton, though, Dorcas has an admiring audience: "Lots of girls here want to be doing this with him. I can see them when I open my eyes to look past his neck. I rub my thumbnail over his nape so the girls will know I know they want him. He doesn't like it and turns his head to make me stop" (191). Dorcas's concern with looks means a kind of call-and-response performance, but one in which both calls and responses mark disconnections. Dorcas marks her distance from the other girls, then Acton marks his distance from her.

In the medium of Morrison's narrative, however, Dorcas's experience pulls together various persons and elements of personal and cultural experience. Dorcas presents herself in images of wrongdoing that have their sources in her private and her public history. Her own history, in which she watched her family's house, with her mother in it, burn up because white people set it on fire, is one of pain. The pain is evident in Dorcas's images of herself swallowing pieces of the burning house, as is her desire to burn with her mother. "Dorcas let herself die," Felice says. " 'Don't let them call nobody,' she said, 'No ambulance; no police, no nobody' " (209). Dorcas in a sense replays the part of her mother as she restages the event of the fire, when no help came (57). And she restages the drama of the song of Frankie and Johnny, taunting Joe and knowing, the night he kills her, that " 'he is coming for me' " (189).

The illicit sexuality of musical lyrics from which Dorcas adopts her images of herself is only one illegitimate element of jazz. To Alice, the music is dangerous because "it made you do unwise disorderly things. Just hearing it was like violating the law" (58). But if the music expresses "outlaw" desires and behavior, Alice as well as most of the black community in *Jazz* seem to identify themselves as, to some degree, outlaw. Although a man has killed her niece and a woman has attacked the body in the funeral home, Alice cannot turn to the law.

"She would have called the police after both of them if everything she knew about Negro life had made it even possible to consider" (74). Law itself is a phenomenon Alice regards critically. Both lawful citizen and outlaw are positions in which she cannot identify herself. Remaining between but outside conventional white alternatives, Alice must maneuver as she has taught Dorcas to move on the streets: "Taught her how to crawl along the walls of buildings, disappear into doorways, cut across corners in choked traffic—how to do anything, move anywhere to avoid a whiteboy over the age of eleven" (55).

The illegitimate form of jazz ("She knew from sermons and editorials that it wasn't real music—just colored folks' stuff" [59]) produces similar improvisations and variations, neither represented as laws nor productive of patterns repeated as laws. Jazz, like Alice's way of walking, does not reproduce established forms but produces a response: what is called for in and by a particular situation. This implies an incoherence if no development has any particular relation to any other. Insofar as black persons live in between the standard forms and laws of behavior, there is no evident means of definition and consistency of identity. But Morrison demonstrates that black music has and produces consistency, sufficient to hold people together and to hold together diverse elements of black experience.

Means of Consistency

The social and communal consistency produced by black music in the novel lies partly in its inclusiveness. Though highly improvisational, jazz and the blues improvise on familiar and traditional techniques and patterns of music and song. Moreover, the music not only represents sexual as political experience but also effects other intersections of public and private, present and past life as what Morrison calls "public secrets" (67).

For those like the seventeen-year-old Dorcas, with a heightened consciousness of sexuality, "the City, in its own way, gets down for you, cooperates" (63).

> The City is smart at this: smelling and good and looking raunchy; sending secret messages disguised as public signs: this way, open here, danger to let colored only single men on sale woman wanted

private room stop dog on premises absolutely no money down fresh chicken free delivery fast. And good at opening locks, dimming stairways. Covering your moans with its own. (64)

Here the double talk characteristic of blues lyrics is read into street signs and other posted public announcements and suggests not only the City's capacity to "get down" but the capacity of interpretation to read sexual implications in the most unlikely places. Yet the double talk of jazz and the blues is of a particular kind. Unlike the ambiguity of language that leads Dorcas to experience her burning sexuality as a substitute for her burning mother and her burning home, this "raunchy" doubleness evokes a self-consciously illicit response.

This process of rereading throws public signs open to private readings, as Michel de Certeau suggests happens when individuals walk through a city.[15] But it is not so much personal freedom that Morrison emphasizes as it is the public expression of illicit behavior. Jazz and the blues publish what white culture consigns to private life; hence white culture denominates jazz and the blues media of entertainment rather than political media. Black culture, Morrison suggests, does not practice that distinction between public and personal, according to which, for example, public debate in white democracy is supposed to be impersonal and disinterested.

Here, the expression of public secrets in black American culture is an expression not only of sexual desire but also of the political views of black persons that have had to be kept secret from white culture. The rereading Morrison's narrator practices on street signs is a particular response to white culture. It insists on the political capacity of black persons to interpret and bring to the surface what white culture keeps secret. This capacity for critical reading provides resistant interpretations of white laws and white pronouncements. Dorcas substitutes, following the rules of white culture, one experience of burning for another; she reproduces destruction. The narrator's reading of public signs instead opens up a realm of response to their destructive and demeaning terms. This realm of response makes the signs seem somewhat ridiculous. It opens up room for refusing to accept them at face value and for meanings that are not apparent in signs.

It is the expression of political secrets that Alice Manfred hears in the drums during the parade down Fifth Avenue that takes place to protest the riots in East St. Louis.

What was possible to say was already in print on a banner that repeated a couple of promises from the Declaration of Independence
and waved over the head of its bearer. But what was meant came
from the drums. (53)

Alice had picked up a leaflet that had floated to the pavement. . . .
She read the words and looked at Dorcas. . . . Some great gap lunged
between the print and the child. She glanced between them strug-
gling for the connection, something to close the distance between the
silent staring child and the slippery crazy words. Then suddenly, like
a rope cast for rescue, the drums spanned the distance, gathering
them all up and connected them: Alice, Dorcas, her sister and her
brother-in-law, the Boy Scouts and the frozen black faces, the watchers on the pavement and those in the windows above. (58)

The drums become for Alice a means of expression and connection
that are not "possible to say." It seems in part the steadiness of sound
and rhythm that allows the drums to be heard as a line or a rope.

But the drums also span the "great gap" between the printed words
of the pamphlet and Dorcas, who says nothing about the riots or about
her parents killed in East St. Louis. They do so, perhaps, because they
recall a lost language.[16] Recalled as a means of communicating over
great distances as well as a means of bringing together a community,
the drums' meaning includes the pain and anger of loss, both past and
present, and the consistency of community, both past and present.
They are a public secret in their open expression of political meanings
that can be heard only by those able to recognize emotional and historical registers of meaning. And Alice always hears these drums when
she hears the blues: "greedy, reckless words, loose and infuriating, but
hard to dismiss because underneath, holding up the looseness like a
palm, are the drums that put Fifth Avenue into focus" (60).

The consistency produced by musical patterns of exchange holds
people together in other ways too. Just as characters are able to read in
public signs their personal desires, characters can perceive reflections
of their own feelings in other people. But such recognitions also depend on reinterpreting white representations. In the long passage
near the end of the novel in Felice's voice, another series of exchanges
takes place, between persons and between the present and the past,
during which views are modified.

Meeting and talking with Violet and Joe after Dorcas's death, Felice changes her perspectives on them, on Dorcas, and on her own parents. Felice has sought out Violet and Joe partly to find out what happened to her mother's ring, which Dorcas borrowed on the night she was killed. Felice does not get the ring, which has been buried with Dorcas, but in the process of tracking it down she changes her feelings about it too. Having heard from Violet about her need to get rid of the image of Golden Gray in order to realize her own identity, Felice thinks about "the way [she] said 'me'"; this leads to thinking about the ring, which her mother stole, differently.

> "The way she said it. Not like the 'me' was some tough somebody, or somebody she had put together for show. But like, like somebody she favored and could count on. . . . Somebody who wouldn't have to steal a ring to get back at whitepeople and then lie and say it was a present from them. I wanted the ring back not just because my mother asks me have I found it yet. It's beautiful. But although it belongs to me, it's not mine. . . . Reminds me of the tricky blond kid living inside Mrs. Trace's head. A present taken from whitefolks, given to me when I was too young to say No thank you." (210–11)

Here the ring becomes of dubious value, and Felice's mother seems dubious too. But both her mother and her ring continue to run through Felice's mind, together with Dorcas, until Felice sees in her mother's theft of the ring something like Dorcas's love of danger.

> "I'll tell my mother the truth. I know she is proud of stealing that opal; of daring to do something like that to get back at the whiteman who thought she was stealing even when she wasn't. My mother is so honest she makes people laugh. . . . So I know how much taking the ring meant to her. How proud she was of breaking her rules for once. But I'll tell her I know about it, and that it's what she did, not the ring, that I really love." (215)

In Felice's thoughts, her mother, Violet, and Dorcas intersect and reveal new perspectives on each other; Felice recognizes their likenesses to each other. These likenesses are below the surface, in feelings, and Felice changes her feelings about all these characters as she thinks about them.

But it is not only an emotional consistency that is produced here but a critical recognition of racial likeness too, and a likeness that is not visual. The consistency of the experiences of Felice's mother, Violet, and Dorcas lies behind the scenes of Felice's memory, in their own memories of pain and loss caused by white people and white culture. Recognizing their pain means that Felice revises the anger she feels toward them. Yet because she recognizes racism as the cause lying behind the pain that led them to act as they did, Felice is bound to them not only by her feelings but also by her consciousness of race. The consistency of race recognized here is an abstract consistency insofar as it is produced by a process of thought that chooses particular elements of the women's experience to consider in relation to one another. Nevertheless, it is an emotional and historical consistency that the critical consciousness identifies.

In *Jazz*, music is a means of consistency not only for black culture but also for black individuals whose parts are otherwise experienced as separated. Coming up to New York on the train, "nervous" and "terrified," Violet and Joe feel themselves dancing.

> The quick darkness in the carriage cars when they shot through a tunnel made them wonder if maybe there was a wall ahead to crash into or a cliff hanging over nothing. The train shivered with them at the thought but went on and sure enough there was ground up ahead and the trembling became the dancing under their feet. Joe stood up, his fingers clutching the baggage rack above his head. He felt the dancing better that way, and told Violet to do the same. (30)

Here the train's shaking is felt as a response to their fears. Once this responsiveness is felt—"they thought it was like them" (30)—the trembling of the train becomes dancing. The train seems to express their bodily symptoms of fear and enables them to give bodily expression to their own responsiveness, "laughing and tapping back at the tracks" (30).[17]

When Dorcas goes to parties, music is experienced again as a medium of consistency among persons and within the body.

> Under the ceiling light pairs move like twins born with, if not for, the other, sharing a partner's pulse like a second jugular. They believe they know before the music does what their hands, their feet are to do, but that illusion is the music's secret drive: the control it tricks

them into believing is theirs; the anticipation it anticipates. In between record changes, while the girls fan blouse necks to air damp collarbones or pat with anxious hands the damage moisture has done to their hair, the boys press folded handkerchiefs to their foreheads. (65)

Here, as on the train, music gives an illusion of control even when bodies are out of control. The desire to control the body resurfaces when the music stops and people try to repair the changes dancing has caused in their appearance; then it is as if they see their bodies in mirrors, as images they need to maintain. The music and their response to the music provide a consistency within and among these persons instead of such unity with an image. Dancing is an experience of sharing, because persons are similarly moved by the music. Though out of rational control, this experience is nevertheless bound by the music, to which persons and parts of the body respond together.

Near the end of the novel, in a passage I have quoted at length earlier, Morrison's narrator, rather than seeing her characters as fading images in a picture, identifies them as "sharply in focus and clicking." She insists on the necessity of hearing these characters, not only in music but also in their responses to music, and in their talk and their responses to talk: *"Talking to you and hearing you answer—that's the kick"* (229). In the novel, because they are both response and motive, talk and music require, as media of cultural identity, not only that people reproduce them but also that people continue to be motivated by them and responsive to them.

The narrator wonders of her characters, "Do they know they are the sound of snapping fingers under the sycamores lining the streets?" (226). The dark clicking fingers, heard in the imagination but not in recordings, could be identified as a lost part of an original work of art: part of the cultural meaning of art that is lost, for example, when works are collected in a museum. But Morrison reverses that trajectory of abstraction, and the inevitability of cultural loss that accompanies it, as she removes the aim of art from representation in a museum to reproduction in the street, in the memory, in the shade. Similarly, she reverses the trajectory of knowledge that separates individual identity from the calls and responses of cultural identity. The "shady" locations of black cultural identity include not only Bunny's and Roseland, which parents warn against (227). They include the not quite or not always visible sharing of identity that is cultivated in the minds, memories, and hands of Morrison's characters. These are necessary black cultural media, because they produce the calls and responses that constitute identity in *Jazz*.

Afterword

Identifying the construction of whiteness as a field of representation, I have focused not only on images but also on a more powerful identification of imagery: as a comprehensive range of representation. The degree to which "looking" and surveillance can produce social order by "inscribing visibility everywhere" has been clarified by critics who have continued Foucault's work on the history and institutions of power in the West.[1] I have given more attention to individual consciousness as a medium of white power that produces order in reflective relations of self and other.

In James's *The Wings of the Dove* and *The Golden Bow* and Faulkner's *The Sound and the Fury* and *Light in August,* whiteness is a theoretically diverse and democratic collective of individuals: a collective, moreover, of self-conscious persons whose public political identity is bolstered by, in effect repeated within, their critical consciousness. The order of whiteness depends on abstracting self and other into internalizable relations of self-as-other.

The self-conscious white person both incorporates otherness and maintains distinction, as a self structured by division. The self-consciously white individual projects the structure of self-division onto a field of racial identity, as Morrison's theory of the white projection of the "not-me" onto a field of darkness has indicated. Racial blackness functions in such a structure to "ground" white identity. Racial darkness is used to visualize or materialize what whites are not, as in *The Golden Bowl,* and thereby marks the freedom of immaterial whiteness. More specifically, as in *Light in August,* racial darkness may mark off particular undesirable and unfree qualities from whiteness. Most significant, I think, racial darkness is identified in novels by James and Faulkner as undifferentiated, unchanging, and nonproductive.

In Morrison's *Sula* and *Jazz*, politically diverse collectives of American blacks produce a racial identity not among self-conscious but among doubly conscious individuals. Individual double consciousness includes an awareness of multiple "views," but the views of the dominant white culture must be comprehended as exclusive rather than inclusive of the self. Thus black double consciousness in Morrison's novels is not strictly identifiable with the workings of a collective identity. But for other reasons, too, the black individual consciousness does not independently reproduce the identity of the black political collective in Morrison's works.

Black identity in these novels is produced in communal exchanges that occur among, not within, characters. Rather than promoting extensions of individualism, these exchanges express a responsiveness among persons that is understood to move relations of self and other beyond the bounds of individual consciousness. Whereas white characters in works of James and Faulkner achieve a diversity and inclusiveness by internally reproducing others' perspectives, black characters in Morrison's novels achieve a diversity that is identified in relations extending beyond the self.

The social responsiveness of persons means that among Morrison's characters even looking is converted into an active relation and takes the form of looking back. Unlike the looking that produces a field of surveillance for Foucault, the looking back that occurs in Morrison's cultures interferes with the capacity of any subject or any single point of view to comprehend or map otherness. In Morrison's novels, even trees may respond to persons, as happens in *Tar Baby*, with opinions that challenge people's thinking and feeling.[2] If objects do not remain objects and become unpredictable in their identity, subjects do not remain subjects either, insofar as subjectivity implies a capacity to internalize otherness. Otherness is produced in these novels in responses by others which are practical and which resist the abstractions that include and comprehend otherness.

If for Morrison neither subjects nor objects remain mere subjects or objects, this variability resembles the transformations of persons and objects into media that occur in James's and Faulkner's works. For James and Faulkner, objects and subjects become media that expand individual white identity. People and objects become means of extensive relation to the world through the production of more and more relations—more differences, more likenesses—within consciousness. These relations may be produced as or with visual metaphors because "vision" is comprehensive. It covers both abstract and material phenomena and is a mode of production as well as a mode of recognition. One person can reproduce or mirror another's meaning or can take another's point of view. The comprehensive reproduction of others' views by the self repeats the assumptions of inclusiveness entailed in critical consciousness and social surveillance both. And both are claimed by whiteness.

Morrison's African American breakdown of the opposition of subjects and objects also has the effect of extending relations among persons and among persons and things. Rather than comprehending one another's points of view, an act that can occur within an individual consciousness, the responses of Morrison's characters produce social and historical extensions of identity, according to which part of the self exists beyond the self. Thus characters are recalled to themselves by Sula, to whom they respond by producing the selves they want to be. Or characters in *Jazz* recall to one another parts of the self that have been missing. Others act as expressions and recalls of missing parts of the self that reconstitute the self. James's wide views extend the self into possibility and open up dimensions of change, but these occur within consciousness and depend on distance from others. Morrison's extensions of identity are social and historical and thereby assume an attachment to persons and events external to consciousness. Characters look and look back—at others and at the past—and these responses produce differences as well as similarities among persons and over time.

By focusing on these various productions of racial identity, I have called attention to interrelations of individual consciousness and collective identity that move the dimensions of racial identity beyond either individual persons or group identities. The ways in which individuals participate in political relations and cultural productions of racial identity in the novels I have considered indicate that particular structures of individual consciousness need to be examined as media of racial production. James's critical consciousness, Faulkner's divided, Lacanian consciousness, and Morrison's double consciousness enter into exchanges between self and other that produce different

kinds of cultural and racial identity. In addition cultural media participate in racial identity, to the extent that no such media can be taken for
granted by critics of race. "Visual culture" in particular is, to some
degree at least, inseparable from the power and production of whiteness. By examining relations between visual media and less sensational modes of cultural production, critics can further clarify the
political meaning and extent of cultural media.

Notes

Introduction Race and Media

1   Two studies of the ethnographic character of James's work focus on white American culture and race. In *The Ethnography of Manners: Hawthorne, James, Wharton* (Cambridge: Cambridge University Press, 1995), Nancy Bentley discusses James's depiction of a white culture of assimilative power. Bentley argues that James, Hawthorne, and Wharton, "rather than either suppressing or celebrating otherness, . . . *cultivate* it, in both senses of that word; they feed it and give it a recognizable life in literature, at the same time as they master it through an ironic assimilation" (23). "An ethnographic diction allowed novelists to domesticate precisely those social facts that would have been ignored discretely [*sic*] in private homes and institutions of high culture," including "an increasing immigration and racial diversity" (21). Reading James's internationalism as a "kind of racial theater" (10), Sara Blair, in *Henry James and the Writing of Race and Nation* (Cambridge: Cambridge University Press, 1996), identifies an assimilative and abstracted perspective with his production of white identity. Even early in his career, Blair indicates, "James's essays experiment with shifting identities and voices, miming and opposing various models and categories—the Anglo-Saxon 'mind,' the American 'character,' the genteel, the European or Continental—of cultural performance. With increasing ingenuity, James mobilizes such unstable models, which inflect and are inflected by ethnographic tenets of race and nation, so as to test and volatilize their limits" (17). Blair's theatrical model of whiteness is similar, in the variability of identity it makes available to white persons, to the collective white American identities I discuss in both James's and Faulkner's novels.

Blair concentrates specifically on James's representations of Jews in her discussion of *The American Scene.* Jonathan Freedman also focuses on James's depiction of Jewish characters in "The Poetics of Cultural Decline: Degeneracy, Assimilation, and the Jew in James's *The Golden Bowl*," *American Literary History* 7, 3 (Fall 1995).

2   The collection edited by Doreen Fowler and Ann J. Abadie, *Faulkner and Race: Faulkner and Yoknapatawpha, 1986* (Jackson: University Press of Missis-

sippi, 1987), includes readings of Faulkner's characterizations of African Americans as well as several discussions of white characterization. In *Faulkner: The House Divided* (Baltimore: Johns Hopkins University Press, 1983), Eric J. Sundquist calls attention to the treatment of race in Faulkner's novels in cultural and historical contexts. Sundquist indicates intersections of public and private experience of a kind important to my own readings of whiteness. He clarifies, for example, how the public obsession with miscegenation in the post–Civil War South is repeated in Quentin Compson's private fear of incest. See Sundquist's discussion of "The Myth of *The Sound and the Fury*," 3–27.

3   Among the many essays and books that address Morrison's work specifically as African American fiction are Hortense J. Spillers, "A Hateful Passion, a Lost Love," in *Toni Morrison: Critical Perspectives Past and Present*, ed. Henry Louis Gates Jr. and K. A. Appiah (New York: Amistad, 1993), 210–35; Valerie Smith, " 'Circling the Subject': History and Narrative in *Beloved*," in *Toni Morrison*, ed. Gates and Appiah, 342–55; Mae G. Henderson, "Toni Morrison's *Beloved*: Re-Membering the Body as Historical Text," in *Comparative American Identities: Race, Sex, and Nationality in the Modern Text*, ed. Hortense J. Spillers (New York: Routledge, 1991), 66; Mae G. Henderson, "Speaking in Tongues: Dialogics, Dialectics, and the Black Woman Writer's Literary Tradition," in *Changing Our Own Words: Essays on Criticism, Theory, and Writing by Black Women*, ed. Cheryl A. Wall (New Brunswick: Rutgers University Press, 1989), 16–37; Farah Jasmine Griffin, "*Who Set You Flowin'?*": The African-American Migration Narrative (New York: Oxford University Press, 1995); and Trudier Harris, *Fiction and Folklore: The Novels of Toni Morrison* (Knoxville: University of Tennessee Press, 1991).

4   Toni Morrison, *Playing in the Dark: Whiteness and the Literary Imagination* (Cambridge: Harvard University Press, 1992).

5   "Black Americans were sustained and healed and nurtured by the translation of their experience into art, above all in the music. That was functional," states Morrison in Paul Gilroy, "Living Memory: A Meeting with Toni Morrison," in Gilroy, *Small Acts* (London: Serpent's Tail, 1993), 175–82. Gilroy cites this passage in his *The Black Atlantic: Modernity and Double Consciousness* (Cambridge: Harvard University Press, 1993), 78.

6   Robyn Wiegman, *American Anatomies: Theorizing Race and Gender* (Durham: Duke University Press, 1995), argues that "visual modernity" is the context in which whiteness has come to be "seen" as a material absence, whereas other racial identities, especially black identities, have been understood to be visible bodies (21).

Among many readings of race in film, Richard Dyer's work has been particularly influential in distinguishing racial whiteness. See "White," *Screen* 29, 4 (Autumn 1988), and *White* (London: Routledge, 1997). See also Michael Rogin, *Blackface, White Noise: Jewish Immigrants in the Hollywood Melting Pot* (Berkeley: University of California Press, 1996), and James A. Snead, *White Screens, Black Images: Hollywood from the Dark Side*, ed. Colin McCabe and Cornel West (New York: Routledge, 1994).

In addition to her numerous essays on films, bell hooks addresses different kinds of visual recognition and visual power practiced by white and black persons in "The Oppositional Gaze: Black Female Spectators," in *Black Looks: Race and Representation* (Boston: South End, 1992), 115–31, and "Representations of Whiteness in the Black Imagination," in *Killing Rage: Ending Racism* (New York: Holt, 1995), 31–50.

7   Morrison is one of a number of African American women writers who have, in the late twentieth century, "undertaken the reconstruction of both history and context for their people." See Justine Tally, "History, Fiction, and Community in the Work of Black American Women Writers from the Ends of Two Centuries," in *The Black Columbiad: Defining Moments in African American Literature and Culture,* ed. Werner Sollors and Maria Diedrich (Cambridge: Harvard University Press, 1994), 358. Most important to my readings of community and history in *Sula* and *Jazz* is Gilroy's *The Black Atlantic,* in which he discusses a black "counterculture of modernity" (36).

8   Dyer, "White," pp. 44, 45. In *White,* Dyer extends this formulation to a comprehensive assertion of the importance of paradox to whiteness. "White identity is founded on compelling paradoxes," and "the paradoxes and instabilities of whiteness also constitute its flexibility and productivity, in short, its representational power" (39–40). He also elaborates on the spiritual expansiveness of whiteness, arguing that the Christian dualism of mind and body allows a transcending of material and historical limits that has been important to empire and to religion (14–17). Such openness or expansiveness is important to my readings of whiteness.

9   Among critics working to particularize varieties of whiteness are Matt Wray and Annalee Newitz, who identify "a growing need for developing our understanding of how the construction of whiteness varies across lines of class, gender, and sexuality and how these constructions vary according to the politics of place and region" in their introduction to *White Trash: Race and Class in America,* ed. Wray and Newitz (New York: Routledge, 1997), 4. Ruth Frankenberg is concerned at "a continued failure to displace the 'unmarked marker' status of whiteness, a continued inability to 'color' the seeming transparency of white positionings," in her "Introduction: Local Whitenesses, Localizing Whiteness," in *Displacing Whiteness: Essays in Social and Cultural Criticism,* ed. Frankenberg (Durham: Duke University Press, 1997), 1.

Frankenberg's historically specific discussion of race in *White Women, Race Matters: The Social Construction of Whiteness* (Minneapolis: University of Minnesota Press, 1993) is part of more recent work that has revised the normative status of whiteness. Howard Winant reviews such changes and argues "that it is no longer possible to assume a 'normalized' whiteness, whose invisibility and relatively monolithic character signify immunity from political or cultural challenge." See "Behind Blue Eyes: Whiteness and Contemporary U.S. Racial Politics," in *Off White: Readings on Race, Power, and Society,* ed. Michelle Fine, Lois Weis, Linda C. Powell, and L. Mun Wong (New York: Routledge, 1997), 40.

10 Jonathan Crary, *Techniques of the Observer: On Vision and Modernity in the Nineteenth Century* (Cambridge: MIT Press, 1990), 96. See also Crary's chapter 5, "Visionary Abstraction," in which he discusses how, in the work of Gustav Fechner and others, "vision, as well as the other senses, is . . . describable in terms of abstract and exchangeable magnitudes" (147).

11 James Lastra, "From the Captured Moment to the Cinematic Image: A Transformation in Pictorial Order," in *The Image in Dispute: Art and Cinema in the Age of Photography,* ed. Dudley Andrew, with Sally Shafto (Austin: University of Texas Press, 1997), 264.

12 Ibid., 278.

13 This mobilized vision has been compared to vision from a moving train. See ibid., and Jacques Aumont, "The Variable Eye, or the Mobilization of the Gaze," trans. Charles O'Brien and Sally Shafto, in *The Image in Dispute,* ed. Andrew, 234–36. See also Sara Blair's discussion in *Henry James and the Writing of Race and Nation* of the importance of trains to James's white identity, 190–210.

14 Aumont, "The Variable Eye," 251, 253. The objective views imply "a generic, abstract, quasi-inhuman eye," whereas subjective shots insist on "the potentially human source of any gaze" (251). Yet the subjective quality of many shots in films does not alter the "self-serving" quality of the images: "points of view that are self-serving to the degree that they must be without rival, so that the spectator may be prevented from occupying anything other than the 'vantage point' offered" (253). This limitation is echoed in the immobility of subjects seated in the cinema (253).

15 Milly is not, however, interested in the view from a train, which she identifies as more confining than liberating. Early in the book (James, *The Wings of the Dove,* ed. J. Donald Crowley and Richard A. Hocks [New York: Norton, 1978]), she feels constrained by Lord Mark, as if she has been "popped into the compartment in which she was to travel for him" (104). She "wished to get away from him" (107), despite his promises that she will "see everything" (104).

16 Henry James, *The Golden Bowl* (London: Penguin, 1987), 548.

17 William Faulkner, *The Sound and the Fury* (New York: Vintage), 371.

18 Frankenberg argues that "the turn to identity and culture" from race entailed in such identifications "simultaneously evades and mystifies the positioning of whiteness in the racial hierarchy"; moreover, ethnic identifications "frequently reify and homogenize whiteness" ("Local Whitenesses," 19). Rogin assesses historical relations between ethnic and racial identities in the United States in *Blackface, White Noise* and contends that "since race created Americans, the ethnocultural perspective should attend to racial history rather than substitute for it" (26). See also Mike Hill's discussion of "the epistemological stickiness" of whiteness that critics must confront (3) in his "Introduction: Vipers in Shangri-la: Whiteness, Writing, and Other Ordinary Terrors," in *Whiteness: A Critical Reader,* ed. Mike Hill (New York: New York University Press, 1997), 1–18.

19 Scholars have insisted on the very different kinds and aims of assimilation in United States history. Noel Ignatiev, *How the Irish Became White* (London: Routledge, 1995), identifies a specific ethnic experience of whiteness while tracing very different social uses of ethnic and racial identities. Alexander Saxton, *The Rise and Fall of the White Republic: Class Politics and Mass Culture in Nineteenth-Century America* (London: Verso, 1990), puts emphasis on the variety of interests, especially class interests, served by constructions of race over a century. These various renegotiations of racial difference have nevertheless, he points out, contributed to the political and ideological powers of whiteness. See, for example, his discussion of the 1890s, 350–77.

20 Cheryl I. Harris's discussion in "Whiteness as Property," *Harvard Law Review* 106, 8 (June 1993): 1709–91, is particularly useful here because of her emphasis on the immaterial and inalienable character of whiteness as property. Harris's legal history of whiteness in the United States focuses on property as "a right, not a thing, characterized as metaphysical, not physical" (1725). Considering whiteness as rights, expectations, privileges, and exclusivity, Harris clarifies that it is not so much what whites have but their assumption of rights to have, their expectations of having, which differentiate them from black persons and which have been consistently affirmed by American courts. What comes with racial identity and what racial identity can be assumed to produce are thereby crucial to an understanding of racial differences in the United States. Harris clarifies that it is not so much the laws governing racial identity as the fact that whites have made them that matters. She insists on the production of rules of racial identity, rather than the racial distinctions produced, as the unrecognized and crucial issue (see especially 1764–66).

21 Jürgen Habermas, *The Structural Transformation of the Public Sphere: An Inquiry into a Category of Bourgeois Society,* trans. Thomas Burger (Cambridge: MIT Press, 1989), 46–47.

22 Michael Warner, "The Mass Public and the Mass Subject," in *Habermas and the Public Sphere,* ed. Craig Calhoun (Cambridge: MIT Press, 1992), 379–80, 381.

23 Ibid., 382.

24 Frankenberg, *White Women, Race Matters,* 231. Frankenberg distinguishes two definitions of culture, one of which is distinct from daily and material life and the other of which forms daily practices (228). "White culture" in the United States is the former kind. Whiteness "as a normative space . . . is constructed precisely by the way in which it positions others at its borders" (231). Yet "whiteness *does* have content inasmuch as it generates norms, ways of understanding history, ways of thinking about self and other, and even ways of thinking about the notion of culture itself" (231).

In "The Universalization of Whiteness: Racism and Enlightenment" (in *Whiteness,* ed. Hill, 281–93), Warren Montag explores, in European philosophy of the eighteenth century, a similar construction of universal norms of human identity, emphasizing the spacing of ideal and actual identities.

Given that [for Rousseau] humanity is not originally human but nonhuman and that the humanness of the human species is not to be found in its actual condition, an ideal emerges out of and against actuality that allows us to assign descending "degrees of perfection" to the individuals or groups we consider. It is the principle not external to humanity but immanent in it as an internal distance that separates humanity as it is from humanity as it ought to be, that receding horizon of perfectibility in relation to which specific anthropological cases may be hierarchized in order of failure. Thus, in appearing to homogenize the human species. . . . such a norm instead furnishes the criteria of its internal differentiation all the way down to the animal who possesses not a single human characteristic except a perfectibility always to be realized. (291)

Montag's elaboration of the internal differentiations within Rousseau's "universal" human identity points more specifically to constructions of knowledge than to the political constructions that interest Warner. Montag's recognition of the normative character of whiteness, however, and his attention to whiteness as a comprehensive collection of differences rather than as a particular difference in identity, parallel Warner's discussion of white male identity in an eighteenth-century American public sphere.

25 Joan W. Scott, *Only Paradoxes to Offer: French Feminists and the Rights of Man* (Cambridge: Harvard University Press, 1996), esp. 5–11. Walter Benn Michaels, too, in "Race into Culture: A Critical Genealogy of Cultural Identity," *Critical Inquiry* 18 (Summer 1992): 655–85, points to the ways in which, more recently, theoretically common identities of persons—in this case their "cultural history"—may appear to ignore race but in fact function as racial distinctions (682–83): "Our sense of culture is characteristically meant to displace race, but . . . culture has turned out to be a way of continuing rather than repudiating racial thought" (684).

26 Warner, in "Mass Public," is careful to identify "white, male, literate, and propertied" persons as the individuals whose particular identities are abstracted in the conception of the democratic individual. Literacy and the ownership of property, however, are conditions a person may be able to change. The more lasting criteria for political power have been those deemed biological and hence unchangeable: race and gender.

27 Michael Omi and Howard Winant, *Racial Formation in the United States: From the 1960s to the 1980s* (New York: Routledge and Kegan Paul, 1986), 23.

28 See bell hooks's discussion of whites' domination of the gaze and their assumption of their own invisibility in "Representations of Whiteness in the Black Imagination": "In white supremacist society, white people can 'safely' imagine that they are invisible to black people since the power they have historically asserted, and even now collectively assert over black people, accorded them the right to control the black gaze" (35).

29 Morrison, *Playing in the Dark*, 39, 37.

30 Ibid., 38, 44.

31 Ibid., 65.

32 In her first novel, *The Bluest Eye* (New York: Plume, 1994), Morrison also gives much attention to the destructive effects of white visual culture on black characters. But in *Jazz* (New York: Plume, 1993) she elaborates more extensive effects of visual culture, as well as clarifying nonvisual media of African American culture.

33 Habermas, *Structural Transformation of the Public Sphere*, 161.

34 Ibid., 200–201. Warner, in "Mass Public," stresses the incompleteness of this transformation, however, and the resulting contradictions in representations of the twentieth-century American public.

> In fact, we have no way of talking about the public without theorizing the contexts and strategies in which the public could be represented. If we believe in the continued existence of a rational-critical public, . . . then it is difficult to account for the counter-democratic tendencies of the public sphere as anything other than the cowardice or bad faith of some journalists. On the other hand, if we believe that the public sphere of the mass media has replaced a rational and critical public with one that is consumerist and acclamatory, then we might expect it to show more consumer satisfaction, more acclaim. (390–91)

> What Warner identifies is "a discourse of publicity structured by deep contradictions between self-abstraction and self-realization" (399).

35 James, *The Golden Bowl*, 161.

36 The emptying out of individuals' positions so that they become convertible is a theoretical practice that has been resisted recently by insistences that positions in social orders be understood in historical and geographical terms. One collection representing such particularizations of position is *Place and the Politics of Identity,* ed. Michael Keith and Steve Pile (London: Routledge, 1993). Angie Chabram-Dernersesian also discusses whiteness from various positions that are excluded from it, in "On the Social Construction of Whiteness within Selected Chicana/o Discourses," in *Displacing Whiteness,* ed. Frankenberg, 107–64.

37 James A. Snead's discussion of "mass-images in our culture" in *White Screens, Black Images,* esp. 141–42, is helpful in clarifying the particular kind of public exchange that I am considering here. Snead points to the ways that "advertising, films and television images establish role-, behavior- and relationship-models that are, through their repetition, even more effective on an unconscious level than rhetorical propaganda on a conscious level." The coding of such imagery has "a 'mythifying' and 'exemplary' impact that gives them a value somewhat higher than truth."

> Stereotypes ultimately connect to form larger complexes of symbols and connotations. These codes then begin to form a kind of "private conversation" among themselves without needing to refer back to the real world for their facticity. The pleasure of recognizing codes displaces the necessity for a viewer

to verify them. Since many mass-media images today claim to be neither reality nor fantasy (witness the docudrama), there are no useful criteria by which to inspect or challenge the claims to truth that these visual images and events constantly make. (141)

38 Warner, considering in detail the relations between consumer behavior and political behavior in the late-twentieth-century American public, argues in "Mass Public" that because everyone experiences only partial representations, everyone is alienated within the public sphere.

No one really inhabits the general public. This is true not only because it is by definition general but also because everyone brings to such a category the particularities from which they have to abstract themselves in consuming this discourse. Of course, some particularities, such as whiteness and maleness, are already oriented to that procedure of abstraction. . . . But the given of the body is nevertheless a site of countermemory, all the more so since statistically everyone will be mapped into some minority or other, a form of positivity minoritized precisely in the abstracting discourse with which everyone also identifies. (396–97)

The television culture that is crucial to the public sphere Warner studies may make the most important difference between his theory of American public life and its representations by James and Faulkner.

39 Anke Gleber discusses the rarity of "female flanerie" in modern urban experience in "Women on the Screens and Streets of Modernity: In Search of the Female Flaneur," in *The Image in Dispute,* ed. Andrew, 55–85. Gleber points to "physical and material obstacles" and also "a psychological containment that often comes in internalized forms of (self-) control" as means of "positioning . . . women on the other side of the gaze" (63).

40 Ibid., 74.

41 Edward W. Said, *Orientalism* (New York: Vintage, 1979), 55. Said uses Bachelard's work *The Poetics of Space,* trans. Maria Jolas (New York: Orion, 1964).

42 Said, *Orientalism,* 55.

43 Helga Geyer-Ryan has argued for a gendered version of such a model, for which she depends on the Lacanian mirror stage, in "Imaginary Identity: Space, Gender, Nation," in *Vision in Context: Historical and Contemporary Perspectives on Sight,* ed. Teresa Brennan and Martin Jay (New York: Routledge, 1996), 119–25. "The anxieties of absence, loss, and castration that lie at the root of xenophobia," Geyer-Ryan writes, "are triggered by the collapse of the fantasy of the whole, unified, undamaged body in a space that is conceived of, metaphorically and metonymically, as the body's extension or double" (121). Geyer-Ryan then argues that because women's bodies are understood to be less unified than those of men, women are differently threatened when they "confront the stranger" (124). My interest is not so much in the space between the self and the mirror image of the self or in issues of boundaries that arise because of the ambiguous self-as-other. I

focus on projections and introjections that occur in a shared cultural space, whose boundaries are less important than the complete coverage of identity provided by the exchanges that occur within it.

44 Said, *Orientalism*, 58.

45 Ibid., 58–59.

46 James, *Wings of the Dove*, 304.

47 See, for example, Eric Lott's "White like Me: Racial Cross-Dressing and the Construction of American Whiteness," in *Cultures of United States Imperialism*, ed. Amy Kaplan and Donald E. Pease (Durham: Duke University Press, 1993), 474–95. Lott argues that "blackface performance reproduced or instantiated a structured *relationship* between the races, racial difference itself, as much as black cultural forms" (481). The identity of white American males, Lott thereby suggests, is dependent on an identification with black males. "The black male and fantasies about him supply the content of the white male Imaginary, they make up its repertoire" (481). One conclusion Lott draws "is that whiteness itself ultimately becomes an impersonation" (491). In *Love and Theft: Blackface Minstrelsy and the American Working Class* (New York: Oxford University Press, 1993), Lott contends that practices of minstrelsy also indicate how "precariously nineteenth-century white working people lived their whiteness" (4). The "articulation of racial difference" in minstrelsy "took the form of a simultaneous drawing up and crossing of racial boundaries" (6). Lott's identification of whiteness with representation and black male characteristics with a repertoire of representations of the white male self suggest the productivity and the hegemonic inclusiveness of whiteness, I think, more than "an exchange of energies between two otherwise rigidly bounded and policed cultures" (6).

Unlike the repertoires of white likenesses that I consider, Lott identifies a repertoire of black images necessary to white identity. I am more closely following Morrison's concept of a playing field, necessary to white identity because within that field the "not-me" can be projected onto darkness. See Morrison, *Playing in the Dark*, 38. In Chapter 3, I argue that a field similar to the Lacanian Imaginary is a distinctly white medium of identity in *The Sound and the Fury*.

In *Racechanges: White Skin, Black Face in American Culture* (New York: Oxford University Press, 1997), Susan Gubar includes minstrelsy as only one of many forms of "racechange" practiced by both white and black persons. Gubar does suggest, however, that, "historically, white posing counters black passing. Often, in other words, the white poser flagrantly exhibits the artifice of the performance, its theatrical falsity, while the black passer seeks to screen or camouflage signs of a discrepancy between hidden identity and outer appearance" (44). Such a distinction between white and black persons' uses of representation is crucial to my readings of racial difference.

48 The moral connotations associated with "black" and "white," "light" and "dark" have a long history in British and American cultures. Winthrop D.

Jordan, *White over Black: American Attitudes toward the Negro, 1550–1812* (New York: Norton, 1977), discusses how much "intense meaning" was attributed to the terms "black" and "white" by the English "long before they found that some men were black." "White and black connoted purity and filthiness, virginity and sin, virtue and baseness, beauty and ugliness, beneficence and evil, God and the devil," and, implicit in all these, an absolute opposition (7). Whiteness also connoted enlightenment; in America, "after the Revolution, Americans would find pressing reason to regard their own whiteness as integral to their emergence as an enlightened nation" (259).

49 Shamoon Zamir, " 'The Sorrow Songs' / 'Song of Myself': Du Bois, the Crisis of Leadership, and Prophetic Imagination," in *The Black Columbiad*, ed. Sollors and Diedrich, 145–66, emphasizes differences between the thinking of white American transcendentalists and that of Du Bois. In an analysis particularly relevant to my argument, she distinguishes between Emerson's and Whitman's reliance on vision for their sense of a prophetic self and Du Bois's need to listen and to write. "*Listening* to the voices singing the spirituals, a more social act than seeing, and sending out into the world his *written* work" are acts that "present . . . a very different ratio of the senses than the one that dominates in Emerson, or even the more 'amative' Whitman, and also a very different conceptualization of visionary action" (162–63).

Chéla Sandoval has also discussed differences between a black and a white critical consciousness in "Theorizing White Consciousness for a Post-Empire World: Barthes, Fanon, and the Rhetoric of Love," in *Displacing Whiteness*, ed. Frankenberg, 86–106. Focusing on Frantz Fanon's and Roland Barthes's critiques of white consciousness in the 1950s, Sandoval argues that these critics differ especially because Barthes's "white solipsism" isolates him, whereas Fanon "sees himself in elective affinity with a revolutionary community" (103). A kind of social extension of self, similar to that Sandoval identifies in Fanon's consciousness, is active, I will argue, in Morrison's characters.

50 Gilroy, *The Black Atlantic*, 56–57.

51 See Gilroy's discussion of political expression on plantations in ibid., esp. 56–57 and throughout chapter 2, in which he argues for the need to reconstruct modernity to include African Americans' experience of it. In chapter 6, Gilroy specifically discusses "active, dynamic processes" of musical performance as well as stories of death and loss that have characterized African political expression in Western locations (200–205).

52 Ibid., 77–79.

53 Gayl Jones, *Liberating Voices: Oral Tradition in African American Literature* (Cambridge: Harvard University Press, 1991), 197. Gilroy stresses the widespread practice of call-and-response: "Antiphony (call and response) is the principal formal feature of these musical traditions [of black culture]. It has come to be seen as a bridge from music into other modes of cultural expression, supplying, along with improvisation, montage, and dramaturgy, the

hermeneutic keys to the full medley of black artistic practices." See *The Black Atlantic*, 78.

54 Among scholars who have studied the history of African American cultures, Charles P. Henry has focused on various continuities of ideology from African as well as early African American to modern political experience. In *Culture and African American Politics* (Bloomington: Indiana University Press, 1990), Henry argues, for example, that "the African influence on the blues" is evident in the pragmatism and specificity of interest of blues songs as well as in their function "to maintain happiness and community spirit" (30). "Blues, while stylistically reflecting the changes that have occurred in the black social world since emancipation, still performs the same function [as singing did among plantation slaves]. It fights oppression not through grand political theory but through the day-to-day overcoming of obstacles" (31).

55 Houston A. Baker Jr., "Critical Memory and the Black Public Sphere," in *The Black Public Sphere*, ed. the Black Public Sphere Collective (Chicago: University of Chicago Press, 1995), 33. Other public images of black persons, especially in music videos, have received attention from critics concerned about the commercial erasure of political meaning from black performances. See Reebee Garofalo, "Culture versus Commerce: The Marketing of Black Popular Music," and Todd Boyd, "Check Yo Self, before You Wreck Yo Self: Variations on a Political Theme in Rap Music and Popular Culture," both *The Black Public Sphere*, ed. Black Public Sphere Collective, 282 and 314, respectively. Gilroy in particular has insisted on the historical and political dimensions of popular black music, arguing that critics have been responsible for ignoring "the phenomenology of musical forms," which "is dismissed in favour of analysing lyrics, the video images that supplement them and the technology of Hip hop production." See "After the Love Has Gone: Bio-Politics and Etho-Poetics in the Black Public Sphere," in *The Black Public Sphere*, ed. Black Public Sphere Collective, 56.

56 In "The Oppositional Gaze," bell hooks argues that "the 'gaze' has been and is a site of resistance for colonized black people globally. Subordinates in relations of power learn experientially that there is a critical gaze, one that 'looks' to document, one that is oppositional" (116). "As critical spectators," moreover, "black women participate in a broad range of looking relations, contest, resist, revision, interrogate, and invent on multiple levels" (128).

57 One critic who has analyzed relations between Morrison's *Jazz* and African American double consciousness is Richard Hardack, in "'A Music Seeking Its Words': Double-Timing and Double-Consciousness in Toni Morrison's *Jazz*," *Callaloo* 18, 2 (Spring 1995): 451–71. Hardack contends that "for many white writers, race is used to express a universal American splitting; for many black writers, universal American fragmentation reflects their specific and representative role in American culture. For Faulkner and Morrison in particular, blackness finally becomes the heuristic emblem of a fragmented American modernity" (452–53). Identifying black double con-

sciousness as "a form of endemically American self-alienation and self-expression" (452), Hardack says that "Jazz, this 'race music,' represents the reified and personified hunger of double-consciousness, of a self which can never be complete in itself" (454). I argue, rather, that Morrison finds a unifying strength in various kinds of doubleness in black culture.

58 Patrick O'Donnell, "Faulkner in Light of Morrison," in *Unflinching Gaze: Morrison and Faulkner Re-envisioned,* ed. Carol A. Kolmerten, Stephen M. Ross, and Judith Bryant Wittenberg (Jackson: University Press of Mississippi, 1997), 225. For example, in representations of race in *Light in August* and *Playing in the Dark,* O'Donnell notes, "what Faulkner dramatizes, Morrison critiques. While, for Faulkner, identity is, 'at the beginning,' indeterminate (non-raced), and then only becomes racially specific in the tragedy of socialization that is played out in Joe Christmas's life and 'apotheosis,' for Morrison, black identity is *determinately non-existent;* it is merely the backdrop upon which the specificity of white identity can be located" (223).

59 Hortense J. Spillers, "A Hateful Passion, a Lost Love," in *Toni Morrison: Critical Perspectives Past and Present,* ed. Henry Louis Gates Jr. and K. A. Appiah (New York: Amistad, 1993), 232.

60 One compelling discussion of the incompatibility of African American experience and constructions of meaning European Americans use to represent that experience is Hortense J. Spillers, "Mama's Baby, Papa's Maybe: An American Grammar Book," *Diacritics* (Summer 1987): 65–81. Spillers clarifies the inapplicability of either matriarchal or patriarchal constructions to African American women and men: "The dominant culture, in a fatal misunderstanding, assigns a matriarchist value where it does not belong; actually *misnames* the power of the female regarding the enslaved community" (80).

61 Morrison, *Jazz,* 59.

62 In "The Souls of Black Folk," Du Bois discusses the double consciousness of the black person, which "only lets him see himself through the revelation of the other world," with no "true self-consciousness." "The history of the American Negro," he asserts, "is the history of this strife,—this longing to attain self-conscious manhood." See W. E. B. Du Bois, "The Souls of Black Folk," in *The Norton Anthology of African American Literature,* ed. Henry Louis Gates Jr. and Nellie Y. McKay (New York: Norton, 1997), 615.

In *The Dilemma of "Double Consciousness": Toni Morrison's Novels* (Athens: University of Georgia Press, 1993), Denise Heinze clarifies in various elements of Morrison's fiction a sustained critical consciousness of black and white cultures. Heinze's discussions indicate, moreover, traditions of double consciousness within African American culture that extend beyond Du Bois's theory of individual consciousness. Recent critics have argued that traditions of double consciousness have been historically central to the production of African American literature and extend back to African as well as African American predecessors. In particular, Henry Louis Gates Jr., *The Signifying Monkey: A Theory of African-American Literary Criticism* (New

York: Oxford University Press, 1988), identifies "signifyin(g)" in both traditions. Gates argues for a complex critical literary heritage, therefore, that is not due simply to relations between black and white cultures. Although "our canonical texts have complex double formal antecedents, the Western and the black" (xxiv), there is also a complex double relation between African American literature and the black vernacular.

A truly indigenous black literary criticism is to be found in the vernacular. What's more, I believe that black writers, both explicitly and implicitly, turn to the vernacular in various formal ways to inform their creation of written fictions. To do so, it seems to me, is to ground one's literary practice outside the Western tradition. Whereas black writers most certainly revise texts in the Western tradition, they often seek to do so "authentically," with a black difference, a compelling sense of difference based on the black vernacular. (xxii)

63 Moreover, their pragmatism may be part of traditional African ideologies. Charles P. Henry, in *Culture and African American Politics*, suggests that early African American pragmatics were a modification of African culture (see p. 15). Henry argues that during Reconstruction, African American pragmatism of a different kind increased. "The sacred worldview of historic dimensions was replaced by a more pragmatic secular outlook concerned with material acquisition and upward mobility" (19).

64 Gilroy, *The Black Atlantic*, 71.

65 Frankenberg, *White Women, Race Matters*, 204.

66 Ibid., 232. Moreover, of the women interviewed for her study, Frankenberg says "that in describing themselves as cultureless these women are in fact identifying specific kinds of unwanted absences or presences in their own culture(s) as a generalized lack or nonexistence" (199). I have argued, on the other hand, that missing is constructive of whiteness, and I would therefore question whether particularizing these women's sense of lack provides a more accurate definition of white culture.

1   Reproducing Whiteness: *The Wings of the Dove*

1 Henry James, "Preface to the New York Edition (1909)," in *The Wings of the Dove*, ed. J. Donald Crowley and Richard A. Hocks (New York: Norton, 1978), 6. All further references to the preface and the novel are to this edition; page numbers are cited in the text.

2 Richard Dyer, "White," *Screen* 29, 4 (Autumn 1988): 45.

3 See chapter 6 of Jürgen Habermas, *The Structural Transformation of the Public Sphere: An Inquiry into a Category of Bourgeois Society*, trans. Thomas Burger (Cambridge: MIT Press, 1989), 181–235. Robyn Wiegman, *American Anatomies: Theorizing Race and Gender* (Durham: Duke University Press, 1995), 50.

4 Ibid., 192.

5   Richard Dyer discusses these transcendent subjectivities in *White* (London: Routledge, 1997), arguing that the Christian dualism of mind and body makes possible the transcending of material and historical limits that is characteristic of whiteness. Christ and Mary "are what one should aspire to be like and yet also what one can never be. This sets up a dynamic of aspiration, of striving to be, to transcend, and to go on striving in the face of the impossibility of transcendence" (17). Among critics who have catalogued such images in literature, Walter Benn Michaels has pinpointed ways in which both American novels and U.S. Supreme Court decisions depict whiteness as invisible and transcendent. For his discussion of imagery of spiritual unity among whites, see "The Souls of White Folk," in *Literature and the Body: Essays on Populations and Persons*, ed. Elaine Scarry, Selected Papers from the English Institute, 1986 (Baltimore: Johns Hopkins University Press, 1988), 190. Note that in her discussion of expectation in "Whiteness as Property," *Harvard Law Review* 106, 8 (June 1993): 1709–91, Cheryl I. Harris identifies whiteness with a more specific transcendence of material identity (1729–31).

6   Michael Omi and Howard Winant, *Racial Formation in the United States: From the 1960s to the 1980s* (New York: Routledge and Kegan Paul, 1986), 14–15.

7   Ibid., 14, 15.

8   Ibid., 14–21.

9   Sara Blair, *Henry James and the Writing of Race and Nation* (Cambridge: Cambridge University Press, 1996), 7. Exploring race in James's work as a performative phenomenon, Blair emphasizes the instability of racial and national identity. "Against more defensive notions of type, James's redirected performances in the internationalist mode concern and themselves depend upon, a whiteness whose currency is 'convertible' rather than fixed" (128). In "The Poetics of Cultural Decline: Degeneracy, Assimilation, and the Jew in James's *The Golden Bowl*," *American Literary History* 7, 3 (Fall 1995), Jonathan Freedman also addresses the instability of James's views of race. "At moments, James seems to embrace a Tainean notion of race as nationality. . . . But he also supplements it with a notion of race as genetic necessity, the scientific ideology that supplemented Taineanism. . . . At still other times . . . James formulates an attempt to move beyond the ideology of race entirely" (495–96).

10   In *Visionary Compacts: American Renaissance Writings in Cultural Context* (Madison: University of Wisconsin Press, 1987), Donald E. Pease discusses the difficulties posed by concepts of freedom as "negative freedom" to white American "cultural legitimation" (7). Pease argues that identifying the United States in opposition to its pre-Revolutionary past "rationalizes an oppositional model more compatible with modern than premodern America" (9). Hawthorne is one writer who reaches into history to provide a richer modern consciousness: "He cannot reflect upon his present life unless he does so from within the realm of the Puritan past" (58).

11   Henry James, *Hawthorne* (New York: Collier, 1966). All references are to this edition; page numbers are cited in the text.

12 Laurence Bedwell Holland, in *The Expense of Vision: Essays on the Craft of Henry James* (Baltimore: Johns Hopkins University Press, 1982), considers two sources for Milly's reproduction: Veronese's *The Supper in the House of Levi* and *The Marriage Feast at Cana*. See 305–13.

13 Anika Lemaire, *Jacques Lacan*, trans. David Macey (London: Routledge, 1977), 87.

14 Julia Kristeva, *Powers of Horror: An Essay on Abjection*, trans. Leon S. Roudiez (New York: Columbia University Press, 1982), 64.

15 Milly Theale might be identified as one of the many female characters who, according to Elisabeth Bronfen in *Over Her Dead Body: Death, Femininity, and the Aesthetic* (New York: Routledge, 1992), "articulate their non-existence in western culture" by "implicit or explicit suicide" (388–89). Like other critics, Bronfen identifies James's cousin Minnie Temple as his model for Milly Theale (368–69). Yet Bronfen's intriguing reading of Alice James (389–92) also suggests striking resemblances between James's sister and Milly Theale. Milly's death might be seen, according to this theoretical identification, as her practicing a "decorporalisation" to destroy the "medium" through which others limit her "subject position" (388–89).

16 Ibid., 97.

17 Laura Mulvey has suggested, in her discussion of the myth of Pandora, that male fetishism produces screens. "The [fetishistic] distortion of signification produces a signifier that has to function as a mask, a means of concealment, that veils and covers over the traumatic moment that cannot be signified. As the traumatic moment was itself born out of a perception of lack, of absence, the fetish object that is 'concealing nothing' is a screen, protecting a void, simultaneously reassuring and terrifying." See "Pandora: Topographies of the Mask and Curiosity," in *Sexuality and Space*, ed. Beatriz Colomina (Princeton: Princeton Architectural Press, 1992), 68. I suggest that females may produce screens to create voids and then maintain those voids as distance from others.

Mulvey argues that "Pandora's curiosity . . . may be interpreted as a curiosity about the mystery that she herself personifies" (66) and so suggests the possibility of the fetishized woman gaining a critical distance from her identity. Such a critical response to the way a person is seen by others who misrepresent her looks has been theorized by bell hooks as crucial to black spectatorship, particularly that of black women. See "The Oppositional Gaze: Black Female Spectators," in *Black Looks: Race and Representation* (Boston: South End, 1992), 115–31.

2 Collective Whiteness in *The Golden Bowl*

1 Richard Dyer argues that "white people—not there as a category and everywhere everything as a fact—are difficult, if not impossible, to analyse *qua* white. The subject seems to fall apart in your hands as soon as you begin.

Any instance of white representation is always immediately something more specific—*Brief Encounter* is not about white people, it is about English middle-class people; *The Godfather* is not about white people, it is about Italian-American people; but *The Color Purple* is about black people, before it is about poor, southern US people." See "White," *Screen* 29, 4 (Autumn 1988): 46. In *The Golden Bowl*, James represents whiteness as a more total abstraction, without particularizing even immediate whiteness.

2   Many critics have focused on the importance of critical consciousness in James's works, but of particular relevance here is Carolyn Porter's discussion "Henry James: Visionary Being," in *Seeing and Being: The Plight of the Participant Observer in Emerson, James, Adams, and Faulkner* (Middletown: Wesleyan University Press, 1981), 121–64. Porter clarifies that "Maggie's power . . . derives from her recognition that she is at once seer and seen" (160).

3   Henry James, *The Golden Bowl* (London: Penguin, 1987), 172. All references are to this edition; page numbers are cited in the text.

4   Jonathan Freedman, in "The Poetics of Cultural Decline: Degeneracy, Assimilation, and the Jew in James's *The Golden Bowl*," *American Literary History* 7, 3 (Fall 1995), argues that assimilation does occur in the novel, with the important exception of the Jewish characters, who function to contain the threat of racial degeneracy. I will return to his argument later in this chapter.

5   Philip Fisher, *Making and Effacing Art: Modern American Art in a Culture of Museums* (New York: Oxford University Press, 1991), 19–21.

6   Ibid., 8–9.

7   Ibid., 249.

8   A process of transformation and fragmentation of objects that has clear parallels to such museum experience has been identified by Jean-Christophe Agnew in his reading of *The Golden Bowl* and commodity culture. See "The Consuming Vision of Henry James," in *The Culture of Consumption: Critical Essays in American History, 1880–1980*, ed. Richard Wightman Fox and T. J. Jackson Lears (New York: Pantheon, 1983), esp. 91–100.

9   Stephen D. Arata, "Object Lessons: Reading the Museum in *The Golden Bowl*," in *Famous Last Words: Changes in Gender and Narrative Closure*, ed. Alison Booth (Charlottesville: University Press of Virginia, 1993), discusses the novel in the context of "the rise of the fine-arts museum in America" in the late nineteenth century (201). Arata argues that James and also Maggie Verver work to call attention to the histories that museum collections erase. "Maggie develops a kind of double vision" and thereby "provides a model for the Jamesian reader, who is also encouraged to attend to the pleasures and values of the text's formal arrangements without being blinded by its enchantments" (220).

10   Nancy Bentley, *The Ethnography of Manners: Hawthorne, James, Wharton* (Cambridge: Cambridge University Press, 1995), provides a different reading of a museum mentality in Edith Wharton's *Age of Innocence*, which she

considers as "a story of culture consciousness and the new social life it produced in the name of cultural preservation" (113). I am considering the museum experience in *The Golden Bowl* less as an experience of objective and authenticating knowledge than as a visionary experience of cultural identity.

11   Beatriz Colomina, *Privacy and Publicity: Modern Architecture as Mass Media* (Cambridge: MIT Press, 1994), 213.

12   Ibid., 226.

13   Fisher, *Making and Effacing Art,* 9.

14   Ibid., 23.

15   See ibid., 166–67.

16   See Stephen Greenblatt, *Renaissance Self-Fashioning: From More to Shakespeare* (Chicago: University of Chicago Press, 1980), especially his discussion of improvisations of imperialism. "What is essential is the Europeans' ability again and again to insinuate themselves into the preexisting political, religious, even psychic structures of the natives and to turn those structures to their advantage" (227).

17   Yet James also recapitulates certain practices of representation that, in the United States, fostered the expansion of empire. In *The Rise and Fall of the White Republic: Class Politics and Mass Culture in Nineteenth-Century America* (London: Verso, 1990), Alexander Saxton demonstrates how much expansionism depended, for example, on representations of vernacular characters who "act out American nationality." Whereas "distinctive speech, lower-class status and egalitarian sentiment . . . enhanced popularity" of a vernacular character, these particular characteristics "tended, initially, to be self-limiting." But "one other major source of vernacular popularity contained no such limitations. . . . In contrast to romantic heroes, all vernaculars (including blackface minstrels) advocated white supremacy" (185). Such representations of a common American identity made easier the task of political parties claiming to be representative.

Expansionism, Saxton argues, accounts, though in different ways, for popular representations of both American Indians and African Americans as enemies of white Americans. Constructing American Indians as enemies effected western expansion. Excluding African Americans from American identity contributed to imperial expansion in the Cuba campaign. Saxton's summary of these politics is on 375–77.

18   Colomina, *Privacy and Publicity,* 312.

19   The expansiveness of the Ververs' identities is indicative of an imperialist perspective at a time when imperialism had reached real limits. See Neil Smith's argument in *Uneven Development: Nature, Capital, and the Production of Space* (Oxford: Blackwell, 1984) that, with "the final partitioning of Africa in the 1880s" (87), capitalism, having run out of natural resources, began to produce nature. "With everything it can muster, this is what capital strives to do: it strives to move from developed to underdeveloped space, then back to developed space which, because of its interim deprivation of capi-

tal, is now underdeveloped, and so on" (150). In *The Rise and Fall of the White Republic,* Alexander Saxton discusses "the hegemonic crisis of the 1890s" in the United States in parallel terms (350–52), noting the closing of the American frontier in 1890 and the "dark visions" of many social observers in that decade (352). Adam Verver's expansive view seems to act similarly to "productions of space" that Smith discusses.

20 If Adam's view were an abstract painting, it might represent means or media. Works of Cubist painters of the early twentieth century, for example, depict various views of a subject, as media of vision: angles along which the eye may travel rather than objects seen. Later abstract painters, too, represent means, as Philip Fisher has argued. See his discussion of Jasper Johns's representation of colors as "means to assemble everything" in *Making and Effacing Art* (86).

21 See Dyer, "White," for a discussion of whiteness as "all colours" (45).

22 Toni Morrison, *Playing in the Dark: Whiteness and the Literary Imagination* (Cambridge: Harvard University Press, 1992), 37–38.

23 In *Playing in the Dark,* Morrison considers how central and marginal racial identities are produced by seeing a blankness of ground where there are figures (38–39, 44–47). She exposes marginality as a cover-up of sorts, whereas the dark prince and the enlightened Ververs both believe in the open and empty identities they produce. For James, the difference between marginal and central social positions is a matter of choice for white Americans. The whiteness of such characters as Milly Theale and Adam Verver, who choose to appear marginal, lies in their ability to assume both positions of marginality and centrality. James seems to insist that this could be a matter of choice for both light and dark persons, including Europeans, although they do not choose to see this, either in *The Golden Bowl* or *The Wings of the Dove.*

One American critic who has discussed political positions of marginality as both historically determined and open to certain choices is bell hooks. See, for example, her discussion of "marginality as position and place of resistance" (150) as well as a site of oppression in "Choosing the Margin as a Space of Radical Openness," in *Yearnings: Race, Gender, and Cultural Politics* (Boston: South End, 1990), 145–53.

24 Freedman argues that the prince is assimilated. See "Poetics of Cultural Decline," 493–95.

25 Sara Blair, *Henry James and the Writing of Race and Nation* (Cambridge: Cambridge University Press, 1996), 129, 187–88. "James's recognition of the plenitude of possibilities that the Jew opens for the reinvention of both American character and 'Anglo-Saxon' tradition is tempered by anxiety about forms of cultural excess that would render his own 'intimate intelligence' irrelevant" (188).

26 Freedman argues that "the imperative affirmed by *The Golden Bowl*" is "the imperative that [Charles] Beresford endorses—the maintenance of an Anglo-American cultural and racial identity under the threat of a seem-

ingly inevitable decline by means of the careful infusion of other racial 'bloods' and cultural experiences. . . . The fear the novel explores, further, issues from Beresford's program: that these processes of transmission will corrupt rather than renew, will contribute to the process of degeneration, not that of regeneration. It is first to express, then to contain, this threat that the Jew is deployed in James's novel." See Freedman, "Poetics of Cultural Decline," 481.

27 Ibid., 487.

28 Freedman, "Poetics of Cultural Decline," 492. Freedman also notes similarities in "the cultural associations invoked by the racial identity of both" the shopkeeper and the prince (490), which to me seem even more extensive than he suggests (490–91).

29 Ibid., 488.

30 This is the second identification in the novel of a European American with a Native American woman. James's comparisons of Fanny to Pocahontas and Maggie to an "Indian squaw" indicate the expanses and the limits of the ways they see American identity. Walter Benn Michaels, in "Race into Culture: A Critical Genealogy of Cultural Identity," *Critical Inquiry* 18 (Summer 1992), discusses a shift in fictional representations of American Indians in the early twentieth century from an "identification with the Indian [that] could function at the turn of the century as a *refusal* of American identity" to one that could "function by the early 1920s as an *assertion* of American identity" by becoming "the unequivocal source of racial difference" (664). Though not wholly either of these, James's figures of American Indian women in *The Golden Bowl* seem closer to the latter alternative than the former. Because no African figure appears among the variety of characters with whom Maggie identifies and because Jewish characters are distinctly excluded from Americanization in the course of the novel, the comparison of Indians to whites seems a special case of assimilation. See also Jane Tompkins's discussion in *West of Everything: The Inner Life of Westerns* (New York: Oxford University Press, 1992), 7–10, of "the absence of Indians in Western movies" (10). In the Westerns she has watched, Tompkins clarifies, American Indian characters either "functioned as props, bits of local color, textural effects" (8) or were played by whites (9).

3 Self-Division as Racial Divide: *The Sound and the Fury*

1 Critics who analyze Faulkner's work in terms of a modern, alienated consciousness include Carolyn Porter, who in *Seeing and Being: The Plight of the Participant Observer in Emerson, James, Adams, and Faulkner* (Middletown: Wesleyan University Press, 1981), 207–76, considers Faulkner's recognition of and responses to alienation and reification; and John Irwin, *Doubling and Incest/Repetition and Revenge: A Speculative Reading of Faulkner* (Baltimore: Johns Hopkins University Press, 1975). Irwin reads Faulkner in the context

of works of Freud and Nietzsche, emphasizing their "tragic awareness that, because of the irreversibility of time, man in time can never get even, indeed, comes to understand that the whole process of getting even is incompatible with time" (4).

The idea that whiteness is an inalienable property is discussed by Cheryl I. Harris in "Whiteness as Property," *Harvard Law Review* 106, 8 (June 1993): 1709–91. On the one hand, Harris notes exceptions to the assumption that property is alienable (see esp. 1731–34). On the other hand, she argues that whiteness is "intrinsically bound up with identity and personhood" (1734). My emphasis here is that Faulkner, employing an alienated modernist consciousness for his white characters, renders them "inalienably," or unchangeably, alienated.

2   Here I follow the argument of Carolyn Porter's Lacanian reading "Symbolic Fathers and Dead Mothers: A Feminist Approach to Faulkner," in *Faulkner and Psychology/Faulkner and Yoknapatawpha, 1991*, ed. Donald M. Kartiganer and Ann J. Abadie (Jackson: University Press of Mississippi, 1994), 78–122. Other recent feminist readings of women's status in Faulkner's work include Minrose C. Gwin, *The Feminine and Faulkner: Reading (Beyond) Sexual Difference* (Knoxville: University of Tennessee Press, 1990). Gwin argues against the absence of Caddy Compson and certain other female characters in Faulkner's novels. For Gwin it is necessary "to free the 'character' of Caddy Compson" and to "begin to hear Caddy's articulation of how ego boundaries may come to evaporate in a maternal space in which self and other are indistinguishable" (27). Deborah Clarke, *Robbing the Mother: Women in Faulkner* (Jackson: University Press of Mississippi, 1994), also uses the work of French psychoanalytic theorists Julia Kristeva and Luce Irigaray to argue that mothers in Faulkner's work are less absences than excessive and disruptive presences. Clarke contends that in *The Sound and the Fury* and *As I Lay Dying*, "the absent maternal presence collapses the distinctions between presence and absence, literal and figurative, bodies and language" (50).

3   One critic who makes this evident is Eric Sundquist, who in *Faulkner: The House Divided* (Baltimore: Johns Hopkins University Press, 1983) focuses on race, and specifically miscegenation, in Faulkner's fiction. Sundquist clarifies that Quentin's obsession with Caddy's purity is due to his interest in the innocence of the South. "Caddy's moral fragility, like her near invisibility as a character, must be seen to portray the violent paradox upon which . . . conceptions of Southern innocence were built" (23). That paradox is evident in the dependence of such innocence on "the unconscious repression or deliberately conscious suppression of the miscegenation of white masters and black slaves" (24).

4   Toni Morrison, *Playing in the Dark: Whiteness and the Literary Imagination* (Cambridge: Harvard University Press, 1992), 44.

5   Irwin, *Doubling and Incest*, 35, 59.

6   The identification of individual and cultural experience in Freud's work

means that "primitive" cultures are identified with children; both are in need of "development." Irwin cites Freud's essay on the uncanny, in which Freud discusses Otto Rank's work on doubles.

[The] invention of doubling as a preservation against extinction has its counterpart in the language of dreams, which is fond of representing castration by a doubling or multiplication of a genital symbol. The same desire led the Ancient Egyptians to develop the art of making images of the dead in lasting materials. Such ideas, however, have sprung from the soil of unbounded self-love, from the primary narcissism which dominates the mind of the child and of primitive man. But when this stage has been surmounted, the "double" reverses its aspect. From having been an assurance of immortality, it becomes the uncanny harbinger of death.

The less "primitive" culture or individual experiences such doubleness as both a gratifying extension of the self and an extension that is frightening because death appears as the destruction of individual identity. Only the more primitive perspective fails to recognize death as the end of individual existence. See ibid., 65–66. The quotation from Freud is taken from *The Standard Edition of the Complete Psychological Works of Sigmund Freud*, trans. and ed. James Strachey et al. (London: Hogarth, 1953), 17:235.

7   In contrast to Freud's universalized conception of consciousness, theorists of double consciousness in black experience have focused more on historical and cultural differences. The relation between W. E. B. Du Bois's concept of double consciousness in *The Souls of Black Folk* and concepts of European modernity has been discussed by Sandra Adell, in *Double-Consciousness/Double Bind: Theoretical Issues in Twentieth-Century Black Literature* (Urbana: University of Illinois Press, 1994), and by Paul Gilroy, in *The Black Atlantic: Modernity and Double Consciousness* (Cambridge: Harvard University Press, 1993). Adell places Du Bois's articulation of African American double consciousness in a Hegelian framework. Gilroy works to "extend [Du Bois's] implicit argument that the cultures of diaspora blacks can be profitably interpreted as expressions of and commentaries upon ambivalences generated by modernity and their locations within it" (117).

8   Walter Benn Michaels, "Race into Culture: A Critical Genealogy of Cultural Identity," *Critical Inquiry* 18 (Summer 1992): 679–80, 682.

9   William Faulkner, *The Sound and the Fury* (New York: Vintage, 1954), 371. All subsequent references are to this edition; page numbers are cited in the text.

10   The grammar is confusing here, but presumably it is Shegog's own physical "insignificance" that is "made of no moment."

11   Gilroy, *Black Atlantic*, 57, 75.

12   Richard Dyer, *White* (London: Routledge, 1997), identifies Christianity with whiteness, in part because of the "dynamic of aspiration, of striving to be, to transcend" that characterizes Christian identification with Christ and Mary (17). Yet Dyer notes Christianity's importance to many nonwhite persons and cultures; thus "it is by no means clear that whiteness is constitutive of

it" (17). Faulkner's representation of the black congregation in *The Sound and the Fury* suggests a Christianity that is incommensurable with whiteness in the novel. Although the black characters experience transcendence, they seem not to internalize transcendence; they transcend individuality, moving into a shared social consciousness that is characterized less by striving than by fulfillment.

13   Joan W. Scott, *Only Paradoxes to Offer: French Feminists and the Rights of Man* (Cambridge: Harvard University Press, 1996), 5–16.

14   Porter, "Symbolic Fathers and Dead Mothers," 81–82, 82, 91.

15   Ibid., 91.

16   Anika Lemaire, *Jacques Lacan*, trans. David Macey (London: Routledge and Kegan Paul, 1977), 73.

17   Olga Vickery, *The Novels of William Faulkner* (Baton Rouge: Louisiana State University Press, 1964), 34.

18   Lawrance Thompson discusses Caddy as "a kind of mirror of all [Ben's] positive values"; see "Mirror Analogues in *The Sound and the Fury*," in *Faulkner: A Collection of Critical Essays*, ed. Robert Penn Warren (Englewood Cliffs, N.J.: Prentice-Hall, 1966), 111. John T. Matthews, *The Play of Faulkner's Language* (Ithaca: Cornell University Press, 1982), discusses "the objects of [Benjy's] collection" (67) as they repeat rather than simply fend off loss (65–70).

19   The Compsons' inability to admit the passing of time was the reason for Jean-Paul Sartre's famous objections to the absence of a future in the novel. For Sartre, the characters act as mere spectators of time: "Everything has already happened. It is this that enables us to understand that strange remark by one of the heroes, '*Fui. Non sum.*' In this sense, too, Faulkner is able to make a man a sum total without a future: 'The sum of his climactic experiences,' 'The sum of his misfortunes.' . . . Faulkner's vision of the world can be compared to that of a man sitting in an open car and looking backward." See Jean-Paul Sartre, "On *The Sound and the Fury*: Time in the Works of Faulkner," in *Faulkner*, ed. Warren 89. It is the consequential relation of past and present that all three Compsons deny. Though Quentin says "*Fui. Non sum*," he also says "*Non fui. Sum*" (216). As able to objectify the present as he is the past, Quentin can observe experience like a tourist or a spectator because the scenes of his life, whenever they occur, are isolated from change.

20   There is no sign in *The Sound and the Fury* of the very different Imaginary presence of black people in the white male's imagination that Eric Lott has discussed in "White like Me: Racial Cross-Dressing and the Construction of American Whiteness," in *Cultures of United States Imperialism*, ed. Amy Kaplan and Donald E. Pease (Durham: Duke University Press, 1993), 474–95. Lott argues that in blackface performance, "to wear or even enjoy blackface was literally, for a time, to become black, to inherit the cool, virility, humility, abandon or *gaite de coeur* that were the prime components of white ideologies of black manhood" (479). Such exchanges, Lott argues, make

evident that "the black male and fantasies about him supply the content of the white male Imaginary" (481).

21 Henri Bergson, *Time and Free Will: An Essay on the Immediate Data of Consciousness,* trans. F. L. Pogson (New York: Harper and Row, 1960), 231.

22 Ibid., 132. It is interesting that for Bergson it is language that threatens to assimilate the "delicate and fugitive impressions" that cannot be reduced to language without losing their inherent character.

4 Playing White Men in *Light in August*

1 William Faulkner, *Light in August* (New York: Modern Library, 1950), 151. All references are to this edition; page numbers are cited in the text.

2 See especially Laura Mulvey, "Pandora: Topographies of the Mask and Curiosity," in *Sexuality and Space,* ed. Beatriz Colomina (Princeton: Princeton University Press, 1992), 53–71.

3 Jürgen Habermas, *The Structural Transformation of the Public Sphere: An Inquiry into a Category of Bourgeois Society,* trans. Thomas Burger (Cambridge: MIT University Press, 1989), 200.

4 See, for example, Jean-Christophe Agnew's discussion of the fragmentation of needs in the modern consumer in "The Consuming Vision of Henry James," in *The Culture of Consumption: Critical Essays in American History, 1880–1980,* ed. Richard Wightman Fox and T. J. Jackson Lears (New York: Pantheon, 1983), esp. 68–74.

5 Eric J. Sundquist, *Faulkner: The House Divided* (Baltimore: Johns Hopkins University Press, 1983), argues that the image of the negative "is a figure of simultaneous concealment and revelation, a figure that marks with explosive precision, at a point of passing from one to the other, the ambiguity of Joe Christmas, who . . . virtually is a *figure* rather than a person" (71). As a figure of passing, Sundquist suggests, Joe is cut off from any material identity. Yet insofar as figuration is, as I argue, a white characteristic in the novel, Joe enters figuration only when he dies, in the last scene.

6 Sundquist notes in particular that if Joe Christmas's " 'passing' between worlds . . . seems nearly a perverse caricature of white racial hysteria," it is "not so perverse . . . as the amendment to a typical 'racial purity' bill introduced into the Virginia legislature in 1925 that would have required all citizens to register, with the state Bureau of Vital Statistics, all racial strains, however remote, that had ever entered their families; and not so hysterical as the climate of anxiety that led to the measure's rejection—because it was clear that many fine Virginians, living and dead, would be classed as Negroes." See ibid., 75–76.

7 That Joanna Burden is confused with blackness is only one of a number of confusions of identity that occur in Joe's relationship with her. In *Faulkner and Southern Womanhood* (Athens: University of Georgia Press, 1994), Diane Roberts notes a number of these confusions, pointing out that "in Joanna

Burden, Joe Christmas confronts both his black and feminine (powerless) selves, as well as his homosexual self" (178). It is interesting to consider these confusions as evidence of the conflations of "blacks and women" which Robyn Wiegman discusses as part of "the nineteenth century's most extreme shaping of the struggle for black liberation within the contours of sexual difference" and which she identifies as "a figure marking the mutual exclusions and contestations between race and gender that governed in a variety of ways the political rights of the public sphere until at least the 1920s." See *American Anatomies: Theorizing Race and Gender* (Durham: Duke University Press, 1996), 46.

8   See bell hooks's discussion in "The Oppositional Gaze: Black Female Spectators," in *Black Looks: Race and Representation* (Boston: South End, 1992), 115–17, of both the historical necessity and the danger of black persons looking back at whites.

9   In *"Light in August* and Rhetorics of Racial Division," in *Faulkner and Race: Faulkner and Yoknapatawpha, 1986,* ed. Doreen Fowler and Ann J. Abadie (Jackson: University Press of Mississippi, 1987), 152–69, James A. Snead focuses on this passage as a place where "the various fatal ambiguities concerning 'white' and 'black' blood come to a head" (166–67) and indicate two different ways of reading the text. Whereas "Jefferson must forget the truth in order to reify and fix its flattering self-image" (168), "the blacks in Jefferson can be expected to remember every nuance of the Christmas story, including the fact that [Joe] was probably white" (167).

5   Black Spaces in *Sula*

1   Houston A. Baker Jr., "When Lindbergh Sleeps with Bessie Smith: The Writing of Place in *Sula,"* in *Toni Morrison: Critical Perspectives Past and Present,* ed. Henry Louis Gates Jr. and K. A. Appiah (New York: Amistad, 1993), 237. Identifying this ordering with female domestic labor and rituals of cleaning, Baker argues that Morrison "places" African American experience by means of "manipulations of the symbolic," countering conventions of displacement by affording "a mirroring language . . . in which we can find ourselves" (258).

2   Toni Morrison, *Sula* (New York: Plume, 1973), 61, 31. All subsequent references are to this edition; page numbers are noted in the text.

3   This historical sense of double consciousness shares with W. E. B. Du Bois's theory of black double consciousness a visionary economy of memory and prophecy. Shamoon Zamir clarifies the nonvisual character of Du Bois's "vision" in " 'The Sorrow Songs' / 'Song of Myself': Du Bois, the Crisis of Leadership, and Prophetic Imagination," in *The Black Columbiad: Defining Moments in African American Literature and Culture,* ed. Werner Sollors and Maria Diedrich (Cambridge: Harvard University Press, 1994), 145–66.

4   Among the critics who have considered Morrison's depictions of lost or

missing experience is Mae G. Henderson, who discusses "the imaginative and reconstructive recovery of the past which characterizes Morrison's fictive process" in "Toni Morrison's *Beloved:* Re-Membering the Body as Historical Text," in *Comparative American Identities: Race, Sex, and Nationality in the Modern Text,* ed. Hortense J. Spillers (New York: Routledge, 1991), 66. Henderson identifies in *Beloved* a particularly female "reconstitution" of a past "along motherlines" (76–77). I point up Morrison's recognition of elements of past experience that cannot be reconstituted or recovered because they never were realized in the past.

Valerie Smith discusses difficulties posed by poststructuralism for historical understanding and argues that in *Beloved* Morrison "asserts and reasserts the subjectivity of the former slaves and the depth of their suffering," largely by excluding that experience from representation. See " 'Circling the Subject': History and Narrative in *Beloved,*" in *Toni Morrison,* 354. I am trying to pinpoint in *Sula* ways in which Morrison practices a more inclusive representation of missing experience, although I agree with Smith that Morrison repeatedly insists on the missing character of missing experience. I would resist, therefore, identifying inclusiveness with fulfillment, and in this I differ from Robert Grant. In his essay "Absence into Presence: The Thematics of Memory and 'Missing' Subjects in Toni Morrison's *Sula,*" in *Critical Essays on Toni Morrison,* ed. Nellie Y. McKay (Boston: Hall, 1988), Grant argues that "memory acts as a cognitive and imaginative synthesizing connector of the lapses, gaps, absences" in the narrative (100). As this synthesis occurs, "lacks become the sources of figurative fulfillment through memory and / or imaginative projection" (96).

5   This inconsistency is reflected in inconsistencies of narrative too. In " 'The Self and the Other': Reading Toni Morrison's *Sula* and the Black Female Text," in McKay, ed., *Critical Essays on Toni Morrison,* Deborah E. McDowell calls attention to the disconnectedness of narrative line in the novel. She argues that *Sula* frustrates various connections that readers are accustomed to making. What occurs in *Sula,* for characters and readers alike, is "a process of self-exploration" (85), in part because the connections on which knowledge depends are unavailable, even thwarted, in the narrative (85–89).

6   In Robert B. Stepto's 1976 interview, Morrison goes on to say: "There's a lot of book after she dies, you know. I wanted them to miss her presence in that book as that town missed her presence." See Stepto's " 'Intimate Things in Place': A Conversation with Toni Morrison," in *Chant of Saints: A Gathering of Afro-American Literature, Art, and Scholarship,* ed. Michael S. Harper and Robert B. Stepto (Urbana: University of Illinois Press, 1979), 218.

7   Kathryn Bond Stockton discusses the importance of toilet and anal imagery in the novel and argues that "Morrison dares to value 'debasement.' " See "Heaven's Bottom: Anal Economics and the Critical Debasement of Freud in Toni Morrison's *Sula,*" *Cultural Critique* 24 (Spring 1993): 82.

8   I am indebted in my discussion of such spacing techniques to Mark Wigley's deconstructive analysis of the relation of architecture to metaphysics

in *The Architecture of Deconstruction: Derrida's Haunt* (Cambridge: MIT Press, 1993). Wigley's analysis of the spatial character of distinctions between inside and outside or self and other follows Derrida in eroding inherent or essential differences within ground and figure and in reconceiving differences in phenomena as spaces between phenomena. In chapter 5, "Throwing Up Architecture," Wigley identifies traditions of domination through domestication as processes of digestion as well as the experience of mourning as an experience of digestion (123–47).

9   Hortense J. Spillers discusses historical difficulties with identifying either African American males or females with conventional symbolic and political orders in "Mama's Baby, Papa's Maybe: An American Grammar Book," *Diacritics* (Summer 1987): 65–80. Spillers argues that "the African-American woman, the mother, the daughter, becomes historically the powerful and shadowy evocation of a cultural synthesis long evaporated—the law of the Mother—only and precisely because legal enslavement removed the African-American male not so much from sight as from *mimetic* view as a partner in the prevailing social fiction of the Father's name, the Father's law" (80).

10   Hortense J. Spillers, "A Hateful Passion, a Lost Love," in *Toni Morrison*, 232.

11   More specifically, Spillers argues that Sula breaks with two conventions of African American female heroism, "uninterrupted superiority on the one hand and unrelieved pathology on the other," evident in Margaret Walker's Vyry Ware and Zora Neale Hurston's Janie Starks, but that "Sula, Vyry, and Janie need not be seen as the terms of an either/or proposition. The three characters here may be identified as subperspectives, or *angles onto* a larger seeing." See ibid., 232.

12   James identifies Adam Verver as a "financial 'backer,' watching his interests from the wing, but in rather confessed ignorance of the mysteries of mimicry." See *The Golden Bowl* (New York: Penguin, 1987), 160.

13   As Mary Ann Doane summarizes differences in gendered spectators, "Male scopophilia has a well-defined and quite specific object—the female body. The male gaze is fixed to the image of the castrated maternal body and obsessed with its implications for the coherence of male identity. . . . The woman, on the other hand, cannot *look* at that body (except in the mirror of her own narcissism) because she *is* it. Female scopophilia is a drive without an object, an undirected and free-floating drive which is conducive to the operation of the phobia." Doane thereby likens female spectatorship to Julia Kristeva's depiction of abjection. See Doane, *The Desire to Desire: The Woman's Film of the 1940s* (Bloomington: Indiana University Press, 1987), 141.

The degree to which such feminist theory can be applied to the experience of African American women has been the subject of much discussion. Patricia Hill Collins suggests that similarities in "values and ideas that Africanist scholars identify as being characteristically 'Black'" and "ideas claimed by feminist scholars as being characteristically 'female'" are due to "the material conditions of oppression." These apparently "can vary dramatically and yet generate some uniformity in the epistemologies of subordinate groups." See "The Social Construction of Black Feminist Thought," *Signs* 14 (Summer 1989): 756–57.

bell hooks, however, in "The Oppositional Gaze: Black Female Spectators," in *Black Looks: Race and Representation* (Boston: South End, 1992), has argued that "mainstream feminist film criticism in no way acknowledges black female spectatorship. It does not even consider the possibility that women can construct an oppositional gaze via an understanding and awareness of the politics of race and racism" (123). hooks theorizes a black female spectatorship whose critical looking breaks with Freudian alternatives of male and female behavior. "As critical spectators, black women looked from a location that disrupted" white positions as viewer and image (123). Sula is certainly a disruptive observer. It seems to me, however, that she fails to produce the critical opposition of hooks's black female spectator of film. Characters in *Jazz* come closer to practicing hooks's critical gaze.

14   See Mae G. Henderson, "Speaking in Tongues: Dialogics, Dialectics, and the Black Woman Writer's Literary Tradition," in *Changing Our Own Words: Essays on Criticism, Theory, and Writing by Black Women,* ed. Cheryl A. Wall (New Brunswick: Rutgers University Press, 1989), 33. Henderson discusses Sula's "deconstructive rereading of the black male text" (34–35) and her ability to transform "unity into diversity, formlessness into form" (36). Henderson's identification in *Sula* of a multivocal and "progressive model for black and female utterance" (35) is in keeping with Deborah E. McDowell's analysis of disruption in the novel. McDowell emphasizes how Sula and her story break connections required of "the 'positive' racial self" as well as those necessary to knowledge. And McDowell argues that because the novel "opposes a single unified image of the black SELF," it allows "metaphors of self" to "glory in difference." See " 'The Self and the Other,' " 77, 87–88.

15   Patricia Klindienst Joplin is one feminist critic to identify weaving as the female antithesis of violent male constructions of meaning. See "The Voice of the Shuttle is Ours," *Stanford Literature Review* 1 (Spring 1984): 51. Jacques Derrida also identifies a "fabric" of differences rather than a fiction of oppositions as the form of meaning in "Differance," in *Speech and Phenomena and Other Essays on Husserl's Theory of Signs,* trans. David B. Allison (Evanston: Northwestern University Press, 1973). Neither present nor absent, *differance* nevertheless always implies something missing. But the sense that "the diverted presentation continues to be somehow definitively and irreducibly withheld" functions as a binding mechanism. "Differance holds us in a relation with what exceeds (though we necessarily fail to recognize this) the alternative of presence or absence" (151).

16   Elisabeth Bronfen, *Over Her Dead Body: Death, Femininity, and the Aesthetic* (New York: Routledge, 1992), 327.

17   Wigley, *Architecture of Deconstruction,* 12, 27.

6 Off the Record: *Jazz* and the Production of Black Culture

1   Toni Morrison, *Jazz*, (New York: Plume, 1993), 33. All further references are
    to this edition; page numbers are cited in the text.

2   Farah Jasmine Griffin calls attention to this passage in *"Who Set You
    Flowin'?": The African-American Migration Narrative* (New York: Oxford Uni-
    versity Press, 1995), because it represents the transformative "impacts the
    migrants have on American cities and American culture" (192–94). Griffin
    discusses *Jazz* as a recent "migration narrative," which she identifies as "a
    dominant form of African-American cultural production in the twentieth
    century" (4). Griffin emphasizes that for Morrison this narrative form is
    transformative in numerous ways. The migration from south to north is
    transformative of both black experience and white experience (192–93).
    Such transformations are achieved, moreover, not by jettisoning the past,
    Griffin argues, but by remembering and representing old and new experi-
    ence. Thus Morrison's text "embodies both the ancestor's orality and the
    modernity of photography. In this way, it is like the migrant, a new subject,
    and like jazz" (196).

3   The reference to trains at the beginning of the passage quoted refers to their
    loudness rather than any view. I have discussed in the Introduction identi-
    fications of trains with the mobile vision of modernity and the viewing that
    is characteristic of white identities. Sara Blair, in *Henry James and the Writing
    of Race and Nation* (Cambridge: Cambridge University Press, 1996), con-
    siders how "the electric car—along with the Elevated, the subway, and the
    Pullman train—provides a stage for James's exploration of the making of
    the American race" and ways in which the Pullman in *The American Scene* is
    "aligned in its phantasmagoric spectacle with visual culture" (191). Mor-
    rison's representations of trains in *Jazz* ally rail journeys with emotional and
    musical more than spectacular experience.

4   Griffin, *"Who Set You Flowin'?"* 194.

5   Feminist theorists have been persistent in their attempts to locate and repre-
    sent experience that exceeds the dimensions of vision and visual media.
    Elizabeth Grosz discusses feminist psychoanalytic resistances to visual do-
    mains of identity in *Volatile Bodies: Toward a Corporeal Feminism* (Bloom-
    ington: Indiana University Press, 1994). See especially her discussion of
    Luce Irigaray's analysis of tactility as a field of experience incommensur-
    able with visuality (103–7). Grosz's project is an exploration of various
    models of bodily identity and bodily differences, and she aims at "new
    methods and models" (210) to address modes of being that have been
    unrepresented or underrepresented. In Morrison's culturally and racially
    specific extensions of identity beyond the limits of visuality, she both calls
    attention to nonvisual cultural media that have been in force within African
    American communities and represents with her own fiction more than
    visual dimensions of experience.

6   In *The Dilemma of "Double Consciousness": Toni Morrison's Novels* (Athens:

University of Georgia Press, 1993), Denise Heinze, in her discussion of the responsive relation Morrison develops between narrator and reader (181–86), identifies characteristics of critical consciousness and responsibility similar to those I identify among characters.

7   Andrea O'Reilly reads the relationship of Alice and Violet more specifically, as one of mothering: "In *Jazz* one woman mothers another and returns her to her lost mother." See "In Search of My Mother's Garden, I found My Own: Mother-Love, Healing, and Identity in Toni Morrison's *Jazz*," *African American Review* 30, 3 (Fall 1996): 372.

8   Gayl Jones, *Liberating Voices: Oral Tradition in African American Literature* (Cambridge: Harvard University Press, 1991), 197.

9   Paul Gilroy, *The Black Atlantic: Modernity and Double Consciousness* (Cambridge: Harvard University Press, 1993), 201.

10 Ibid., 203.

11 Ibid., 56–57.

12 Jones, *Liberating Voices*, 202.

13 See also Craig Hansen Werner's *Playing the Changes: From Afro-Modernism to the Jazz Impulse* (Urbana: University of Illinois Press, 1994), 301–3, for a brief discussion of Morrison's narrative responsiveness in *Jazz* to African voices as well as voices of gospel and the blues.

14 It is the importance of such reflections in Violet's choice of identity that qualifies, I think, the importance that Derek Alwes assigns to individual choice in *Jazz*. See his "The Burden of Liberty: Choice in Toni Morrison's *Jazz* and Toni Cade Bambara's *The Salt Eaters*," *African American Review* 30, 3 (Fall 1996): 353–65. Alwes argues that Morrison "wants to engage the reader in the conscious, individual process of evaluation and selection of issues, of 'truths,' of the things that constitute the construct known as identity" (363).

15 In *The Practice of Everyday Life*, trans. Steven R. Rendall (Berkeley: University of California Press, 1984), Michel de Certeau discusses "a contradiction between the collective mode of administration and an individual mode of reappropriation" (96) of the spaces of city life. One mode of individual reappropriation of city space is walking through the city, choosing one's route. Another is the naming with proper names of streets and spaces. "The magical powers proper names enjoy" occur in part because a "rich indetermination gives them, by means of a semantic rarefaction, the function of articulating a second, poetic geography on top of the geography of the literal, forbidden or permitted meaning" (104, 105).

16 See Jones's discussion in *Liberating Voices* of African drumming as part of the heritage on which jazz draws, with respect to Ann Petry's "Solo on the Drums" (96–98).

17 Morrison has earlier identified the rhythm of trains with music. "Railroad blues" were an important dimension of the blues tradition. Hazel Carby briefly discusses blues of migration and the railroad as sung by women in "It Jus Be's Dat Way Sometime: The Sexual Politics of Women's Blues," in

Gender and Discourse: The Power of Talk, ed. Alexandra Dundas Todd and Sue Fisher (Norwood, N.J.: Ablex, 1988), 233–35.

Afterword

1   The quotation is from Robyn Wiegman, *American Anatomies: Theorizing Race and Gender* (Durham: Duke University Press, 1995), 38.
2   Toni Morrison, *Tar Baby* (New York: Plume, 1982), 127.

Index

Derrida, Jacques, 233 n.15
Doane, Mary Ann, 232 n.13
Du Bois, W. E. B., 21, 216 n.49,
    218 n.62, 227 n.7, 230 n.3
Dyer, Richard, 3, 11, 209 n.8, 220 n.5,
    221–22 n.1, 227–28 n.12

Faulkner, William: on blackness, 7, 28;
    on gender, 15–16, 18–19; on race, 2;
    on whiteness, 1–2, 4, 6–8, 14–16,
    17–21, 25, 28–30, 188–90, 203–4. *See
    also individual works*
Fetishism, 62–63, 75, 221 n.17
Fisher, Philip, 66–69, 72, 75, 84,
    224 n.20
Foucault, Michel, 202, 203
Frankenberg, Ruth, 8, 30, 209 n.9,
    210 n.18, 211 n.24, 219 n.66
Freedman, Jonathan, 90–93, 96,
    220 n.9, 222 n.4, 224 n.24, 224–
    25 n.26, 225 n.28
Freud, Sigmund, 21, 58, 225–26 n.1,
    226–27 n.6, 227 n.7

Gates, Henry Louis, Jr., 218–19 n.62
Gender, 10, 214 nn. 39, 43, 232–33 n.13.
    See also Blackness; Whiteness
Geyer-Ryan, Helga, 214–15 n.43
Gilroy, Paul, 23, 27–29, 103–4, 191,
    216 n.51, 227 n.7
Gleber, Anke, 214 n.39
The Golden Bowl (James): American
    character in, 75–76, 77, 80–82, 97–
    98; assimilation in, 38, 89, 90–94;
    cultural production in, 14–15, 19,
    158–59; darkness in, 7, 87–89, 97;
    European character in, 82–86, 88–
    89; gender in, 18, 97; history in, 77–
    78, 85–88; imagery in, 70–73, 78,
    225 n.30; improvisation in, 77, 79–
    80; Jewish characters in, 90–94,
    222 n.4, 224 nn. 24, 25, 224–25 n.26,
    225 n.30; museum culture in, 64, 66–
    73, 78, 222 n.9, 222–23 n.10; and

race, 2, 90–94, 220 n.9, 223 n.17,
    224–25 n.26; whiteness in, 20–21,
    64–66, 68–82, 94–98, 224 n.23
Grant, Robert, 231 n.4
Greenblatt, Stephen, 80, 223 n.16
Griffin, Farah Jasmine, 178, 234 n.2
Grosz, Elizabeth, 234 n.5
Gubar, Susan, 215 n.47
Gwin, Minrose C., 226 n.2

Habermas, Jürgen, 9–10, 14, 28, 29,
    31–32, 35, 128
Hardack, Richard, 217–18 n.57
Harris, Cheryl I., 211 n.20, 220 n.5,
    225–26 n.1
Hawthorne, Nathaniel, 40–42, 46–47,
    49, 63, 220 n.10
Heinze, Denise, 218 n.62, 234–35 n.6
Henderson, Mae G., 159, 230–31 n.4,
    233 n.14
Henry, Charles P., 217 n.54, 219 n.63
Hill, Mike, 210 n.18
Holland, Laurence Bedwell, 221 n.12
hooks, bell, 208–9 n.6, 212 n.28,
    217 n.56, 221 n.17, 224 n.23, 230 n.8,
    232–33 n.13

Ignatiev, Noel, 211 n.19
Irigaray, Luce, 226 n.2, 234 n.5
Irwin, John, 100–101, 225–26 n.1, 226–
    27 n.6

James, Henry: on American character,
    40–43; on blackness, 20–21, 28; on
    gender, 18–19; on Hawthorne, 40–
    42, 46–47, 49, 63, 65; on whiteness,
    1–2, 4, 7–8, 14–16, 17–21, 25, 28–30,
    147, 188–90, 203–4, 220 n.9. *See also
    individual works*
Jazz (Morrison): blackness in, 5, 173–
    91; city in, 173–76, 178, 179–80, 185,
    196–97; community in, 173, 190–91,
    198–201; cultural production in, 21–
    27, 176–80, 189–201; double con-

sciousness in, 178, 186–87, 190, 192–99, 203; images in, 174–76, 188–89, 192; looking in, 192–94; loss in, 178–79, 179–87; migration in, 234 n.2; missing in, 180–87, 190–91, 204; mothering in, 235 n.7; music in, 175, 176–78, 190–91, 195–97, 199–201, 235 n.13, 235–36 n.17; narrative form of, 234 n.2; public sphere in, 176, 178, 189–91, 195–97; race in, 2; railroad in, 199–200, 234 n.3; visual culture in, 213 n.32

Jones, Gayl, 191, 216–17 n.53, 235 n.16

Joplin, Patricia Klindienst, 233 n.15

Jordan, Winthrop D., 215–16 n.48

Keats, John, 15, 72, 73, 95

King, Martin Luther, Jr., 24

Kristeva, Julia, 60, 226 n.2, 232 n.13

Lacan, Jacques, 6, 26, 59, 105–6, 114, 121, 156, 179, 204, 214 n.43, 215 n.47

Lastra, James, 6

Le Corbusier, 68

LeMaire, Anika, 59

Light in August (Faulkner): blackness in, 131–40, 143–44, 229–30 n.7, 232 n.9; female corruption in, 137–40, 141–42; gender in, 126–28, 132–33, 137–40, 229–30 n.7; history in, 126–27, 131–33, 145; imagery in, 15–16, 124–29, 133–36, 138–40, 140–45, 177, 299 n.5; public sphere of, 19–20, 123–31; race in, 2; theatricalization in, 123–31; whiteness in, 124–33, 140–45, 232 n.9

Lott, Eric, 215 n.47, 228–29 n.20

Matthews, John T., 228 n.18

McDowell, Deborah E., 231 n.5, 233 n.14

Michaels, Walter Benn, 102, 212 n.25, 220 n.5, 225 n.30

Montag, Warren, 211–12 n.24

Morrison, Toni: on blackness, 3, 21–30, 203–5; on history, 231 n.4; on music, 208 n.5; on whiteness, 2, 11–13, 20, 202. *See also individual works*

Mulvey, Laura, 221 n.17

Newitz, Annalee, 209 n.9

O'Donnell, Patrick, 25, 218 n.58

Omi, Michael, 38–39

Pease, Donald E., 220 n.10

Playing in the Dark (Morrison), 2, 11–13, 21–22, 88–89, 100, 176, 202, 215 n.47, 218 n.58, 224 n.23

Poe, Edgar A., 88–89, 95

Porter, Carolyn, 105–7, 108, 112, 222 n.2, 225–26 n.1, 226 n.2

Public sphere, 8–10, 13–16, 17–21, 22–24, 31–32, 35, 121–22, 123–31, 213 n.34, 214 n.38, 217 nn. 54, 55, 230 n.7

Race, 1–2, 29–30, 38–39, 210 n.18, 212 n.25, 220 n.9. *See also* Blackness; Whiteness

Roberts, Diane, 229–30 n.7

Rogin, Michael, 210 n.18

Said, Edward W., 16–17

Sandoval, Chela, 216 n.49

Sartre, Jean Paul, 228 n.19

Saxton, Alexander, 211 n.19, 223 n.17, 223–24 n.19

Scott, Joan W., 10, 105

Smith, Neil, 223–24 n.19

Smith, Valeris, 213 n.4

Snead, James A., 213–14 n.37

The Sound and the Fury (Faulkner): assimilation in, 102–5; blackness in, 7, 99, 102–4, 114–22, 227–28 n.12; gender in, 27, 104–7, 226 n.2; history in, 100–102, 103, 107–8; loss in, 111–14, 184; missing in, 106–7, 111–13; self-

Patricia McKee is Professor of English at Dartmouth
College and author of *Public and Private: Gender, Class,
and the British Novel, 1764–1878* (1997) and *Heroic
Commitment in Richardson, Eliot, and James* (1986).

Library of Congress Cataloging-in-Publication Data

McKee, Patricia
Producing American races: Henry James, William
Faulkner, Toni Morrison / Patricia McKee.
p. cm. — (New Americanists)
Includes bibliographical references and index.
ISBN 0-8223-2329-X — ISBN 0-8223-2363-X (pbk. : alk.
paper)
1. American fiction—20th century—History and criticism.
2. Race in literature. 3. Literature and society—United
States—History—20th century. 4. Faulkner, William, 1897–
1962—Political and social views. 5. James, Henry, 1843–
1916—Political and social views. 6. Morrison, Toni—
Political and social views. 7. Whites—United States—Race
identity. 8. Afro-Americans—Race identity. 9. Afro-
Americans in literature. 10. Whites in literature.
I. Title. II. Series.
PS374.R32M38 1999
813.009'355—dc21   98-32346